STUDY HELPS ON THE HEIDELBERG CATECHISM

Revised edition

Rev. Norman L. Jones

*The Reformed Church
in the United States
2009*

Study Helps on the Heidelberg Catechism
By Rev. Norman L. Jones
Revised Edition, 2011

© 1981, 1987, 1995, 2009, 2011 by
The Reformed Church in the United States
All rights reserved.

Produced by the Publications and Promotions Committee
of the Reformed Church in the United States

Design by Eric D. Bristley

Scripture quotations taken from:
The Holy Bible, New King James Version
© 1984 by Thomas Nelson, Inc.

Preface

These studies are intended to help lead our covenant youth into the riches of the *Heidelberg Catechism*. They are by no means exhaustive, and they are not a substitute for the actual memorization of the Catechism. This must be emphasized. Rather, we offer these helps for the purpose of stimulating thought and helping to clarify some of the points of the Catechism for both students and lay teachers.

The Catechism is a very profound theological book, and study aids can be helpful in bringing out its riches of truth. There has been an effort made to show the relevancy of the Catechism to the religious and social scene, to show the student many practical applications of God's truth to his own life.

Attention is called to the glossary of theological terms by Dr. Alexander De Jong at the end of the book, which will prove helpful when these terms are encountered.

It is left to the teacher to determine the assignments and to work out periodic examinations. Each teacher will have his own program for covering the Catechism. It seems advisable, however, to go through half the Catechism in a catechism season.

I acknowledge my indebtedness to many Reformed catechetical writers in the writing of these lessons. Especially am I grateful to Professor Merle Meeter for many helpful suggestions. Also, a word of special thanks to the Baker Book House of Grand Rapids, Michigan, for permission to use the glossary from Dr. Alexander C. De Jong's manual, *An Introduction to Biblical Truths* (1978, originally entitled *What I Confess*).

Norman L. Jones
Pierre, South Dakota

The translation of the Heidelberg Catechism used in this workbook is a revision of the 1950 translation of the Heidelberg Catechism by a Special Committee of the Eureka Classis, Reformed Church in the U.S. in 1978, and first printed in 1986. It is referred to as the Modern Version. All Bible quotations are taken from the New King James Version.

The Publications and Promotions
Committee of the RCUS

Contents

Introduction
to the Catechism

❦ *The Heidelberg Catechism*

What does the word "catechism" mean?

The word has come to mean "instruction by questions and answers."

Who wrote the Heidelberg Catechism?

The Catechism is the work of two men, Zacharias Ursinus (a seminary professor) and Caspar Olevianus (a minister), who lived over 450 years ago in Heidelberg, Germany. They were asked by Frederick III, ruler of a German state called the Palatinate, to prepare a catechism. Frederick III wanted this Catechism to help the churches in his land to be *Reformed* in their doctrine rather than Roman Catholic or Lutheran or Baptist.

The little book was published in 1563, first in German and then in Latin. It has since been translated into many languages. This Catechism has become famous as the official creed (belief) for Reformed denominations in various countries.

Why should we learn the Heidelberg Catechism?

Many churches today do not require the children to learn their catechism. In fact, many churches do not even have a catechism. Perhaps you do not see why it is important that you learn the Catechism. Here are two reasons why we must study the *Heidelberg Catechism:*

1. *Our Catechism explains the message of the Bible correctly.*

Because there are so many wrong interpretations of the Bible in our day, it is important for us to know how the Reformation Church, following the early Apostolic Church, interpreted the Scriptures. The godly Reformers were devout students of Scripture and of the history of theology. The Heidelberg Catechism gives us the *true interpretation* of the Bible over against many false interpretations. Therefore, we must learn the Catechism to have the correct understanding of the Bible.

2. *The Catechism is an aid to confessing Christ properly.*

To be a communicant (confirmed) member of the Reformed Church, we must give a good confession of our faith in Jesus Christ (see Matthew 10:32 and Romans 10:9-10). The Catechism gives the teaching of the Bible in a concise, systematic way; and as we learn the Bible and the Catechism together, we see the wonderful plan of salvation unfold before our eyes, and the doctrinal statements stick in our minds. This helps us to understand our salvation and prepares us to make an intelligent confession of our faith in Christ.

For these reasons, then, we need to learn the Catechism, and learn it well. It must be strongly stressed, however, that merely repeating the Catechism does not save you! Only as you personally trust in Jesus Christ and commit yourself to Him will you be saved. Pray that the Holy Spirit of God will bring you to a saving knowledge of the Savior, the Lord Jesus Christ.

Questions:

1. What does the word "catechism" mean? _____

    _____

2. Who were the two men who wrote the Heidelberg Catechism?
    a) _____
    b) _____

3. What was the name of the ruler who requested these men to write the Catechism? _____

4. Why did he want such a catechism to be written? _____

    _____

    _____

5. Do the Lutheran and Roman Catholic Churches also teach our Catechism? ☐ Yes ☐ No ▶ *Explain:* _____

    _____

6. The Reformed Church in the U.S. is the only Reformed Church which teaches the Heidelberg Catechism. ☐ True ☐ False

7. Give two reasons why you should learn the Heidelberg Catechism:
    a) _____

    _____

    b) _____

    _____

8. If a person can recite the answers in the Catechism correctly, he is truly a Christian. ☐ True ☐ False ▶ *Explain:* _____

    _____

    _____

    _____

9. Who is needed to bring you to a saving knowledge of Jesus Christ?

_____

10. Write out 2 Timothy 2:15. _____

_____

_____

_____

❧ *The Theme of Comfort*

Q1. What is your only comfort in life and in death?

That I, with body and soul, both in life and in death, am not my own, but belong to my faithful Savior Jesus Christ, who with His precious blood has fully satisfied for all my sins, and redeemed me from all the power of the devil; and so preserves me that without the will of my Father in heaven not a hair can fall from my head; indeed, that all things must work together for my salvation. Wherefore, by His Holy Spirit, He also assures me of eternal life, and makes me heartily willing and ready from now on to live unto Him.

This first question of the Catechism is really a summary of all the questions that follow. We may say that it introduces the great truths which are to be explained more fully in the next 128 questions and answers. This question and answer is a very beautiful statement of the Christian gospel, and we should memorize it so as never to forget it.

Notice that the gospel (good news) of salvation is concerned with three great matters: misery, redemption, and gratitude. Our misery is the misery of *sin* (not physical pain): We are guilty of sin, and have corrupt, sinful natures, and are under the awful curse of God.

But God has not left us to perish in the misery of sin. Rather, secondly, He has graciously provided redemption (salvation) for us, and this is our *comfort*. Comfort is to have strength, hope, and thankfulness in the midst of trouble. And what is this redemption that gives us so much comfort?

Salvation is being taken by God to Himself, so that we no longer belong to the Devil. Each of the three Persons of the Trinity saves us. The *Father* planned our salvation in every detail; the *Son* purchased our salvation by giving His life for us; the *Holy Spirit* applies the benefits of Christ's work to us, gives us personal assurance of salvation, and makes us willing and ready to live in obedience and love to God.

Your attention is called to the fact that the Catechism is written very *personally*. It constantly speaks of "me," "my," "I," and "our." This does not mean, we repeat, that every one who reads or memorizes these answers is truly saved and knows the comfort of salvation. No, not at all, for this is a textbook and Bible instruction book only for *believers*. Are baptized *children* believers? The promise of God made to Abraham and to all Christian parents is that their children are also part of the visible church (see Q74); thus you covenant children are considered as part of the church unless you should turn away from the Lord. Some baptized children of the Church do turn away from Christ, but they are the exception rather than the rule, according to Scripture. May God use His Word, and the instruction of this Catechism, to give you faith and to strengthen your faith.

Questions on Number 1

1. This first question is really a _Summary_ of the whole catechism.

2. The Christian gospel is concerned with three great matters. They are:
    a) _misery_
    b) _redemption_
    c) _gratitude_

3. Sin brings misery, salvation brings _Comfort_.
    What is salvation? _Strength, hope, and thankfullness_
    in the midst of trouble

4. The Christian's "body and _Soul_ both in _life_
    and in _death_ .... belong to (his) faithful Savior, Jesus Christ."

5. Each of the three Persons of God saves us.
    a) The Father _planned_ our salvation.
    b) The Son _purchased_ our salvation.
    c) The Holy Spirit _applies the benefits to_ our salvation.

6. The Savior's blood (death) does three things for us:
    a) it fully _allows me to cleanse my sins_
    b) it _protects_ me from all the power of the Devil
    c) and so _Cleanses_ me.

7. What does the word "redemption" mean? (See the Glossary)
    Sinners pay bondage for their
    sins via ransom. This ransom

is Jesus Christ's blood

8. Who assures you that you belong to the Savior and have eternal life?
   The holy Spirit

9. Can you truly say you belong to Christ if you are not willing to live for Him? ☐ True ☑ False

10. Baptized young people, even if they do not repent and do not believe and obey Christ, may say truthfully, "I am not my own but belong to my faithful Savior." ☑ True ☐ False ▶ Explain: _They are an exception in Scripture_

11. Write out 1 Corinthians 6:20. _~~For get~~ you were bought at a price. Therefore honor God with your body._

🔥 The Christian's Three-fold Knowledge

Q2. How many things are necessary for you to know, that in this comfort you may live and die happily?

Three things: First, the greatness of my sin and misery. Second, how I am redeemed from all my sins and misery. Third, how I am to be thankful to God for such redemption.

Christian comfort depends on knowing certain things. A person does not have to know a great deal to become a Christian, but our Christian progress and happiness depend very much on our gaining more knowledge. Christians who never seem to learn much about the Bible and the Christian life are weak Christians and in the "baby" stage of their spiritual lives. How do we grow to be strong, happy, and useful Christians, having true Christian comfort? The Catechism speaks of a three-fold knowledge which we must learn in order to be Christians, and which will increase as we learn the Bible and apply it to our own lives.

1. We must know our great sin and misery.

This is not a pleasant experience; but, nevertheless, we must first learn that we have a deadly disease—sin—or we shall never seek the remedy for it. Sin makes us guilty before God and arouses His anger against us.

2. We must learn how we are redeemed from our sin.

Our assurance of being saved is dependent on our learning about Christ and the Holy Spirit and their work for us and in us.

3. We must show our thankfulness to God for His saving us.

If you were rescued from a burning building by someone, you would certainly thank that person; and we must thank the Lord for saving us from sin by living as He wants us to live.

We must not think that we learn these things only once and that that is the end of the matter. Our whole life on earth is to be devoted to learning more about our sinfulness, our redemption, and what it means to be thankful to God. We must read God's Word each day, hear it preached regularly, and ask God to plant it in our hearts in order that we may grow in this three-fold knowledge and the comfort that it brings.

This answer gives the main outline of the Catechism:

1. *My sinfulness (sin): questions 3-11*

2. *My redemption (salvation): questions 12-85*

3. *My thankfulness (service): questions 86-129*

Questions on Number 2

1. A person can be a Christian and know nothing about the Bible.
   ☑ True ☐ False

2. To grow in faith and gain deeper Christian happiness and comfort, it is necessary that you gain more ___knowledge___

3. What are the three key-words of Christian knowledge?
   a) Sinfullness
   b) Redemption
   c) Thankfulness

4. Why is it necessary to learn of our sinfulness? If we don't know our sins, we will never search for a remedy

5. How many questions in the Catechism deal with the subject "my sinfulness"? ___8___

6. The threefold knowledge which comforts us in Christ is received (*check one*):

☐ a. by merely reading or hearing the Bible

☐ b. by studying other religions

☑ c. by the Holy Spirit's applying the gospel to our hearts

7. This question teaches us that we must first experience for a long time our misery only, then at a later period experience redemption, and then still later learn to be grateful. ☑ True ☐ False

8. Are sinners in misery even if they do not *feel* miserable?
☑ Yes ☐ No

9. A Christian may learn of his sinfulness and of salvation through Jesus Christ, but refuse to learn to live a thankful life.
☑ True ☐ False

10. Write out Ephesians 5:8. _For you were once darkness, but now you are light in the Lord. Live as children of light._

Part 1.
How Great is My Sin

❦ *The Definition of Sin*

Q3. From where do you know your misery?

From the Law of God.

Here we learn *the source of our knowledge of sin*. Question 2 taught us that we must learn of our sin and misery. Here we find out *how* we learn of them. The Law of God tells us the truth about ourselves; it exposes the ugliness of our hearts and convinces us that we are not good, but evil in the sight of the Lord. His Law teaches us what is required of us in our thoughts, in our words, in our actions, in our relation to both God and our fellow man. The Law speaks first to our hearts, and demands purity of love and obedience there; for without a pure heart that seeks only God's glory, neither our words nor our actions will be pure. "Out of the *heart* spring the issues (sins or good acts) of life" (Proverbs 4:23).

What do we mean by the Law of God? The word "law" is used in various ways in Scripture. Sometimes it refers to the Old Testament laws of worship (the tabernacle ritual, the priesthood, etc.). Those laws do not apply to us today. Sometimes it refers to the Books of Moses, or to the whole Old Testament. We may also speak of the whole Bible as being the Law of the Lord. Often the "Law" means the Moral Law, called the Ten Commandments, which is God's will for all men at all times. The Moral Law is God's revelation of right and wrong which never changes. Question 3 is referring specifically to the Ten Commandments, which require perfect love to God, as the next question teaches.

The Holy Spirit reveals to us that in our hearts we have never kept any of the Ten Commandments perfectly; and, therefore, we are convicted as sinners, and we deserve damnation. Thus the Law shows us our sin and misery.

We understand, of course, that God, being our Creator, has the perfect right to give us His Law and tell us what He wants us to do. God is the Almighty Lawgiver, and we must obey Him without murmuring or questioning His authority.

Questions on Number 3

1. This question tells us the _____ of our knowledge of our sin.

2. We get our knowledge of sin *first,* by: (*check one*)
   ☐ a. looking at the evil things people do.
   ☐ b. by examining our own thoughts.
   ☐ c. by learning the Law of God.

3. The Law of God speaks first to our _____ , for out of _____
   _____ are the issues of life.

4. The phrase "the Law of God" is used in the following three ways:
   a) _____
   b) _____
   c) _____

5. All the laws found in the Bible require our obedience now.
   ☐ True   ☐ False

6. The "Moral Law," also called the _____ , is:
   ☐ a. only for the Jews in the Old Testament.
   ☐ b. only for Christians now.

☐ c. for all men now.

☐ d. only for unbelievers now.

7. Should the minister read the Ten Commandments in the worship service? ☐ Yes ☐ No ▶ *Explain:* _____

_____

_____

8. *Who* must teach us that we have never kept the law of God perfectly in our hearts and that we are worthy of damnation? _____

9. A person can never feel guilty of sin and know his misery if he has never learned the Law of God. ☐ True ☐ False

10. Write out Romans 3:19. _____

_____

_____

_____

_____

❧ *The Requirement of the Law*

Q4. What does the Law of God require of us?

Christ teaches us in sum, Matthew 22: "Thou shalt love the Lord thy God with all thy heart, and with all thy soul, and with all thy mind, and with all thy strength. This is the first and great commandment. And the second is like unto it, thou shalt love thy neighbor as thyself. On these two commandments hang all the law and the prophets."

Here we learn what the Law of God requires of us, namely, *perfect love* to God and to our fellow man. Our Lord Himself, quoting from Deuteronomy 6:5, explained that only perfect love is acceptable to God. This means our heart, mind, soul, and strength—in other words, *our whole being*—must be completely dedicated to God. Our thoughts, words, and deeds must be always perfect in love to God, or we are accounted as sinners. To be imperfect in love is to be a lawbreaker, a transgressor.

Our Lord divides the Ten Commandments into two parts or tables: the first part (Commandments 1 through 4) is the "first and great commandment" of love to God, and the second part (Commandments 5 through 10) is the commandment of love to men out of love to God.

This Law of love to God is the basis of all morality in the Old Testament (law and prophets) and in the New Testament, and it is the charter of true religion, the biblical, covenantal faith.

Questions on Number 4

1. Give the Bible reference in Matthew where Christ explains what the Law of God requires from us: _____

2. Is it possible to keep any of the Ten Commandments without also loving God? _____

3. Have you always loved God perfectly in *every* thought, word, and deed? ☐ Yes ☐ No

4. If you have failed in any way to love God perfectly, you deserve God's ☐ a. praise ☐ b. anger ☐ c. sympathy ☐ d. punishment (*check one*).

5. Some people have true love for their friends even though they do not love God. ☐ True ☐ False ▶ *Explain:* _____

   _____

   _____

6. Four words are used to tell us how much we should love God:
   a) "with all our _____
   b) "with all our _____
   c) "with all our _____
   d) "with all our _____."

7. What Old Testament verse is Jesus quoting? _____

8. How many commandments are in the *second* table of the Law?

   _____

   _____

9. A person who truly loves God may forget about the commandments, as they are not necessary in such a case.
   ☐ True   ☐ False

10. Write out Romans 13:10. _____

   _____

   _____

_____

_____

❧ *The Fact of Sin*

Q5. Can you keep all this perfectly?

No, for I am prone by nature to hate God and my neighbor.

Having seen what the Law of God requires of us, we now see what we actually *are*. Question 5 teaches us that we are entirely sinful. Instead of being God-lovers, we are God-haters! Our hearts are so full of sin that we are utterly unable to keep the Law of Love.

The Bible teaches us, and the Holy Spirit convinces us, that as we are *by nature* we cannot please God. We call this condition our *total depravity*. Our hearts are always turned away from God and toward the service of ourselves and the world and Satan. Nor do we love our neighbor, because to love our neighbor we must love him for God's sake and seek his salvation. And this the God-hating sinner cannot do.

Does this truth mean that the natural man (apart from God's grace) can do no good at all? That he cannot keep the Law in any way? The natural man does have an outward observance of the Law in that he usually does not kill, steal, lie, and commit adultery. But this outward obedience is not true obedience, for it is done from the wrong motives. Such "obedience" is for selfish reasons only and is therefore unacceptable to God.

So, by nature, the sinful heart of man cannot do spiritual good, cannot please God (Romans 8:8), and cannot keep the Law (Romans 8:7). Is the Holy Spirit teaching you that you were born with a sinful, God-hating heart and that your best works while unconverted are as "filthy rags" in the sight of God (Isaiah 64:6)?

Questions on Number 5

1. What does "prone" mean? (See your dictionary.) _____

   _____

2. It is true that our natural "hearts" (with which we are born) are full of hatred, instead of love, for God. ☐ Yes ☐ No

3. Many unconverted people think they love God, but the "god" they love is not the God of the Bible. ☐ True ☐ False

4. Our natural hatred for God is called our "total _____."

5. The Law of God requires not only outward obedience, but also obedience from proper _____

6. Because we cannot keep the Law of love to God and man, since we were born sinful, God does not require it anymore. ☐ True ☐ False

7. An atheist who gives a thousand dollars to the community hospital has done a good work in the sight of God. ☐ True ☐ False

8. Since unbelievers can do no good, they should not be required to keep any of the Ten Commandments, even outwardly.
☐ True ☐ False

9. Do converted Christians keep the Law of love perfectly?
(See Catechism Q62) ☐ Yes ☐ No

10. Write out Romans 3:10–12. _____

_____

_____

_____

_____

❦ *God Created Man in His Image*

Q6. Did God create man thus, wicked and perverse?

No, but God created man good and after His own image, that is, in righteousness and true holiness, that he might rightly know God his Creator, heartily love Him, and live with Him in eternal blessedness, to praise and glorify Him.

In questions 6 and 7 we learn of the *origin* or cause of our sinful natures. First, we learn who is *not* to blame—God is not to blame! Would anyone blame God for his own sinfulness? Yes, sinful man blames His Creator for his own sins. Remember Adam's excuses when he sinned? He said to God, "The woman whom *You* gave to be with me, she gave me of the tree, and I ate" (Genesis 3:12). In other words, Adam blamed God for giving Eve to him. When people are caught doing wrong, they usually have some excuse and do not blame themselves for their evil. Or they will say, "I can't help it, I did not make myself."

The Catechism teaches that instead of God creating man sinful, God created man good. Indeed, we were created in the holy image of God

Himself. What is this "image" of God that Adam and Eve had when they were created? The image of God is that part of man that makes him like God and different from the animals. The image of God is an *eternal spirit nature having personality.* This personality includes a *mind, affections,* and a *will.* Adam was created so that with his *mind* "he might rightly know God, his Creator." With his *affections* he could "heartily love Him," and with his *will* Adam could choose righteousness and holiness. Having this image of God, Adam as created could "live with God in eternal blessedness, to praise and glorify Him."

Therefore, God is not in the least to blame for the fact that man is now by nature wicked and perverse. (See James 1:13–18)

Questions on Number 6

1. In number 6 we learn ☐ a. *who was* ☐ b. *who was not* to blame for man's sinfulness (*check one*).

2. People usually try to excuse themselves and blame someone else if they are caught doing wrong. ☐ True ☐ False

3. Since God did not create us wicked and perverse, we are not born sinful. ☐ True ☐ False

4. What is the "image of God" which makes man different from the animals? _____

   _____

5. Name 3 parts of the human personality which are aspects of the image of God:
   a) _____
   b) _____
   c) _____

6. Man, being a perverse sinner now, no longer has any of the image of God in him. ☐ True ☐ False

7. Until the moment that they sinned, Adam and Eve could "rightly

   _____

   _____

   _____."

8. According to Ephesians 4:24, it is possible for man *now* to choose righteousness and holiness (living unto God according to His will).
    ☐ True   ☐ False

9. God is not to blame for Adam's sinfulness nor for our sinfulness.
    ☐ True   ☐ False

10. Write out Genesis 1:27, 31. _____

    _____

    _____

    _____

    _____

    _____

❧ The Origin of Sin

Q7. From where, then, does this depraved nature of man come?

From the fall and disobedience of our first parents, Adam and Eve, in Paradise, whereby our nature became so corrupt that we are all conceived and born in sin.

Having seen in question 6 that God is not to be blamed for our corrupted, depraved natures (hearts), here we learn just who *is* to be blamed—Adam and Eve. Our first parents willfully fell into sin by their disobedience in Paradise, the Garden of Eden. The sinfulness of Adam's heart came by his own action. We read the story of Adam's sin in Genesis, chapter 3.

But not only did Adam's nature become completely sinful, his sinful nature has been passed on to all mankind. We must confess that "our nature" is also corrupt, even from our very birth. Yes, our nature is sinful from its formation in our mother's womb. David said, "In sin my mother conceived me" (Psalm 51:5). In Romans 5:12 we read, "through one man sin entered the world, and death through sin, and thus death spread to all men, because all sinned." This verse teaches that through Adam's *one act of sin* all of us become guilty and corrupted by sin. We call this sin of Adam, which became our sin, *Original Sin*.

Yes, mankind has taken a fall! Unbelievers think that human nature is good and getting better all the time—all that is needed for man to improve himself is education, money, and pleasant surroundings. But the Word of God teaches the exact opposite. Adam was created perfectly holy and happy; he was very exalted. But by his willful sin he fell very low; he became unholy and unhappy.

We are now corrupted like a completely rotten apple, so that our thoughts and actions—our whole life—are by nature only evil and wicked.

Just how could Adam, the perfect human being, sin in the first place? This is a question impossible for us to answer. We know it happened; and we know that it was part of God's plan in order that He might save us by His Son Jesus Christ. But the entire blame and guilt of sin rested on Adam, and now on ourselves—not on God.

Questions on Number 7

1. The question of where we got our depraved (sinful) nature is impossible to answer. ☐ True ☐ False

2. We call Adam's sin in the Garden:
   ☐ a. God's fault ☐ b. Eve's fault ☐ c. Original Sin ☐ d. the Fall

3. The reason Adam disobeyed God is that God did not create Adam and Eve holy and sinless. ☐ True ☐ False

4. A baby, when it is born today, is (*check one*):
   ☐ a. naturally sweet and sinless.
   ☐ b. partly corrupted by sin.
   ☐ c. entirely corrupted and depraved.

5. The Modernists and others who reject the Bible say that people are

   _____.

   All that people need is _____

   _____.

6. When Adam ate the forbidden fruit, he acted (*check one*):
   ☐ a. only for himself.
   ☐ b. only for himself and Eve.
   ☐ c. for himself and the whole human race.

7. How many of Adam's sins are charged against the human race?

   _____

8. Check the two results of Adam's sin for himself and for us:
   ☐ a. Man became guilty before God.
   ☐ b. Man has a fear of snakes and strange fruit.

☐ c. Man needs education to be happy.

☐ d. Man's heart is corrupted.

9. It is not fair to mankind to be charged with the sin of the first man.
    ☐ True ☐ False ▶ *Explain:* _____

    _____

    _____

    _____

10. Write out Romans 5:19. _____

    _____

    _____

    _____

    _____

❧ *The Extent of Sin: Total Depravity*

Q8. But are we so depraved, that we are completely incapable of any good and prone to all evil?

Yes, unless we are born again by the Spirit of God.

Having seen in question 7 that the origin or source of our sinfulness is to be found in man alone—not in God—we now are told the *extent of sin in our hearts*. This question tells us that we are "wholly incapable of any good and prone to all evil." That is how wicked we really are!

This corrupted condition of our souls, inherited from our parents, is called our "total depravity." The noun "depravity" comes from the Latin word *depravare* which means "to be crooked, perverse." To be depraved means to be crooked, to be out of line with what is right.

Our hearts are completely out of line with what is right. They are unable to obey God's Law. Sin has so taken over our hearts that all our powers are twisted to hate God and to rebel against Him. Until we are born again (regenerated), our hearts are always directed away from God and toward this world. By nature we are *ungodly*, we are *godless*; we are "without God in the world" (Ephesians 2:12). Until we are born again, we cannot have one holy thought or one desire to love God and to obey His holy Law of love. We are *totally* depraved; not even our *will* or *conscience* is free from the power of sin.

This total depravity does *not* mean, however, that every unbeliever actually does all possible evil; it means that he is prone (inclined) to it.

Actually, many unbelievers do many things which appear to be "good" in the sight of man. They serve as doctors, give money to the poor, act like decent citizens, and so on. But all man's so-called "good works" come from an evil heart and thus are not good in God's holy eyes. The "goodness" and "kindness" of the natural man are always directed toward man, *never* toward God.

This inability to do good, please note, does not leave us free to do evil. We are still required to love God perfectly, and God never excuses our total depravity.

Our only escape from the power of sin in our hearts lies in our being born again by the Holy Spirit—that is, having spiritual life brought to our dead hearts by the power of God's Spirit.

Questions on Number 8

1. Question 8 tells us the _____ of sin, or how bad we really are.

2. Does it make us popular when we tell people that they are inclined to all evil? _____ Is it true? _____

3. "Depravity" comes from the Latin word _____, which means _____.

4. Total depravity means (*check two*):
   - ☐ a. Some people are totally evil and wicked, like Stalin and Hitler.
   - ☐ b. Our hearts are constantly inclined to hate God and resist Him.
   - ☐ c. All men do all possible acts of evil.
   - ☐ d. Sin has corrupted every part of our mind and soul.

5. People are not born with totally depraved hearts; this comes later as they learn to do evil. ☐ True ☐ False

6. When any person helps others and lives as a good citizen, he shows that he is not totally depraved but has at least some love for God and His Law. ☐ True ☐ False

7. Being totally depraved and inclined only toward evil excuses us from loving God and being sinless. ☐ True ☐ False

8. The "new birth," also called _____ , breaks the power of sin in our souls, so that we are no longer totally depraved.

9. The "new birth" of our souls is accomplished by (check one):
    ☐ a. ourselves   ☐ d. confirmation
    ☐ b. the minister   ☐ e. the power of the Holy Spirit
    ☐ c. baptism   ☐ f. religious education

10. Write out Jeremiah 17:9. _____

    _____

    _____

    _____

11. Write out Romans 8:7. _____

    _____

    _____

    _____

    _____

❦ *The Responsibility for Sin*

Q9. Does not God, then, do injustice to man by requiring of him in His Law that which he cannot perform?

No, for God so made man that he could perform it; but man, through the instigation of the devil, by willful disobedience deprived himself and all his descendents of this power.

The question here asked is often posed by people when they hear that God requires perfect obedience from man, even though man is incapable of any true obedience to God. They ask, "Is it fair of God to demand that which I cannot give?"

The Bible teaches that God still does require of man that he love God perfectly, according to the Law. Jesus repeated the Great Commandment to the lawyer in Matthew 22:36–40 and in Matthew 5:48. He said, "Therefore you shall be perfect, just as your Father in heaven is perfect."

The reason that God still can demand of totally depraved sinners perfect love and obedience is that *man is entirely to blame for his present predicament*. If a boy should deliberately skip school when he was scheduled to take a test, could he blame the teacher for flunking him? Likewise, God's requirements remain the same for man as they were for Adam when he was first created.

Our total depravity resulted from *our* Fall from righteousness into sin in the Garden of Eden. Adam was created in the *image* of God and was capable of obeying God (see Q6 again), but by listening to Satan and obeying Satan, he sinned and brought himself under God's curse and *lost* his spiritual power to love God.

It is true that you and I were not in the Garden, but Adam acted as our representative, and what he did was imputed (charged) to us, his posterity. Adam's disobedience was *willful* (not done in ignorance), and the awful consequences of his Original Sin are passed on to us. We must confess before God that *we* are to blame for our depravity, not God, and that every moment that we fail to love and obey perfectly, we increase our guilt!

Questions on Number 9

1. Question 9 answers a question about the (*check one*)
   ☐ a. justice of God   ☐ b. love of God   ☐ c. patience of God

2. We may truthfully say that man being human was never capable of obeying God perfectly. ☐ True ☐ False

3. If people question the "fairness" of God in requiring of them what they cannot do, they are ignorant of what? _____

   _____

4. Man was created in the _____ of God, which is explained in question _____, and this means that man was able to love and serve God perfectly.

5. What do you think is meant by "the instigation of the Devil"?

   _____

   _____

6. Are we charged with Adam's willful disobedience? _____
   ▶ *Explain:* _____

   _____

   _____

7. Give Scripture references that prove that God still requires perfect love and service from sinful man: _____

   _____

   _____

8. The idea of having someone else *represent* us is not approved of in human affairs today. ☐ True ☐ False

9. It is proper for us to blame Adam and not ourselves for our guilt and total depravity. ☐ True ☐ False

10. Write out Romans 5:12. _____

_____

_____

_____

_____

_____

❧ *God's Curse and Punishment on Sin*

Q10. Will God allow such disobedience and apostasy to go unpunished?

Certainly not, but He is terribly displeased with our inborn as well as our actual sins, and will punish them in just judgment in time and eternity, as He has declared: "Cursed is every one that continueth not in all things which are written in the book of the law to do them."

Having seen in question 9 that the responsibility for sin lies in man, not in God, we now learn in questions 10 and 11 the *consequences* of sin. The necessary result of sin is its punishment. Question 10 tells us that God is "terribly displeased with our sins" and He *must* punish them. Question 11 tells us *why* God is so terribly displeased, namely, because He is *just.*

His justice demands that His perfect righteousness and holiness be honored by the punishment of all sin that is committed against His righteous nature and His holy Law. Sin is *rebellion against God,* and He hates it with a perfect hatred. *It is an attack against His sovereignty,* and it must be duly punished.

Here we learn: (1) *which* sins God will punish and (2) *when* God will punish them.

First, we are sinners in two ways. We have an "inborn" depravity— our sinful nature—inherited from Adam through our parents. Our depraved *nature* is hateful to God and brings His wrath down upon us. We are also sinners by our *acts* of sin in thought, word, and deed. These are the corrupt fruits of our depraved hearts. Each one of these distinct acts of sin deserves God's eternal curse. Thus we are sinful in a double manner.

Secondly, when will the Holy God punish our sins? The Catechism says that the punishment is received in *time* (now) and in *eternity* (hell). The person whose sins have not been forgiven through Christ is even now experiencing a foretaste of God's wrath: He lives in *spiritual death,* not knowing the favor and love of God; he experiences all manner of evils in this world such as sickness, suffering, wars, accidents, natural disasters (floods, fires, tornados, etc.), and many other unpleasant things. These are God's judgments against unbelievers in this world.

At death, the unforgiven person is sent into the everlasting punishment of hell, where there is weeping and wailing and gnashing of teeth forever (Matthew 8:12; 13:42, 50). Is there anyone who will escape God's just punishment? No one will escape who has only his works to rely upon, because all the works of the depraved sinner are wholly unacceptable when judged by the Book of the Law of God.

Questions on Number 10

1. In questions 10 and 11, we are told of the _____ of sin.

2. The reason why sinful man must expect punishment from God is because of what kind of Person God is. He is _____

3. What is sin that makes it so displeasing and *hateful* to God? _____
    _____

4. It is always wrong to hate. ☐ True ☐ False

5. According to God's Word, the only sins that God will justly punish are wicked thoughts, words, and deeds, that is, our actual sins.
    ☐ True ☐ False

6. Another name for our "inborn sin" is (*check one*):
    ☐ a. our secret sinful thoughts
    ☐ b. our totally depraved nature
    ☐ c. the sins which come from our hearts.

7. Every sin, no matter how "small," is deserving of God's everlasting curse, simply because it is *sin.* ☐ True ☐ False

8. What are some ways by which God punishes sinners in this present life? _____
    _____
    _____

9. What does the word "apostasy" mean? (consult the Glossary.)
    _____
    _____

10. Write out Romans 1:18. _____

_____

_____

_____

_____

_____

_____

_____

❧ *The Consequences of Sin: Everlasting Punishment*

Q11. But is not God also merciful?

God is indeed merciful, but He is likewise just; His justice therefore requires that sin which is committed against the most high majesty of God, be punished with extreme, that is, with everlasting punishment both of body and soul.

Continuing with the *consequences* of sin, we are here taught that the justice of God does not conflict with His mercy. Many people are not concerned about their sins because they have the mistaken idea that God is so loving that He would never punish any of His creatures in hell. But this is a false hope. God's love and mercy do not cancel out His wrath against sin. God must punish the guilty sinner, who alone is responsible for his own sin, or God would cease to be holy and righteous and just. God is not only a Heavenly Father, but He is also the "most high Majesty."

Jesus spoke more about the punishment of hell than He spoke of heaven, but many people do not know this because they have never actually read the Bible. They are trusting in false preachers.

Let us be clear as to what we mean when we speak of God punishing *sin*. We mean that He punishes the *sinner* who commits it. Sin is never separated from a person; it is not something which can be punished by itself apart from a person. Likewise, when the Bible speaks of God hating sin, it means that God hates the *person* who sins. "God is angry with the wicked every day" (Psalm 7:11). It is only by our sins being charged to the Person of Christ that we can be spared from the punishment which we deserve.

Again, we are reminded of God's everlasting punishment of the sinner who dies with the guilt of sin. The Bible teaches that there will be *different degrees* of punishment in hell, because each person will have a different measure of guilt (Luke 12:47–48); but everyone's punishment in hell will be unspeakably awful. It is the place of "outer darkness," where there is "weeping and gnashing of teeth" (Matthew 8:12). That is, the light of God's mercy will be totally absent; only His wrath will be manifested. It is the place of fiery torment (Matthew 13:42, Revelation 20:10), where the sinner's conscience and God's Law will gnaw as a painful worm forever (Mark 9:48). Truly, hell is fearful to think about. Make sure *you* do not go there! And be faithful to warn others of it also.

Questions on Number 11

1. Many people are not worried about a hell of eternal suffering because, they say, God is only a God of love. ☐ True ☐ False

   Are they right? _____

   _____

2. The mercy of God and the wrath of God are in conflict with each other. ☐ True ☐ False

3. What is the justice of God? (consult the Glossary under "the Righteousness of God.") _____

   _____

   _____

4. The Bible speaks of God hating (*check one*):
   ☐ a. sin   ☐ c. sin apart from the sinner
   ☐ b. the sinner   ☐ d. people apart from sin.
   Give a Bible reference for proof: _____

5. The sins of ☐ unconverted sinners ☐ converted sinners deserve eternal punishment. (check one)

6. To whom is God merciful and why? _____

   _____

   _____

   _____

7. Can you love a God who would punish people in hell forever and ever?_____

   _____

8. Match the following verses with these five awful facts about hell:

    Revelation 14:11   There are degrees of punishment there.

    Matthew 25:46   It is a place of blackness and darkness forever.

    Luke 12:47–48   It is a place of smoking torment.

    Jude 13   The punishment is everlasting.

    Matthew 25:41   It will be the abode of the Devil and his angels.

9. The body of the sinner is punished only in this life; the soul of the sinner will be punished in hell forever.   ☐ True   ☐ False

10. Write out Revelation 20:14–15. _____

    _____

    _____

    _____

    _____

    _____

    _____

Part 2.
How I Can Be Redeemed

◖ *The Nature of Redemption:*
Satisfying God's Justice

Q12. Since, then, by the righteous judgment of God we deserve temporal and eternal punishment, how may we escape this punishment and be again received into favor?

God wills that His justice be satisfied; therefore, we must make full satisfaction to that justice, either by ourselves or by another.

How thankful we should be that the Bible does not end with the message of man's condemnation and that the Catechism does not end with question 11!

We now begin our study of the second main part of the Catechism which teaches us the gospel—good news—of salvation from our sin and condemnation. In the following 73 questions, we shall learn of the nature of our redemption; we shall learn *Who* the Redeemer is; and we shall learn *how* we receive the redemption that He provided for us— through faith.

We shall learn what the gospel is by studying the Apostles' Creed (numbers 23-58), and then by studying in detail the great truth of justification by faith (numbers 59-64). The last part of this section explains the sacraments (baptism and the Lord's Supper) and the key-power of the Christian Church, which are means used by God to strengthen our faith and keep us in the way of salvation.

In question 12 we learn that there can be no escape from the punishment of God apart from God's justice being satisfied. If man's salvation is to be accomplished at all, it can only be in accordance with God's perfect justice. God, being just and righteous, cannot ignore or excuse our sins. His justice and wrath demand that our sins be perfectly punished, as question 11 explained to us.

Question 12, then, teaches the *necessity of Divine satisfaction;* that is, of God's justice being satisfied by the full punishment of our sins. There can be no salvation for us until the sin problem is settled.

Now the important question is, "How can this sin problem be solved?" Who or what can be a substitute for us and bear God's wrath against our sins and in so doing permit us to escape? If no substitute can be found for us, then we shall have to make full satisfaction to God's justice ourselves. This will require both temporal (this present world) and eternal punishment (hell)!

How to save man from the just punishment due to him is no easy problem. Only the wisdom of God could devise the answer—see Ephesians 1:7-8.

Questions on Number 12

1. The second part of the Catechism is the _____ part of the Catechism, consisting of _____ questions.

2. What do these words mean in reference to the gospel?
   (*Consult the glossary*)
   a) Wrath of God _____

   _____

   b) Salvation _____

   _____

   c) Satisfaction of Christ _____

   _____

d) Propitiation _____

_____

3. What great creed is explained in our Catechism? _____

4. The sacraments and the key of church discipline have something to do with our salvation. ☐ True ☐ False

5. If salvation is possible at all for us, it ☐ a. *must be* ☐ b. *must not be* ☐ c. *ought to be* ☐ d. *need not be* in accordance with the perfect and holy justice of God (*check one*).

6. Question 12 teaches us the _____

_____

7. The question of how man is to be saved is (*check one*):
   ☐ a. easy   ☐ c. impossible for man to answer
   ☐ b. rather difficult

8. We may escape God's punishment, but our sins cannot possibly escape God's justice and wrath. ☐ True ☐ False

9. If we were to make satisfaction to God by *ourselves*,
   we: ☐ a. *could* ☐ b. *could not* escape punishment.

10. If we were to make satisfaction to God by *another*,
    we: ☐ a. *could* ☐ b. *could not* escape punishment.

11. Write out Romans 2:11–12. _____

_____

_____

_____

_____

_____

_____

❦ *The Impossibility of Self-Redemption*

Q13. Can we ourselves make this satisfaction?

Certainly not; on the contrary, we daily increase our guilt.

We have seen that in order for us to be restored to God's favor and be fit to live with Him in heaven, there must be a satisfaction made for our sins. The righteousness and justice of God require that every sin be punished perfectly. If God should overlook sin, then He Himself would be an unrighteous God, and His own holy Law would be worthless.

Now we face the question, "how is this satisfaction of God's justice going to be accomplished for us?"

Question 13 asks if we ourselves can perform this great task, and the answer is emphatically, No! *Self-redemption or self-salvation is utterly impossible.* How could any sinner pay off his debt to God without spending an eternity in hell? And even then it would not be paid off, because those who suffer in hell are also adding to their guilt by their continued hatred of God. (How awful that those suffering in hell are also increasing their guilt!)

Secondly, we cannot satisfy the justice of God—which requires perfect love and obedience to Him—because of our depraved hearts. It is impossible for any human being on this earth to live a single day without sinning in thought, word, and deed. To save ourselves not only requires paying the full penalty of past sins, but it also requires that we begin rendering perfect love to God each moment of our lives.

These two things, then, make self-redemption impossible for us:

1. All our sins must be punished with everlasting punishment (Question 11).

2. We are not able to live in perfection the remainder of our days on earth. We daily increase our guilt apart from daily forgiveness through our Lord Jesus Christ.

This question and answer condemns all forms of religion which teach that good works can save a person. The so-called "good works" of sinful men are not good, and they cannot satisfy the justice of God for past sins and guilt. Those who trust in their "good works" to get them to heaven will find that they have to be punished in hell forever first!

Questions on Number 13:

1. The _____ of God must be satisfied.

2. It is impossible for any sinner to fully pay the debt of punishment for his sins in this life. ☐ True   ☐ False

3. It is possible for a sinner to fully pay the debt of punishment for his sins in hell. ☐ True   ☐ False

4. Question 13 teaches us that _____ is utterly impossible.

5. The justice of God requires not only punishment for past sins, but it also requires *what* from us the rest of our days on earth?

   _____

   _____

6. Why is it impossible to keep from sinning every day?

   _____

   _____

7. The Roman Catholic Church teaches that a person who is punished in Purgatory after death may finally receive enough punishment for his earthly sins to satisfy the justice of God and thus be eligible for heaven. Why is this teaching wrong? _____

   _____

   _____

   _____

8. We daily increase our guilt by sins of thought, _____
   and _____ .

9. Modernists and others who teach salvation by good works are (*check all that apply*):
   ☐ a. wrong about sin, good works, and salvation
   ☐ b. denying the necessity of punishment for past sins
   ☐ c. right about good works
   ☐ d. insulting our Savior.

10. Write out Psalm 130:3–4. _____

    _____

    _____

    _____

    _____

❦ No Mere Creature Can Make Satisfaction

Q14. Can any mere creature make satisfaction for us?

None; for first, God will not punish any other creature for the sin which man committed; and further, no mere creature can sustain the burden of God's eternal wrath against sin and redeem others from it.

Question 14 answers another question about who can make satisfaction for us. We have seen in the previous question that we ourselves cannot save ourselves, but is it possible for another *creature* to take our place as a substitute? Again, the answer is, NO!

By "mere creature" the Catechism is speaking of something that is created by God, but is not God Himself.

First, we are taught that only a human being can be punished for human sins. God could not remain just if He punished some creature other than man for the sins committed by man. This excludes *angels*, which are above man, and *animals*, which are below man. Besides, angels do not have bodies, and animals do not have souls, both of which must be punished. Only a true human nature can be a proper substitute for man the sinner.

And, yet, there is no mere man who could qualify as a proper substitute for you to satisfy the justice of God. Why not? Because a fellow human being would himself be a sinner and deserve to be punished by God forever for his own sins. And, further, even if this were not the case, no mere man could have a surplus of perfect obedience to God to give for someone else. No man can gain extra merit to pass on to someone else who lacks any merit before God.

But let us suppose that God would create a new man without sin. Could that new sinless person be your substitute to receive your punishment in hell? Again, the answer is, No. Even if God did create such a person, that person could not take the burden of God's eternal wrath against sin for even a moment without breaking under it and hating God. Thus, the punishment administered to him would cause him to become a sinner, and he would then deserve the punishment himself. Besides this, a mere perfect man could only try to take the place of just one other human being. He could not try to be a substitute for two or more people.

It is very obvious, then, that there is absolutely no hope of redemption for us either by ourselves or by any other mere creature. No other human being can begin to take our punishment or love God for us. Our case is hopeless indeed. Only God could devise a method of salvation for us which satisfies His perfect justice with respect to both our sins and our obligation of perfect obedience. That method is the giving of His own Son, Jesus Christ, in the atoning death of the cross.

Questions on Number 14

1. This question and answer gives us some ray of hope that perhaps it could be possible for some other mere creature to be a substitute for us and purchase our salvation. ☐ True   ☐ False

2. God would be just but not loving if He made one of His holy angels take your place in hell. ☐ True   ☐ False

3. Believers in the Old Testament days offered animal sacrifices (*check one*):
   ☐ a. as sufficient substitutes for them
   ☐ b. as types and pictures of Jesus Christ, their only real substitute
   ☐ c. as partial payments for their sins

4. Another mere human being could be your substitute and take your punishment in hell if he were sinless. ☐ True   ☐ False

5. Jesus Christ is God, not a man, and therefore He could be a substitute for sinners. ☐ True   ☐ False

6. To "sustain the burden of God's eternal wrath against sin" means to take the full punishment for sin and love God perfectly while being punished. ☐ True   ☐ False

7. Jesus Christ satisfied God's justice as our substitute in two ways:
   a) He obeyed God's _____ perfectly for us.
   b) He suffered the torments of _____ perfectly for us.

8. Our Savior actually loved God perfectly while He was being punished for our sins. ☐ True   ☐ False

9. The Roman Catholic Church teaches that some men (the "saints") were extra holy and good and that they are able to give to others some of their "left-over" obedience. Why is this teaching wrong?

   _____

   _____

10. Write out Ezekiel 18:20. _____

    _____

    _____

❦ *The Kind of Redeemer We Need*

Q15. What kind of a mediator and redeemer, then, must we seek?

One who is a true and righteous man, and yet more powerful than all creatures, that is, one who is also true God.

Questions 15, 16 and 17 tell us *exactly what kind of Substitute-Redeemer we need* to satisfy the justice of God in our place.

As we have already seen (Question 14), a substitute for man must be a perfect man himself. And yet, such a substitute must be more than a mere man. He must be God also. Now this means that our substitute must be a supernatural person, some unique Person such as has never before appeared on earth. This Redeemer must be especially provided by God, quite apart from any ability of the human race to produce Him. The human race could not possibly produce a substitute to take the place of even one sinful man before the justice of God.

But God has provided for us a Mediator and Redeemer exactly suited to the problem that confronted us—a Substitute who is *both* God and man. Question 18 identifies Him as Jesus Christ.

Two words in this question need a little explanation if we are to understand the rest of the Catechism and the Bible. They are "Mediator" and "Redeemer" ("Deliverer" in some translations).

1. Mediator

A "mediator" is a person who stands between two other persons, who are at odds with one another, and brings them together. We read, "For there is one God and one Mediator between God and men, the Man Christ Jesus" (1 Timothy 2:5). In the Old Testament, the prophets, priests, and kings acted as mediators between God and man. But they only pictured Jesus Christ the true Mediator who alone can bring us to God and God to us through the putting away of our sins and the establishment of the New Covenant of Grace (see Hebrews 8:6; 9:15; 12:24).

2. Redeemer

A "redeemer" is a person who buys back a slave or captive by the payment of a ransom. God is the Redeemer of His people because He purchased them for Himself by paying a price for them. God redeemed Israel from Egypt through the payment of the bloody Passover sacrifices and His great strength (Exodus 6:6; 15:13) He redeems us from sin and frees us from the power of Satan by paying the price of the life of His Son Jesus Christ. His blood purchased our redemption (Ephesians 1:7). The price was paid to the justice of God, however, and not to the Devil!

Our Savior is both Mediator and Redeemer. He was appointed by God for this great task, and He willingly acted as the God–Man to satisfy the justice of God for us.

Questions on Number 15

1. Questions 15 through 17 tell us exactly _____

   _____

   we need to satisfy God's justice.

2. The two qualifications needed by a Substitute are that He be:
   a) One who _____
   b) and yet One who is _____

   _____

3. The Savior who appeared to save us from our sins was produced by the human race. ☐ True ☐ False

4. It is proper to speak of Jesus Christ as (*check one*):
   ☐ a. true and sinless man only
   ☐ b. true God only
   ☐ c. true man and true God together.

5. A Mediator is a Person who does what? _____

   _____

   _____

6. Christ as Mediator brought together whom? _____

   _____

   _____

7. A Redeemer is a Person who does what? _____

   _____

   _____

   _____

   _____

8. Match the following:

    "Your Redeemer"   Exodus 15:13

    Prophets, priests, kings   Galatians 3:20

    Hebrews in Egypt   Job 9:33

    "not a mediator of one"   Isaiah 60:16

    He wanted a Mediator   point to Christ the true Mediator

9. _____ _____ is our Mediator and Redeemer,
    and therefore our Savior. He purchased us with _____
    from the power of _____.

10. Write out Isaiah 9:6. _____

    _____

    _____

    _____

    _____

    _____

❧ *The Kind of Redeemer We Need:*
A True and Righteous Man

Q16. Why must he be a true and righteous man?

**Because the justice of God requires that the same human nature
which has sinned should make satisfaction for sin; but one who is
himself a sinner, cannot satisfy for others.**

Question 16 explains why the Redeemer must be a true and righteous
man. We have already learned from questions 14 and 15 that the
qualifications the Redeemer must possess are both *true humanity* and
true Deity and *why* this must be so.

It is not necessary to repeat here all that was said in our lessons
on questions 14 and 15, other than to emphasize the point that our
Substitute had to have our human nature, and yet not have our sinful
nature. Therefore, he must not be an ordinary child of Adam. "In Adam
all die" (1 Corinthians 15:22), because in Adam all are sinners. The
human race, we repeat, could never have produced the sinless Man,

Jesus Christ.

Jesus was conceived in a virgin by the Holy Spirit so that His human nature was preserved from the guilt and corruption of Adam's sin. To Mary the angel said, "The Holy Spirit will come upon you, and the power of the Highest shall overshadow you; therefore, also, that Holy One who is to be born will be called the Son of God" (Luke 1:35). The holy conception and the virgin birth of our Redeemer are basic Christian truths and the Apostles' Creed includes them (see Q35).

As a true (real) man, the Savior was able to take the place of true (real) men. It would have been impossible for an angel to be our substitute, because an angel's nature cannot be put to death. On the other hand, an animal—lacking a soul—could not receive *spiritual* punishment, which the justice of God requires.

As a *righteous* man, our Lord was Himself sinless and thus free from any self-deserved punishment. So a perfect human nature (body and soul) was used by God to make satisfaction for the sinful human nature of others.

Questions on Number 16

1. Question 16 explains why the Redeemer must be _____
    _____.

2. The true human nature of Jesus Christ means that he has
    (*check one*):
    ☐ a. a human body only
    ☐ b. a human soul only
    ☐ c. both a human body and human soul.

3. The justice of God requires that human nature must make
    satisfaction for sinful human nature. ☐ True   ☐ False

4. Being a true man, Jesus Christ was a son of Adam as are all of us.
    ☐ True   ☐ False

5. Jesus Christ received his human nature from (*check one*):
    ☐ a. the Holy Spirit working in Mary
    ☐ b. from Mary alone
    ☐ c. from Mary and Joseph

6. The many preachers today who deny the miracle of the Virgin Birth
    of Jesus may still be considered Christian ministers. ☐ True ☐ False

7. What do you think happened to Christ's human nature when He died:

   a)To His body? _____

   _____

   b) To His soul? _____

   _____

8. If Jesus had sinned even once against God's Law of love, He could not have been our Savior. ☐ True   ☐ False

9. By "true man," the Catechism is referring to Jesus as a _____ man, possessing both _____ and _____. As a "righteous man," it is referring to what characteristic of our Lord's human nature? _____.

10. Write out Hebrews 2:14. _____

    _____

    _____

    _____

    _____

    _____

    _____

❧ *Our Redeemer Must Be True God*

Q17. Why must he also be true God?

That by the power of His Godhead He might bear in His manhood the burden of God's wrath, and so obtain for and restore to us righteousness and life.

Question 17 repeats the truth of question 14 concerning the necessity of our Savior's being no less than God Himself.

The reason that the Substitute-Redeemer must also be God is that a mere human nature, even though sinless, could never bear up under the crushing burden of God's wrath, His awful anger.

Being "true God" means that Jesus Christ is none other than the Second Person of the Almighty Eternal Trinity, co-equal with God the Father and God the Holy Spirit. Modernists and many cults today (such as Jehovah's Witnesses, Christian Science, and Mormons) deny that

Jesus is actually equal to God the Father. But to deny the Deity of Christ is to be anti-Christ and be lost.

The Apostle John begins his Gospel, "In the beginning was the Word, and the Word was with God, and the Word was God" (John 1:1). That Word is, of course, Jesus Christ, as verse 14 explains. The "Word" is the Creator, along with the Father and the Spirit (vss. 3 and 10), and He fully "declared" (revealed) the invisible God (vs. 18). Only God can reveal God.

The union of the Divine Son with the human nature of Jesus is called the "Incarnation" (God in the flesh). This union of the two natures is a mystery to us, but we believe that it truly happened, and had to happen if we are to be redeemed!

In the first few centuries of the Christian Church, several influential teachers taught wrong views of the relationship of the Divine and human natures of our Lord. These *wrong* views are four in number and they were properly condemned by the Church Councils as being unbiblical. These views are:

1. **Arianism.** Arius taught that Jesus is the greatest of God's creations, but He is not actually God. He denied the Divine nature of Christ.

2. **Apollinarianism.** Apollinarius taught that Christ was God, but He was not fully human. He denied the human nature of Christ.

3. **Nestorianism.** Nestorius taught that Jesus is two separate persons (God and man), rather than one Divine person with two natures (divine and human). He denied the oneness of Christ's person.

4. **Eutychianism.** Eutyches taught that Christ was one person, but that He had only one nature; and this one nature of Jesus was a mixture of both God and man so that He was neither fully God nor fully human. He denied the two natures of Christ.

The truth is that our Lord is the one person of the Son of God and that He has two distinct natures: the nature of the Son of God (deity) and the nature of a perfect human being (body and soul). We do not pretend to be able to understand these things fully, but we believe them because the Bible teaches them about the Savior.

The God-nature of Jesus gave strength to the man-nature of Jesus so that He was able to suffer under the awful wrath of God and not develop hatred or bitterness toward God. While taking all the punishment of hell that all believers deserved, our Lord loved the Father perfectly. It was the power of the Divine nature that enabled Christ to suffer the infinite wrath of God in His human nature.

We have only a little understanding of the union of the two natures of Christ and His unspeakable sufferings. No man has ever suffered or will ever suffer as our Redeemer suffered for us. He had to be God to endure it!

By His perfect life and His perfect sufferings unto death, eternal righteousness and life were *purchased* for us.

Questions on Number 17

1. The "Godhead" of Jesus means (check one):
    ☐ a. His righteous human nature   ☐ c. The Holy Spirit in Jesus
    ☐ b. His divine nature

2. The doctrine that Jesus is actually God is believed by all groups that call themselves Christians. ☐ True ☐ False

3. In the first chapter of the Gospel of _____,
    we have proof that Jesus is no less than _____.
    a) In verses 1 and 14, Jesus is called the _____.
    b) Verses 3 and 10 tell us that Jesus _____
    _____
    c) Verse 14 tells us that Jesus reveals the _____
    of the Father, and is full of _____and _____.

4. The word that describes the union of the Divine nature to the human nature in Jesus is _____ (*God in the flesh*).

5. The union of God and man in Jesus Christ is difficult but not impossible to understand fully. ☐ True ☐ False

6. When did the incarnation take place? _____

7. What did the Divine nature do for the human nature of Christ when He suffered? _____
    _____
    _____

8. If Jesus had been a sinless man *only*, what would have happened when He began to receive the punishment of hell in His body and soul? _____
    _____
    _____

9. By His perfect death under the wrath of God, our Savior did *what* for us, according to the last part of this answer? _____
    _____

10. Write out Philippians 2:6 and 8. _____

_____

_____

_____

_____

_____

_____

❦ *The Redeemer Identified*

Q18. But who now is that Mediator, who in one person is true God and also a true and righteous man?

Our Lord Jesus Christ, who is freely given unto us for complete redemption and righteousness.

Having seen in questions 15 through 17 what qualifications the Substitute must have in order to redeem us from our sins, we now have that Redeemer *identified*. Our Lord Jesus Christ, born of the virgin Mary over 2,000 years ago is that Mediator-Savior.

Notice three matters that are emphasized in this question:

1. Christ is *freely* given to us.

This statement stresses the fact that God sent His Son to us out of free grace. He was under no obligation to send His Beloved Son to us sinners, but He did so solely out of love and mercy. That famous text, John 3:16, teaches us why God sent His Son for us: "For God *so loved* the world that He gave His only begotten Son." Romans 5:8 says, "But God demonstrates *His own love* toward us, in that while we were still sinners (undeserving of His favor), Christ died for us." Not only did the Father freely send the Son, but the Son freely came to be our Savior. Ephesians 5:2 teaches that "Christ also has loved us and given Himself for us." (See also Galatians 2:20 and 1 John 3:16.)

We must understand that sinful man did not desire Christ, did not ask for Him, did not deserve Him, and did not accept Him: "He is despised and rejected by men, ... and we hid, as it were, our faces from Him; He was despised, and we did not esteem Him (Isaiah 53:3).

2. In Christ we have complete redemption and righteousness.

(*Compare this statement with question 30.*) Christ is a complete and all-sufficient Savior. Nothing can be added to His work of salvation. He fully satisfied the justice of God on behalf of each one of the elect. All that is required for our full restoration to fellowship with God and everlasting life was purchased for us by the Savior's death and resurrection. Even repentance and faith are gifts given to us by the ascended Lord of glory (Acts 5:31; Ephesians 2:8).

3. The Mediator is *One Person.*

(*Notice the phrase in the question.*) The orthodox (true) Christian Church has always believed that though Jesus Christ has *two natures,* He is only *one Person*—Divine, and not human. Here again we have a mystery; yet we must insist that Christ is not two persons, but one. When He spoke of Himself, He always said "I" and not "we."

As noted in our last lesson, the heretic (false teacher) Nestorius taught that Jesus Christ is *two* persons, and the Church had a great discussion about this subject. Finally it was decided that Nestorius was wrong. The Church wrote a creed called the Creed of Chalcedon (AD 451) to teach the truth of Scripture about Christ. Can you locate this famous creed and find the statement in this Creed about the relationship of the two natures of Christ?

Questions on Number 18

1. In question 18 we have the Redeemer _____.

2. Three important matters pointed out in this question are these:

    a) _____

    _____

    b) _____

    _____

    c) _____

    _____

3. Give some Bible references which prove that the Father freely gave the Son. _____

    _____

4. Give some Bible references which show that the Son freely gave Himself for us. _____

    _____

5. Jesus came to this world of lost sinners because men wanted Him so very much. ☐ True ☐ False

6. What famous Old Testament passage tells us how sinful man feels
    about the Savior? _____

    _____

7. Because our Mediator purchased salvation for us, all we need to add
    to it of ourselves is our repentance and faith. ☐ True   ☐ False

8. The Savior, being both God and man, is two persons.
    ☐ True   ☐ False

9. Being true God, the Redeemer does not have a human soul.
    ☐ True   ☐ False

10. The truth about the natures and person of Christ was explained in
    the year _____ by church teachers, in the Creed of _____.
    This Creed condemned the teachings of _____,
    who taught that Jesus Christ is two _____.

11. Write out 1 Corinthians 1:30. _____

    _____

    _____

    _____

    _____

    _____

    _____

❧ *The Redeemer Revealed in the Gospel*

Q19. From where do you know this?

From the Holy Gospel, which God Himself revealed first in Paradise,
afterwards proclaimed by the holy patriarchs and prophets, and
foreshadowed by the sacrifices and other ceremonies of the law,
and finally fulfilled by His well-beloved Son.

Question 19 tells us *where the Redeemer is revealed*, that is, how He is
made known to us. He is taught to us by God in one place alone—in the
Holy Scriptures. The Scriptures teach the "gospel"—the "good news" of
salvation.

   When God is pleased to teach mankind about Himself, that teaching
is *revelation*. We can only know God as He *reveals* Himself to us. There are

two revelations that God has given to mankind. They are the following:

1. General Revelation

This refers to God's teaching about Himself in nature, the creation. This universe is God's "handiwork" (Psalm 19:1), and it shows us something of God's glory and wisdom and power. What we call "nature"—the sky, stars, earth, seas, trees, plants, animals, and especially man—reflects the greatness of the Creator. All men everywhere are faced with God's presence in nature and, therefore, are responsible to worship and glorify Him (Romans 1:19-20). When we study the world (science, etc.), we study God's *general revelation* of Himself. Has your science teacher told you this?

2. Special Revelation

Even though nature reveals God, no person can be saved by studying nature. The creation does not tell us about the Gospel of our Redeemer, Jesus Christ. The message of salvation is found only in the Bible, and this we call *special revelation*. The Bible is our *final* source of knowledge about God, Christ, salvation, and even general revelation, also. The Bible, God's *Special Revelation,* is our *only* rule for faith and practice.

The whole Bible tells us about Christ, from Genesis through Revelation. This question emphasizes that the Old Testament teaches Christ. Even in the Garden of Eden, God promised the Savior. In Genesis 3:15 He is called the "Seed of the woman," and the remainder of the Bible is but a gradual unfolding of this promise of the Seed of the woman. The "holy Patriarchs" (literally, "old fathers") are the great men of God mentioned in the Book of Genesis. God spoke to them of the Savior who would come as the seed of Abraham, Isaac, and Jacob, and Judah.

The "prophets" are all those people in the Old Testament who spoke by inspiration of God and gave further details of the Christ who was to come. Malachi was the last prophet of the Old Testament to write Scripture, though John the Baptist was really the last of the Old Testament kind of prophets.

Also, in the Old Testament God taught much about the work of the coming Christ by the many sacrifices and rituals of Mosaic worship. The people were taught that God would provide a Redeemer who would give Himself as a sacrifice—even as their lambs and goats were sacrificed—for their sins. The Old Testament prophets, priests, and kings were also "pictures" of Jesus Christ who was to come as the Prophet, Priest and King.

The Old Testament teachings about Christ were at first very simple and few, then more and more information was given, until finally a great book of special revelation had been produced at the close of the Old Testament age.

Jesus Christ, when He was born, was the great Fulfillment and Object of that Old Testament special revelation. He was brought forth by God when all things had been made ready (Galatians 4:4).

This rather long lesson is still not complete without a little explanation about the inspiration of the Bible. (Our Catechism could well use a separate question on this subject!)

How do we know that the Bible is truly the Word of God—the Special Revelation of God? We answer:

1. The Bible *claims* to be the very Word of God. All through the Old Testament we read, "and the Lord said," and similar expressions. Luke 1:68–70, 2 Timothy 3:16, and 2 Peter 1:21 also speak of the Old Testament writings as the Word of God.

2. Christ always spoke of the Old Testament Scriptures as the Word of God (Matthew 4:4; John 10:35).

3. Christ promised His Apostles that they would be given supernatural ability to write New Testament Scripture after the Holy Spirit was given to them. (John 14:26; 15:26–27).

4. The New Testament writers claimed to write the Word of God (1 Corinthians 2:13; 1 Thessalonians 4:8, etc.).

Thus, the authority of Christ and the authority of the Bible go together. To reject the Bible is to reject Jesus Christ. Therefore, we confess that the Scriptures are *infallible* (fully reliable) and *inerrant* (without error).

Of course, we must realize that no one will ever accept the Bible as the very Word of God unless the Holy Spirit gives him a spiritual mind to understand and believe what the Bible says about itself (1 Corinthians 2:14).

Lastly, when we speak of the Bible as being God's inspired and perfect words, we are referring to the Hebrew and Greek words that were first given. Our various *translations* of the Bible are never perfect, but they can be extremely accurate and trustworthy.

Questions on Number 19

1. What is meant by the word "revelation" when used about God?

_____

_____

2. What are the two kinds of revelation about God?
   a) _____
   b) _____

3. The *source* of our information about Christ and salvation is what?

_____

4. If we did not have the Bible, we could still find out how to be saved by studying other religions. ☐ True ☐ False

5. The word "gospel" means _____

_____

6. The gospel of Christ was(*check one*):
   ☐ a. completely revealed in the Old Testament
   ☐ b. not completely revealed in the Old Testament
   ☐ c. not revealed in the Old Testament at all.

7. Match the following:

   The first promise of the Savior   spoke the Words of God

   Patriarchs   Hebrews 9:12

   Prophets   John the Baptist

   Ceremonies   Genesis 3:15

   The last O.T. prophet   "pictures" of Christ

   Redeemer   "old fathers"

8. The Old Testament gives us a slowly developing picture of the work of Christ, though Adam and Eve knew enough of the gospel to be saved. ☐ True ☐ False

9. Give three reasons why you believe the Bible is the very Word of God.
   a) _____

   _____

   b) _____

   _____

   c) _____

   _____

10. Write out John 5:46–47. _____

_____

_____

_____

❧ *The Necessity of Faith*

Q20. Are all men, then, saved by Christ as they have perished in Adam?

No, only those who by true faith are engrafted into Him and receive all His benefits.

The next three questions of our Catechism (20, 21, 22) tell us of the *place of faith in our redemption.* We have seen in questions 12 through 19 what redemption from sin and Satan is, namely, our deliverance from the curse of God's law, and the punishment due to us, by means of the Substitute who took our place. Further, we have seen who that Substitute is, Jesus Christ, who is both perfect God and perfect man.

Now we must ask: Will everyone be redeemed by the death of Christ? Did Jesus take the place of everyone in the world, of everyone who has ever lived in the long history of mankind? Will all men be saved by Christ even as all men are lost in Adam?

The answer is an emphatic NO! The Bible does not teach a universal salvation for every human being. There is a popular teaching today called "Universalism," which says that all men are lost in Adam and also that all men are saved in Christ (We must beware of both Modernism and Universalism).

The truth is that all men who remain in Adam shall die, and all who enter Christ from Adam shall live. (See 1 Corinthians 15:22.)

This question teaches the *necessity of faith.* The "connecting link" between Christ and our souls is a living faith. Apart from it we cannot partake of the saving benefits of the atonement of Christ. Faith is like a spiritual hand which reaches out and grasps Jesus Christ and clings to Him.

Notice other important matters in this question:

1. Faith is the *means* appointed by God to receive Christ's benefits. But it is not a *power* which man has of himself. Faith is a *gift* of the Holy Spirit (Ephesians 2:8).

2. Man does not graft himself into Christ, but he is engrafted by God. Remember, a farmer grafts a branch into a tree; the branch does not do this by itself! The Holy Spirit puts us into Christ by giving us a true faith in Christ.

3. This grafting into Christ, which means being joined to Christ by the Holy Spirit, results in our receiving *grace and life continuously* from

Christ. We receive all the benefits of Christ's work for us through this living faith. We might also liken our faith to a "pipeline," as well as a "hand," by which the resurrected Christ gives His life and grace to us moment by moment.

Apart from Christ the "Vine, " there is no life for the "branches" (see John 15:1-8); and without a true faith given to us by the Holy Spirit, we are dead branches, still united to Adam unto death. Remember, it is not church membership, but a true faith that removes us from Adam's tree, and puts us into Christ's tree of life.

Questions on Number 20

1. Questions 20, 21, 22 tell us about _____

    _____

2. Jesus as Substitute took the place of (*check all that apply*):
    ☐ a. all men   ☐ c. some men of the Old Testament age.
    ☐ b. some men   ☐ d. all the men of the New Testament age

3. *Universal salvation* is taught by the Catechism. ☐ True ☐ False

4. A *true* _____ in Christ can be likened to a
    "_____ link," or a "pipe- _____ ,"
    or the "spiritual _____" of our hearts that reaches
    out and grasps Christ.

5. The word "engrafted" speaks to us of what activity done by "tree
    surgeons"? _____

    _____

6. John 15:1–8 likens Christ and His people to a Vine and branches.
    a)Who is the Husbandman? _____
    b) The branches are grafted into the Vine in order to do what?

    _____

    _____

    c) The branches need what in order to bring forth more fruit
    (v. 2)? _____
    d) To abide in the Vine, the branches must have what in them
    (v. 7)? _____

7. Branches that are pruned and destroyed were never really engrafted
    properly. ☐ True ☐ False

8. We are grafted into Christ by (*check one*)
    ☐ a. true faith alone
    ☐ b. faith and works
    ☐ c. faith, works, and church membership

9. Faith is necessary for men to be united to Christ, because faith is possible for all men to have by an act of will. ☐ True   ☐ False

10. According to question 8, we must be regenerated, "born again," by the Spirit of God. What is the correct order of these blessings: *Faith, New Birth, Benefits of Christ, Grafting into Christ?*
    a) _____
    b) _____
    c) _____
    d) _____

11. Write out Ephesians 2:8. _____
    _____
    _____
    _____

❧ The Nature of Faith

Q21. What is true faith?

True faith is not only a sure knowledge, whereby I hold for truth all that God has revealed to us in His Word, but also a hearty trust, which the Holy Ghost works in me by the Gospel, that not only to others, but to me also, forgiveness of sins, everlasting righteousness, and salvation are freely given by God, merely of grace, only for the sake of Christ's merits.

Having seen the *necessity* of faith in question 20, we are now taught *the nature of true faith*. It is very important that we know what the Bible teaches about faith, as there are many wrong ideas about this subject. Many people think that they are Christian believers, when really they are not true believers at all. We must not let Satan deceive us on this matter.

Reformed theologians (Bible scholars) have found in Scripture that there are three kinds of counterfeit or false faith. Before examining question 21, which describes true faith, let us briefly mention those three kinds of false faith, so that we will be on our guard against deceiving ourselves.

1. Historical Faith

A person who has this kind of faith, merely accepts the facts of the Bible as true. He claims that he believes that Jesus lived, that He performed miracles, etc., but he does not really trust in Christ personally, pray to Christ, or seek grace to live for Him. Even the Devil and his evil angels have this kind of faith. See Mark 5:6–10; James 2:19. Many people know the facts of the Bible but are not saved.

2. Temporary Faith

This kind of false faith seems to be true at first, but then, as Jesus explained in the parable of the four soils (Matthew 13:4–23), it lasts for only a little while. The person with a temporary faith, like the seed on the stony place or the seed in the thorny ground, does not bear fruit unto eternal life. Such a person may be happy and joyful to be a convert to Christ (Matthew 13:20), but then when troubles and persecution or the desire for worldly things gets too strong, he leaves his "faith" behind. We see him no more among the people of God.

3. Miraculous Faith

This is a superstitious kind of faith in supernatural things. People with this kind of faith believe in miracles and often say that they have seen a miracle or have experienced one. They only want a "Christianity" which emphasizes present-day miracles such as healing, speaking in tongues, etc. (See Matthew 7:22, 23; Acts 8:18–20; 1 Corinthians 13:2). They want a miracle worker, but are not really interested in the Christ who saves from sin.

In none of these cases does the "believer" really love the Word of God and seriously seek to apply all of it to his life.

Now let us see what *true* faith is, as the Bible describes it. Two things are present in true faith, which is the gift of God's Spirit.

1. "A certain knowledge"

There must be a proper knowledge of the Word of God and especially of the facts of sin, of the Savior, and of Christian service. There can be no salvation if a person lacks essential information about the gospel. Our knowledge must be certain and firm (Hebrews 11:6).

We see here the importance of having good Bible instruction in our church and of doing missionary work outside our church to teach people the Scriptures.

2. "A hearty trust"

The next step, after being convinced by the Holy Spirit that the Word of God is true, is to *personally commit ourselves* to this truth. We must, from our hearts, personally surrender ourselves to the Lord and personally ask Him to forgive us our sins and give us His righteousness. True faith involves personal commitment. The Holy Spirit works this hearty trust "*in me.*"

One of the greatest examples in the Bible of this true faith is Abraham. Romans 4:20–22 tells us that Abraham (1) "did not waver at the promise of God through unbelief." He had a firm knowledge of God's promise, and (2) "being fully convinced that what He had promised, He was able to perform"—Abraham heartily trusted God to keep His promise to him even to the point of attempting to sacrifice his son Isaac on an altar.

The personal *benefits* of this true faith are also listed in our question: (1) forgiveness of sins; (2) everlasting righteousness; (3) eternal salvation. The *basis* for receiving these benefits is not our faith (see Q61), but (1) the free grace of God and (2) the merits of Christ. Do *you* have this true faith and this eternal salvation? If you are assured of it, give thanks to God!

Questions on Number 21

1. Everybody who says he is a Christian believer really does have true, saving faith in Christ. ☐ True   ☐ False

2. Name the three counterfeit "faiths" which are mistaken for true faith.

   a) _____

   b) _____

   c) _____

3. If a person should say, "Sure, I'm a Christian. I've been through Catechism and learned all that stuff," he might have only what kind of faith? _____

4. What do you think of the common saying that it does not matter what religious teachings you believe, just so long as you are sincere?

   _____

   _____

   _____

5. A true knowledge of Scripture means "I hold _____
   _____that _____ in His Word."

6. Since a correct knowledge of Scripture is so necessary for a true faith, I should choose the following activities (*check all that apply*):

☐ a. Sunday School

☐ b. TV program instead of Midweek Bible Study

☐ c. visiting friends instead of attending Youth Fellowship

☐ d. the Peace Corps

☐ e. Christian missions

☐ f. playing on the internet

☐ g. the daily reading of God's Word

7. "A hearty trust" means (*check one*):

☐ a. personal commitment ☐ d. temporary faith

☐ b. some interest ☐ e. joining the church

☐ c. faith but not obedience

8. True faith in Christ is (*check one*):

☐ a. easy for most people

☐ b. rather difficult for many people

☐ c. impossible apart from the working of the Holy Spirit in us.

9. *True faith* is always very strong and never has any doubts.

☐ True ☐ False ▶ *Explain:* _____

_____

_____

10. Write out John 20:31. _____

_____

_____

_____

_____

_____

❧ *The Content of Faith*

Q22. What, then, is necessary for a Christian to believe?

All that is promised us in the Gospel, which the articles of our catholic, undoubted Christian faith teach us in sum.

This last question on the place of faith in redemption deals with the *content of true Christian faith.* The "certain knowledge" referred to in question 21 includes all the truth contained in the Apostles' Creed, here spoken of as the "Articles of our catholic, undoubted Christian Faith."

True faith is based upon the Word of God, particularly the great truths of Creation, Sin, Redemption, and Judgment, which we call the Gospel. These things are all mentioned in the Creed.

It is interesting that our Catechism does not use the expression "Apostles' Creed." Perhaps the reason it does not is because at the time of the Reformation, the Roman Catholic Church taught that the Apostles themselves had written it. This, of course, is not true. Rather, this creed was gradually developed in the first centuries of the Christian Church as a baptismal confession. When a person was baptized, the minister would ask, "Do you believe in God the Father Almighty?" The person being baptized would answer, "I believe in God the Father Almighty." There were also questions and answers about Christ the Son of God and about the Holy Spirit. We can see how this "creed" (from the Latin *credo* which means "I believe") came from the baptismal formula in Matthew 28:19.

Notice four things about this creed:

1. It is "catholic."

This creed is catholic (universal) in that all Christian churches hold to it. It is the faith of God's people in all ages.

2. It is "undoubted."

That is, the truths of this creed may not be questioned or doubted if one wishes to call himself a Christian believer. It is clearly based on the Word of God, which is truth.

3. It is "Christian."

This creed teaches the fundamental truths of Christianity. Christianity is first of all a system of beliefs, and apart from these truths there is no true Christianity.

4. It is a "Faith."

All religion is based on a faith, or commitment of the heart which directs the life. Indeed, all of life issues from the faith of the heart. Even the non-Christian has a basic faith in his heart. But it is a mistaken and misdirected faith in false gods. Our faith is in the Triune God of Scripture. And our Christian faith is manifested by walking in covenant fellowship with our Redeemer-King, who says, "If you love Me, keep My commandments" (John 14:15).

Remember, the Reformed Church in the U.S. is committed to the Apostles' Creed as interpreted by the Heidelberg Catechism. Do you know the twelve articles of this creed? And when you recite this creed, is it really the faith of your heart?

Questions on Number 22

1. What is necessary for a Christian to believe? _____

   _____

   _____

   _____

2. This question tells us the _____ of true faith. In
   short, it is the great _____ of the _____ of
   God: Creation, _____ , Redemption, and _____

   _____ .

3. The Apostles' Creed must surely be believed because it was written
   personally by the Apostles. ☐ True   ☐ False

4. What connection, if any, does Matthew 28:19 have with the
   Apostles' Creed? _____

   _____

   _____

   _____

5. "Creed" comes from the Latin word _____ ,
   which means _____

6. What are the four characteristics of the religion of the Apostles'
   Creed?

   a) _____

   b) _____

   c) _____

   d) _____

7. We should avoid calling our faith "catholic," as we do not belong to
   the Roman Catholic Church. ☐ True   ☐ False

   ▶ *Explain:* _____

   _____

   _____

   _____

   _____

   _____

8. Match the following:

    I believe   baptismal formula

    catholic   a system of beliefs and a Christ-centered life

    Matthew 28:19   creed

    Christianity   believed by all

9. Every person in the world has a faith in his heart which directs his life. ☐ True   ☐ False

10. Write out Romans 6:17. _____

    _____

    _____

    _____

    _____

    _____

❦ *The Apostles' Creed*

Q23. What are these articles?

I believe in **God the Father**, almighty, maker of heaven and earth. And in **Jesus Christ**, His only begotten Son, our Lord; who was conceived by the Holy Ghost, born of the virgin Mary, suffered under Pontius Pilate, was crucified, dead and buried; He descended into hell; the third day He rose from the dead; He ascended into heaven, and sitteth at the right hand of God the Father almighty, from thence He shall come to judge the living and the dead. I believe in the **Holy Ghost**, the Holy Catholic Church, the communion of saints, the forgiveness of sins, the resurrection of the body, and the life everlasting.

This question gives us the twelve articles of the Apostles' Creed. We repeat again that this creed was not written by the Apostles, nor by any one man, but, rather, was gradually formed as additional articles were added to the three basic articles on the Trinity. One phrase, "He descended into hell," was added in the sixth or seventh century A.D. Most of the articles of this Creed were put together by the third or fourth century.

Some "Fundamentalist" Christians use the expression "No creed but Christ," and they reject such creeds as the Apostles' Creed and the Heidelberg Catechism. They say that they want only the person of Christ and the Bible, not a man-made creed. What should one say to their argument?

We should reply to these people that a creed is simply a statement of belief as to what the Bible teaches about God and salvation. The motto, "No creed but Christ" is actually a creed itself—it is a statement of one's faith. But what a poor creed it is, as it does not tell us anything *about* Christ. And Jesus Himself asked His disciples: "What do you think about the Christ? Whose Son is He?" (Matthew 22:42). As a matter of fact, there may be several early "confessions of faith" put into the Scriptures by the Apostles. 1 Timothy 3:16 was originally an early Christian hymn or confession. It begins, "And, confessedly, great...." ("Without controversy" is a poor translation).

A biblical creed, carefully developed from the teachings of Scripture, serves the following important purposes:

1. A creed helps to unite believers.

Those who have the same faith declare that faith to one another by means of their common creed.

2. A creed is a standard of belief for a church.

It becomes a test of doctrine for both those in the church and those who wish to enter the church.

3. A creed helps to preserve the truth for the following generations.

We have received a precious treasure of faith *from* others, and we must pass it on *to* others.

4. A creed is a useful tool for teaching the faith of the church.

We must ever remember that creeds are man-made, but they are made by holy men who with the aid of the Holy Spirit have carefully studied the Bible to find out what it really teaches. Creeds may be changed by the church, but only after the most careful study by all the church.

The Apostles' Creed, since it is made up of expressions from the Scripture has stood the test of time, and has been confessed by the churches for about fifteen centuries. Any "church" or "Christian" who would refuse to confess this creed is not Christian!

But to confess this creed only with the mouth and *not* from the heart is not Christian either! Is your confession *Christian?*

Questions on Number 23

1. The present form of the Apostles' Creed has how many articles?

   _____

2. Which phrase was the last one added? _____

   _____

3. When were most of the articles in use by the Christian Church?

    _____

4. The common motto: "No creed but Christ," is
    (*check all that apply*):
    ☐ a. perfectly proper
    ☐ b. only a man-made creed
    ☐ c. a wrong view of the Christian faith.

5. A creed is simply a statement of one's understanding and faith in
    God and the gospel. ☐ True ☐ False

6. Give four uses of a creed by the church:
    a) _____

    _____

    b) _____

    _____

    c) _____

    _____

    d) _____

    _____

7. The Reformed, the Lutheran, and the Roman Catholic churches all
    use the Apostles' Creed and interpret it in the same way.
    ☐ True   ☐ False

8. A creed, or confession, of a church may never be changed or added
    to, because it is as perfect as Scripture itself. ☐ True   ☐ False

9. A person should be admitted into the membership of a Reformed
    Church if he pays his "dues," even if he refuses to accept our
    confession, the Heidelberg Catechism, as true. ☐ True   ☐ False

10. Everyone who repeats the Apostles' Creed in church is a born-again
    Christian. ☐ True   ☐ False

11. Write out 1 Timothy 3:16 in the correct translation:

    _____

    _____

    _____

_____

_____

_____

❧ Trinitarian Division of the Creed

Q24. How are these Articles divided?

Into three parts: the first is of God the Father and our creation; the second, of God the Son and our redemption; the third, of God the Holy Ghost and our sanctification.

Questions 24 through 58 give us a thorough explanation of the twelve articles of the Apostles' Creed. Questions 24 and 25 give us the outline of the Creed and show us that it is based on the Triune God. The Christian's basic confession is that the true and living God is a Trinity: Father, Son, and Holy Spirit. This God is the source of creation, redemption, and sanctification.

The truth of the Trinity is the most basic truth of all. Unless we understand who God is, we shall never know the truth properly about anything else. The Triune God is the basic reality, and all other truths must be seen as coming from God.

The Creed is divided into three parts, one each for the Father, the Son, and the Holy Spirit. You will note that the longest section is devoted to the Son (Articles 2 through 7) and there is only one short article on the Holy Spirit: "I believe in the Holy Spirit" (Article 8).

The Catechism, however, properly teaches that Articles 8 through 12 also come under the work of the Holy Spirit. So, actually, the section about the Father is the shortest of the Creed:

The 12 articles are as follows:

"God the Father and our creation"

1. *I believe in God the Father, Almighty, Maker of heaven and earth.*

"God the Son and our redemption"

2. *And in Jesus Christ, His only-begotten Son our Lord,*

3. *Who was conceived by the Holy Spirit, born of the Virgin Mary,*

4. *Suffered under Pontius Pilate, was crucified, dead and buried; He descended into hell;*

5. *The third day He arose from the dead:*

6. *He ascended into heaven, and sitteth at the right hand of God the Father Almighty:*

7. *From thence He shall come to judge the living and the dead.*

"God the Holy Spirit and our sanctification"

8. *I believe in the Holy Spirit;*

9. *The holy catholic church, the communion of saints;*

10. *The forgiveness of sins;*

11. *The resurrection of the body;*

12. *And the life everlasting.*

The order of the three Persons of the Trinity is not that of worth or dignity. As the next question and question 53 teach, the three Persons are One God, co-equal and co-eternal. But the *works* of God are always *from* the Father, *through* the Son, and *by* the Holy Spirit. None of the Persons ever acts independently from the other two.

Questions on Number 24

1. Questions 24 and 25 give an _____

   _____

   and _____questions in the Catechism are
   devoted to explaining the Apostles' Creed.

2. The creed has _____ main sections, one each for the_____
   Persons of the Godhead. There are _____ articles.

3. What is the basic truth of all knowledge? _____

   _____

4. The longest section of the Creed is devoted to _____
   The shortest section is devoted to _____.

5. Match these:

   Holy Spirit   Redemption

   The Father   Sanctification

   The Son   Creation

6. Write out the ninth article: _____
   _____
   _____

7. Which articles refer to the work of the Holy Spirit? _____

8. The order of Father, Son and Holy Spirit is the order of greatness.
   That is, the Father is greater than the Son and the Son is greater than
   the Holy Spirit. ☐ True ☐ False

9. The Father always works _____ the Son and _____
   _____ the Holy Spirit.

10. Write out 1 Peter 1:2. _____
    _____
    _____
    _____
    _____

❧ *God the Trinity*

Q25. Since there is but one Divine Being, why do you speak of three persons: Father, Son, and Holy Ghost?

Because God has so revealed Himself in His Word, that these three distinct persons are the one, true, eternal God.

The basis of our Christian Faith is the Triune God, and this fact underlies the Apostles' Creed. When we think about the true God who has revealed Himself in nature and in Scripture, we are faced with a mysterious Being.

The gods of the pagans are quite simple gods, not too different from man himself, and are often more sinful than man himself! But the true God is so great and glorious, so powerful and wise and just, that we are soon blinded by His greatness and majesty. Isaiah asked the question "To whom then will you liken God? Or what likeness will you compare to Him?" (Isaiah 40:18) The Apostle Paul speaks of God—including the Son—"Who alone has immortality, dwelling in unapproachable light, whom no man has seen or can see, to whom be honor and everlasting power. Amen" (1 Timothy 6:16).

No, we cannot search out God; we can only bow before Him in Jesus Christ and worship. "Oh the depth of the riches both of the wisdom and knowledge of God! How unsearchable *are* His judgments, and His ways past finding out!" (Romans 11:33).

We cannot now present a thorough discussion of the attributes of God, but the main thing we must learn here is that God is a Trinity.

There are especially two things that we must believe about God's nature.

1. God is One.

Both Old and New Testaments teach that there is only one true and everlasting God. See Deuteronomy 6:4; Mark 12:29; 1 Timothy 2:5. (Heathen people believe in many gods. This is called polytheism: *poly* = many; *theism* = gods.) God is one in His nature; He is pure Spirit, not having a body and parts. He is *one* in His purpose and will and cannot change.

2. God is Three Persons.

Here we have further mystery. In the one God there are three Persons: Father, Son, and Holy Spirit. A "person" is an "I," someone who can speak to others and listen to others. God can speak to Himself in three ways: The Father can speak to the Son and to the Holy Spirit. The Son can speak to the Father and to the Holy Spirit. And the Spirit can speak to the Father and to the Son. The three Persons of the Trinity have forever enjoyed this Divine fellowship with each other as the One God.

Now the Triune *(tri* = three, *une* = one) God is mysterious to us. We do not understand how one God can be three Persons. Why, then, do we believe it? And why, then, does the Apostles' Creed affirm it? The answer is simply that the Bible teaches this about God. God speaks of Himself in the plural (more than one) in the first chapter of the Bible (Genesis 1:26), as well as in other passages (Isaiah 6:3; 48:16).

The New Testament gives us a fuller understanding of God as Father, Son and Holy Spirit, each of Whom is a Person; but altogether they are only one God. Read Matthew 3:16-17; Matthew 28:19; John 8:19; 10:30, 33; Acts 5:3-4; 20:28; 1 Corinthians 13:14; 1 Peter 1:2.

It follows from this proof of the Trinity that Modernists, Jehovah's Witnesses, Mormons, and other cultists who deny the Trinity do not worship the God of the Bible. They have a false god—1 John 2:23; 2 John 9.

To deny the Trinity is to deny the most basic fact of the Bible and to believe in Him is to believe the most important truth of the Bible and to live in Him Who gave it.

Questions on Number 25

1. The reason Christians believe in the God of Scripture is that He is such a simple God to understand. ☐ True   ☐ False

2. If God is a mysterious Being, it follows that we cannot really know Him enough to have fellowship with Him. ☐ True ☐ False

3. The doctrine of the Trinity is (check all that apply):
   ☐ a. a questionable doctrine
   ☐ b. the basic Christian truth
   ☐ c. a doctrine that divides true Christianity from false religion

4. The biblical doctrine of the Trinity includes two basic truths which we take by faith in Scripture. They are these:
   a) _____
   b) _____

5. The doctrine of the Trinity is a mystery to us because we do not understand how one God can really be three Gods. ☐ True ☐ False

6. Match the following:

   The Father is God   John 1:1

   The Son is God   1 Corinthians 3:16

   The Holy Spirit is God   Colossians 1:3

7. What does the word "triune" mean? _____
   _____

8. The doctrine of a Triune God is (*check all that apply*):
   ☐ a. clearly revealed in the O.T.
   ☐ b. hinted at in the O.T.
   ☐ c. more clearly revealed in the N.T. than in the O.T.

9. We may consider other people to be Christians who say they believe in God, even though they do not accept the teaching that Jesus is actually God. ☐ True ☐ False

10. Write out 2 Corinthians 13:14. _____
    _____
    _____
    _____
    _____

🕯 *God's Work of Creation and Providence*

Q26. What do you believe when you say: "I believe in God the Father Almighty, Maker of heaven and earth"?

That the eternal Father of our Lord Jesus Christ, who of nothing made heaven and earth with all that in them is, who likewise upholds and governs the same by His eternal counsel and providence, is for the sake of Christ, His Son, my God and my Father, in whom I so trust, as to have no doubt that He will provide me with all things necessary for body and soul; and further, that whatever evil He sends upon me in this troubled life, He will turn to my good; for He is able to do it, being Almighty God, and willing also, being a faithful Father.

Questions 26, 27 and 28 explain the first article of the Creed: "I believe in God the Father Almighty, Maker of heaven and earth." This article speaks of God, especially the Father, as the Almighty Creator (Maker) of all things, and also the Father of Christ and our Father.

God the Father is "Father" in three ways, according to Scripture and our Catechism.

1. God is the Father of Creation.

When the Creed speaks of the Father creating all things, it means the entire Godhead: Father, Son, and Holy Spirit. Sometimes the Scriptures mean all three Persons when they speak of God as "Father."

The doctrine of creation is a basic doctrine of Christianity; for apart from this doctrine there is no Christianity. Yet, today, there are many who deny it. Creation means that all things came into existence by the Word of God (Psalm 33:6; Hebrews 11:3). To "create" means "to make something out of nothing." Only the Almighty power of God can truly create.

Only in the Bible do we find the truth of the *origin* of all things. Apart from a belief in Genesis, chapters one and two, which give the creation story, men must believe that all things came from chance and that matter is eternal. But this theory explains nothing. It is simply a false *religious* belief.

Many people hold to the doctrine of *biological evolution,* that is, that all life (plant, animal, and human) gradually developed out of some simple form of life which appeared by accident many thousands or millions or billions of years ago! This theory is taught as fact in almost every school textbook in our public schools today, and even in many churches. But this is a lie, and Christians must reject it and protest that it is anti-Scriptural.

2. God is the Father of Jesus Christ.

The first Person of the Trinity is called the Father, and the second Person is called the Son in Scripture. There is a *procession of life* in the Trinity. The Son's life comes from the Father. This is why the Son is called the "only-begotten Son" (John 1:14, 18; 3:16; see Q33 of the Catechism). The Holy Spirit's life comes from both the Father and the Son. Christ is the eternal, natural Son of God, having no beginning or ending.

3. God is the Father of Believers.

The Father of creation and the Father of Jesus Christ also calls Himself our "heavenly Father." We are not sons of God as Christ is, but, rather, we are sons by adoption. The Modernists, however, say that Jesus and all mankind are sons of God in exactly the same way.

This question emphasizes the Fatherhood of God to *believers,* as God is *not* the Father of Satan's children (John 8:44). As our gracious God and Father through Christ, He (1) "provides me with all things necessary for body and soul;" and (2) "turns all evil into good for me." Only the Almighty God who created all things can control them for our good and His own glory.

Let us never be afraid of anything in God's creation, but rather let us worship the Creator and serve Him only.

Questions on Number 26

1. Questions _____ explain the _____ article of the Creed which explains the _____ Person of the Godhead (*fill in the blanks*).

2. The Heavenly Father is "Father" in three ways. They are the following:

   a) _____

   _____

   b) _____

   _____

   c) _____

   _____

3. The first Person of the Trinity is the only Person of the Trinity who was active in creating the universe. ☐ True　☐ False

4. God created the heavens and the earth out of the basic chemicals and energy which have always existed. ☐ True　☐ False

5. What do the following words mean?
    a)Almighty _____

    _____

    b) Create _____

    _____

    c) "Eternal counsel" _____

    _____

    d) "Troubled life" _____

    _____

6. A Christian can believe both the doctrine of Creation and the theory
    of evolution at the same time. ☐ True   ☐ False
    ▶ *Explain:* _____

    _____

7. God the Father is the Father of Christ and our Father in exactly the
    same way. ☐ True   ☐ False
    ▶ *Explain:* _____

    _____

8. Since God created all men, He is the "heavenly Father" of all men.
    ☐ True   ☐ False

9. As our heavenly Father, what two things does God do for us,
    according to this question?
    a) _____

    _____

    b) _____

    _____

10. Write out Colossians 1:16. _____

    _____

    _____

    _____

    _____

    _____

❧ *The Providence of God*

Q27. What do you understand by the providence of God?

The almighty, everywhere present power of God, whereby, as it were by His hand, He still upholds heaven and earth with all creatures, and so governs them that herbs and grass, rain and drought, fruitful and barren years, meat and drink, health and sickness, riches and poverty, indeed, all things come not by chance, but by His fatherly hand.

Questions 27 and 28 deal with the doctrine of God's *providence,* which is closely related to the doctrine of creation. In creating the world, God caused all things (other than Himself) to come into being. Creation was a once-for-all series of acts in six days. The providence (from the Latin *providere* = "to see before") of God refers to His upholding, governing, and maintaining the work of creation. Providence is the continuous working of God's power in all things to keep them from vanishing back into nothingness! Providence is, therefore, as important as creation itself.

The providence of God also includes sin and evil. Sin and evil could not exist if God did not also include them in His eternal plan and use them to bring glory to Himself. But though sin is included in God's decree and providence (Amos 3:6), we must never forget that God always *hates* sin (Deuteronomy 25:16).

No accidents or chance happenings occur in a universe that is governed in its every detail by the providence of God. The vast creation, from the starry heavens to the smallest atom—and especially our lives— are directed not by chance, nor by fate, nor luck, nor the stars, but by an Almighty Person—our Heavenly Father (Matthew 10:29–31)!

If God created all things in six days and then ceased from this activity, we may ask: What are the *miracles*—are they acts of creation or acts of providence? It would seem that in the type of miracles wherein God brought matter into being that did not previously exist, such as the oil for the widows (1 Kings 17:8ff; 2 Kings 4:1ff) or the food for the 5,000 (John 6), we have additional acts of creation by Almighty power. Also, when we speak of the "laws of nature" (such as gravity, etc.), we must never forget that God is the Creator of those laws and He can supersede them whenever He so pleases. We may not expect miracles today, however, but we should expect God to bless us by His loving providence (Matthew 6:33; 1 Timothy 4:8).

Questions on Number 27

1. Questions 27 and 28 teach the _____ of God.

2. Providence comes from the Latin *providere,* which means

_____

_____

3. Providence means that (*check one*):
   ☐ a. God is still creating.
   ☐ b. God's power is operating in some things.
   ☐ c. God upholds and governs all things moment by moment that
   they may serve His glory.

4. What would happen to any object of creation if God should suddenly
   withdraw His providence from it? _____

   _____

5. What kinds of things do people speak about when they do not
   believe in the providence of God? _____

   _____

   _____

6. The sinful acts of Satan and men are not included in God's overall
   plan or His providence because God hates these things.
   ☐ True   ☐ False

7. Miracles are impossible now because they are contrary to the laws of
   nature. ☐ True   ☐ False

8. If "barren years," "sickness," and "poverty" come not by chance but
   by God's Fatherly hand (*check one*):
   ☐ a. we should not try to avoid these things
   ☐ b. we should receive them with thankfulness
   ☐ c. we know God hates us when He sends them to us.

9. God's providence and the laws of nature are contrary to each other.
   That is, if one is true, the other cannot be true. ☐ True ☐ False

10. Write out Acts 14:17. _____

    _____

    _____

    _____

❧ *The Comfort of God's Providence*

Q28. What does it profit us to know that God created, and by His providence upholds all things?

That we may be patient in adversity, thankful in prosperity, and for what is future have good confidence in our faithful God and Father, that no creature shall separate us from His love, since all creatures are so in His hand, that without His will they cannot so much as move.

This last question on the first article of the Creed directs us to the *comfort* that we may have in knowing that God is the sovereign Preserver, Provider, and Controller of all things. It makes a great difference in our lives whether we believe in the providence of God or not, whether we believe that our Heavenly Father rules all things in our lives or not.

We are here taught to develop three Christian attitudes towards God's providence:

1. *We must be patient in adversity.*

2. *We must be thankful in prosperity.*

3. *We must have good confidence in the future.*

The same God who created us and has redeemed us will never fail us nor forsake us. His providence is always directed to our eternal good and His eternal glory.

"No *creature* shall separate us from His love." By "creature" is meant any created thing, living or non-living; animal, human or angel. Nothing can even move, whether the sun in the heavens or the thoughts in a man's mind, apart from our heavenly Father's will. What a blessed comfort this is—especially in deep distress, trouble, or sorrow.

But we are here faced with a problem. Do living, *thinking* creatures, such as men, have a will? Do you make choices and decisions? Of course you do! Then are the will of God and the will of man independent of, and separated from, each other?

The answer is NO. God's secret will, or will of predestination, and providence controls all other created wills, so that God's will is always done in every act of man's will. Yes, even when men sin, and when they murdered the Son of God, they were fulfilling the will of God (Acts 2:23; 4:26, 28).

This is a mystery to us, but "without His will they cannot so much as move." See also Proverbs 19:21; Acts 17:28a. But there is another expression of the will of God, also: His *revealed* will, or the will of His commandments. And this second will of God is *never* kept by sinful man. So we must understand that there is a double will of God, His *predestinating* will, and His *revealed* will, and we cannot fully understand their mysterious relationship to each other (see Deuteronomy 29:29).

Questions on Number 28

1. It is a comfort for the ☐ *believer* ☐ *unbeliever* to know that God completely controls all things. (*check one*)

2. The providence of God is mysterious, and sometimes even the best Christians are cursed by God in His providence. ☐ True ☐ False

3. What does the Catechism mean by "creature"? _____

   _____

   _____

4. If God does not control all things at all times, then some other power would be equal with God. ☐ True ☐ False

5. Match the following:

   thankful   in adversity

   good confidence   in prosperity

   patient   in the future

6. We ought to thank God for health, prosperity, and good crops, but not for drought, barren years, sickness, and poverty.
   ☐ True ☐ False

7. The two wills of God are:
   a) _____
   b) _____

8. We ☐ *can* ☐ *cannot* understand how they are both true. There is ☐ *mystery* ☐ *no mystery* to this subject.

9. The *secret* will of God is the same as
   ☐ a. His revealed will

☐ b. His predestinating will

☐ c. His will of providence

10. Men are *not* responsible for their sinful actions, for even man's sin is included in the secret will and providence of God. ☐ True ☐ False

11. Many are telling us that all life on earth may be destroyed by nuclear war or global warming. Can man thus destroy the future which God has planned for His Church? ☐ Yes ☐ No

▶ *Explain:* _____

_____

_____

12. Write out Romans 8:28, 35. _____

_____

_____

_____

_____

_____

_____

❦ *The Name of Jesus*

Q29. Why is the Son of God called "Jesus," that is, Savior?

Because He saves us from our sins, and because salvation is not to be sought or found in any other.

Questions 29 through 52 in the Catechism explain Articles 2 through 7 of the Apostles' Creed. These articles deal with *God the Son and our redemption.* The Catechism divides this subject into three parts:

1. *Christ's names and titles 29-34*

2. *Christ's five steps of humiliation 35-44*

3. *Christ's four steps of exaltation 45-52*

We shall now begin our study of Christ's names.

The Bible gives *many* names to God and Christ. Some are taken from the *heavenly bodies*—"Morning Star," "Sun of Righteousness" (Revelation 22:16; Malachi 4:2). Some are taken from the *plant* kingdom—"Rose of Sharon," "Lily of the Valley" (Song of Solomon 2:1). Some are from the *animal* kingdom—"Lamb of God," "Lion of Judah" (John 1:29; Revelation 5:5). Many more such names could be given. All these names for our Savior are meaningful and describe the richness and greatness of His Person and Work.

The most common names for the Savior are "Lord," "Jesus," and "Christ." In this question, the name Jesus is explained. Jesus is the New Testament form of the Old Testament name Joshua, which means "the Lord saves." The angel told Joseph (Matthew 1:21) that Mary's child should be given the *personal name Jesus,* because "He will save His people from their sins." Whenever you hear or read the name "Jesus," remember it means that your salvation from sin is only by the Son of God. Just as the Old Testament Joshua led Israel into the promised land of Canaan, so the New Testament "Joshua"—Jesus—leads us to the heavenly Canaan. Jesus is the only Savior and He is the complete Savior as the next question will teach us.

Questions on Number 29

1. Beginning with question 29 and extending through question 52 we have an explanation of which articles of the Creed? _____

2. What do these articles deal with? _____

   _____

3. Questions 29 through 34 explain the most common _____ of Christ.

4. The various names for Jesus are "meaningful and show the

   _____

   _____

5. The name "Jesus" means " _____ " and comes from the Old Testament name _____.

6. "Why is the Son of God called Jesus, that is, Savior?" _____

   _____

   _____

7. Jesus is the *personal name* of Christ, just as some boys are called "Charles" and some girls "Alice." ☐ True ☐ False

8. Which people did the angel say Jesus would save from their sins (Matthew 1:21)? _____

9. Does this mean everybody or the chosen ones? _____

10. The name "Jesus" indicates that: (*check one*)

☐ a. God saves us   ☐ c. Israel saves us

☐ b. the O.T. Joshua saves us   ☐ d. we must help save ourselves

11. Write out Acts 4:12. _____

_____

_____

_____

_____

❧ Christ is the Only Mediator

Q30. Do those also believe in the only Savior Jesus, who seek their salvation and welfare from "saints," themselves, or anywhere else?

No, although they make their boast of Him, yet in their deeds they deny the only Savior Jesus; for either Jesus is not a complete Savior, or they who by true faith receive this Savior, must have in Him all that is necessary to their salvation.

This question gives further explanation of the name Jesus—"The Lord Saves." To say that Jesus saves means that Jesus is the *only* Savior. There are many today, just as when the Catechism was written, who claim to believe in Jesus as Savior, but who *deny that He is the only Savior.* The Roman Catholics add the "saints" to Jesus, especially the Virgin Mary, and they pray to these people as well as to Jesus.

Others, such as *Arminians* (those who follow the teachings of James Arminius, a Dutch heretic in the 16th century), add their own "free will" to Jesus and say that Jesus cannot save except they themselves help Him by using their own *natural faith and free will.*

Many others also trust in their "good works" and church membership to save them. We call them Legalists, as they believe that salvation is obtained by belief in Christ and by keeping the law. The epistle to the Galatians was written to oppose legalism (See Galatians 2:16–21).

All these people are really *denying* Jesus as the *only* Savior and the *complete* Savior. Ask your Lord to help you trust in Him alone for all that is necessary for your salvation. Even your *faith* must be a gift to you from Jesus (Ephesians 2:8).

Questions on Number 30

1. This question is a further explanation of what?

    _____

2. Everyone who says that he believes in Jesus really does believe that Jesus is the only and the complete Savior. ☐ True ☐ False

3. Do you think it is possible for a person even to boast (brag) about Jesus and, yet, in deeds, deny Him as the only Savior? ☐ Yes ☐ No
    ▶ *Explain:* _____

    _____

4. The Catechism says that to have Jesus as Savior, we must "by true faith _____ "
    and "have _____
    our _____ ."

5. We can think of three types of people who call themselves "Christians" but who deny that Jesus is the complete Savior. They are (*Check three*):
    ☐ a. Legalists   ☐ e. Baptists
    ☐ b. Calvinists   ☐ f. Arminians
    ☐ c. Roman Catholics   ☐ g. Reformed
    ☐ d. Presbyterians

6. What is an "Arminian"? _____

    _____

7. Name a famous "saint" to whom Roman Catholics pray:

    _____

8. True faith in Christ comes from: (*check one*).
    ☐ a. our natural ability   ☐ b. from the Holy Spirit

9. Do you think it is possible for a person in a Reformed Church to boast about Jesus and yet *not* trust in Jesus *alone* and *completely* for his salvation? _____
    ▶ *Explain:* _____

    _____

10. Write out Colossians 2:10. _____

_____

_____

_____

❧ Christ the Anointed

Q31. Why is He called "Christ," that is, Anointed?

Because He is ordained of God the Father and anointed with the Holy Ghost to be our chief Prophet and Teacher, who has fully revealed to us the secret counsel and will of God concerning our redemption; and our only High Priest, who by the one sacrifice of His body, has redeemed us, and ever lives to make intercession for us with the Father; and our eternal King, who governs us by His Word and Spirit and defends, and preserves us in the redemption obtained for us.

Questions 31 and 32 explain and apply the name Christ. This name was not given to the Savior by His parents. Rather, this is His *official title* given by God which describes Jesus' offices and duties as Redeemer. (Note: those who rejected Jesus refused to call Him "Christ"—they were looking for another Christ.)

The name "Christ" is from the Greek title *Christos* which means "The Anointed One." In the Old Testament, the Hebrew title is "Messiah." Both "Messiah" (Hebrew) and "Christ" (Greek) mean the same thing—"The Anointed One."

The Catechism teaches us that the Christ—God's Anointed One—has *three* offices to perform: the offices of Prophet, Priest, and King. These were the three main offices instituted by God in the Old Testament. The prophets (such as Moses, Elijah and Isaiah), the priests (such as Aaron and Eli), and the kings (such as David and Solomon) were appointed and anointed by God. The anointing was performed by having oil poured on the head, and it was a picture of the Holy Spirit's filling the person with wisdom and strength for his job.

God gave to Jesus all three offices—Prophet, Priest and King— to fulfill. At Jesus' baptism (Matthew 3:16), He was anointed by the Holy Spirit (who came as a dove) to carry out these three duties. In Jesus Christ, we have God's greatest Prophet, His greatest Priest, and His greatest King, greater than those of the Old Testament.

The Catechism teaches the separate duties of these three offices:

1. As *Prophet*, Jesus fully declared the truth of God to us (John 15:15).

2. As *Priest,* Jesus offered a sacrifice (Himself) and prays for us (Hebrews 7:25–27).

3. As *King,* Jesus rules over us, defends us and preserves us forever (Luke 1:33).

Jesus performed these three offices of the Christ on earth, and He continues to perform them in heaven.

Questions on Number 31

1. The name "Christ" was given to Jesus by:

    ☐ a. His parents   ☐ b. God   ☐ c. men

    It is His ☐ a. *official*   ☐ b. *personal* name.

2. The name "Christ" is the N.T. Greek title for the O.T. Hebrew title

    _____,

    which means _____.

3. In the New Testament, everyone referred to Jesus as "Jesus Christ."

    ☐ True   ☐ False ▶ *Explain:* _____

    _____

4. Check the office (prophet, priest, king) that is found in the following references:

1 Sam. 16:13	☐ prophet	☐ priest	☐ king
Hebrews 8:1	☐ prophet	☐ priest	☐ king
Jeremiah 1:5	☐ prophet	☐ priest	☐ king
1 Timothy 6:15b	☐ prophet	☐ priest	☐ king
Leviticus 8:12	☐ prophet	☐ priest	☐ king
John 4:17–19	☐ prophet	☐ priest	☐ king

5. When was Jesus anointed with the Holy Spirit to do the work of the Christ? _____

6. As our chief Prophet and Teacher, Christ "has _____
    revealed to us the _____ and will of God _____
    our _____."

7. As our High Priest, Christ does two things for us. What are they?

    a) _____

    b) _____

8. What three things does the Catechism mention that Christ does for us as our King?

   a) _____

   b) _____

   c) _____

9. A person may have Christ as his only Savior, but refuse to obey Christ his only King. ☐ True ☐ False

10. Write out John 1:41b. _____

   _____

   _____

   _____

   _____

   _____

❧ *Meaning of the Name "Christian"*

Q32. But why are you called a Christian?

Because by faith I am a member of Christ and thus a partaker of His anointing, in order that I also may confess His Name, may present myself a living sacrifice of thankfulness to Him, and that with a free conscience I may fight against sin and the devil in this life, and hereafter in eternity reign with Him over all creatures.

Would you like to hold an office? Politicians aspire to hold public offices, and will often work very hard in order to get them. But the greatest honor that can be conferred on any man is conferred on the children of God. We have been given the *office* of Christian!

The name "Christian" literally means "a follower of Christ;" and as the name *Christ* was an official title and office, so Christians are those who partake in the offices of Christ because we are partakers of His anointing to office. The name Christian, which has become so significant and important, was originally given to the disciples of Christ by their enemies as a term of reproach and scorn! The term is found only three times in the New Testament (Acts 11:26; 26:28; 1 Peter 4:16). Now we glory in the name and wear it proudly!

Following the three-fold office of Christ (see Q31), we also have the same three-fold office of prophet, priest and king. In reality, Adam, our first parent, was given the three-fold office at his creation. But by his fall, he became a prophet, priest, and king in the service of Satan—*speaking* the lie of the Devil, *consecrating* himself to the Devil's work and *exercising dominion* over the world on behalf of the Devil.

In Christ, our three-fold office is restored. As Christians we are once again prophets, priests, and kings unto God.

1. **As prophets,** we are to confess the Name of Christ and declare His truth to others (Acts 2:17; Romans 10:9; Ephesians 4:25).

2. **As priests,** we are to present ourselves as living sacrifices to Christ and consecrate all that we are and have to the service of God. This includes our talents and our money (Romans 12:1, 2; 1 Peter 2:9).

3. **As kings,** we are to exercise dominion by the Word of God over ourselves, our homes, our churches and society. We are to fight the good fight against sin and the Devil and reign with Christ both now and forever (Genesis 1:28; Romans 8:37; Revelation 1:6; 5:10).

When we begin to grasp the real meaning of being a Christian, life becomes a wonderful, new challenge. How exciting to be the officers of God under the Chief Officer, Jesus Christ! We must never ignore our high calling in Christ, nor act contrary to our holy offices of prophet, priest and king. And for this great task we must depend on the strength and wisdom of the Holy Spirit Who has anointed us (Acts 2:38; 1 John 2:20, 27).

Questions on Number 32

1. Because we are united to Christ by His Holy Spirit and are followers of Him, it is proper that we be called "Christians." ☐ True ☐ False

2. What does "Christian" mean? _____
   _____

3. This name was first given to believers by whom? _____

4. How many times is this name mentioned in the New Testament?
   _____

5. As "prophets" of Christ we are to " _____ Name."

6. To be a Christian prophet, we must tell people the truth even if they do not like to hear it. ☐ True   ☐ False

7. As you "present yourself a living sacrifice of thankfulness" to Christ, you are being a _____ of Christ.

8. To consecrate ourselves to Christ we must: (*check one*)
   ☐ a. serve Christ once in a while when we feel like it

☐ b. give a little of our money to Christ if we have plenty to spare

☐ c. try to be decent citizens but not take our religion too seriously

☐ d. try to attend church meetings if there are no other activities

☐ e. none of these

9. As "kings" of Christ we are expected to take a strong stand and fight for the true Gospel even if others disagree.   ☐ True   ☐ False

10. Write out Revelation 1:6. _____

_____

_____

_____

_____

❧ Christ is the Eternal Son of God

Q33. Why is He called God's "only begotten Son," since we also are the children of God?

Because Christ alone is the eternal, natural Son of God; but we are children of God by adoption, through grace, for His sake.

The third name of the Savior in the Apostles' Creed is "only begotten Son." In this question this name is explained. A father "begets" a child; he gives life to a child. You were "begotten" by your father. The Son of God is said to be "begotten" by the Father (See the Gospel of John 1:14, 18; 3:16). This means that there is the closest possible relationship between God the Father and God the Son. The Son's life comes from the Father. It does *not* mean that the Father is older or greater than the Son. The Son is *eternal* as is the Father. The Son is also the *natural* Son of God; that is, He is of the same Divine Substance and of the same Being as the Father. But the Life of God proceeds *from* the Father *to* the Son and *to* the Spirit. A diagram may help (*see below*).

Though Modernists like to call Jesus the "son of God," they do not mean what the Bible and our Catechism mean; rather, they say that *we are all the sons of God in the same way.* Jesus is like us and we are like Jesus as "sons of God."

The truth is that we are sons only by "adoption," not by nature, as is Jesus. To say that Jesus is "the only begotten Son of God" is to say that Jesus IS God! To say that we are "adopted sons of God" is to say that we are only humans saved by grace and brought into God's family and household.

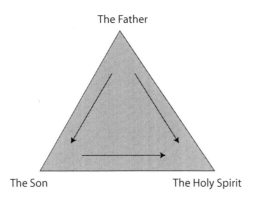

The Father

The Son   The Holy Spirit

How God's Life Flows Among the Three Persons

Questions on Number 33

1. Only God the Father "begat" a son. Human fathers do not "beget" children. ☐ True   ☐ False

2. To say that Jesus is the "only begotten Son of God" is to say that the Father is older than the Son and greater. ☐ True   ☐ False

3. Jesus is the "natural" Son of God. This means that all believers in Christ are the natural sons of God also. ☐ True   ☐ False

4. Give some references where the name "Only Begotten" is used of the Son: _____

    _____

5. To say that Christ is the "eternal, natural Son of God" is to say that He is God. ☐ True   ☐ False

6. Draw a diagram showing how the Life of God flows among the Persons of the Trinity.

7. What group of people today say that Jesus is the "son of God" but deny that He is *actually God?* _____

8. Mere human beings can never be considered "sons of God" in any sense. ☐ True ☐ False ▶ *Explain:* _____

   _____

9. Look up John 1:12 and Romans 8:14–16.
   a) What do you think is meant by adoption into God's family through grace? _____
   b) Who receives this "adoption?" _____
   c) When does it take place? _____

10. Write out Ephesians 1:5–6. _____

   _____

   _____

   _____

   _____

   _____

❧ Christ is the Lord

Q34. Why do you call Him "our Lord"?

Because not with silver or gold, but with His precious blood, He has redeemed and purchased us, body and soul, from sin and from all the power of the devil, to be His own.

The fourth and last title of Christ mentioned in the Creed is here explained, the title "Lord." The title "Lord" is given to one who possesses authority and power over others. Jesus Christ is the *supreme* Lord. He is "Lord of lords and King of kings" (Revelation 17:14; 19:16).

The reason that Jesus is Lord over our bodies and souls is because He has redeemed us from the lordship of our former masters. By our willful disobedience in Adam, we came *under the power* of sin, death, the Devil, and hell, as God's just punishment for our sin.

Now Christ has *redeemed* us, that is, He has purchased our freedom from slavery by paying a ransom price for us—His own precious blood (1 Peter 1:18–19). In the Old Testament, a slave could be freed if a ransom were paid to his master. Our Savior freed us from the slavery of sin and Satan, by paying the greatest ransom, His own life.

By redeeming us with His blood, Jesus made us His servants or slaves. *You can* only include yourself in this phrase *"our* Lord" if you have put your trust in Jesus Christ as your only Lord and Savior. If Christ is your *Lord* then you will not live as unbelievers do, who are still slaves of the Devil. Read again question and answer number one.

Questions on Number 34

1. The "Lordship" of Jesus is not important to us. ☐ True ☐ False

2. When did man become a servant of Satan? _____

3. Man must be a servant of either Satan or Jesus Christ.
   ☐ True ☐ False

4. The Bible pictures our slavery to Satan in which of these Bible stories?
   ☐ a. In Adam and Eve working in the Garden of Eden.
   ☐ b. In the Israelites' toiling for Pharoah in Egypt.
   ☐ c. In the Israelites' building the temple of Solomon.
   ☐ d. In the Israelites' serving the King of Babylon.

5. To "redeem" means
   ☐ a. to sell   ☐ c. to imprison
   ☐ b. to buy back   ☐ d. to punish.

6. What did Jesus pay to redeem us so that *He* could be our Lord and Master? _____
   Give a Bible reference for this: _____

7. "Not with _____ or _____,
   but _____ blood,
   _____ body and soul, _____, to be His own."

8. Because Christ is our Master, we owe Him our (*check all that apply*):
   ☐ a. love   ☐ c. reverence
   ☐ b. obedience   ☐ d. gratitude

9. If we belong to Jesus, to whom do our time, money, talents, and homes belong? _____

10. Write out Titus 2:14. _____

_____

_____

_____

❦ *The Virgin Birth of Christ*

Q35. What is the meaning of "conceived by the Holy Ghost, born of the Virgin Mary"?

That the eternal Son of God, who is and continues true and eternal God, took upon Himself the very nature of man, of the flesh and blood of the Virgin Mary, by the operation of the Holy Ghost; so that He might also be the true seed of David, like unto His brethren in all things, except for sin.

Having studied the four names of Jesus Christ, we now begin a study of the *five steps of Christ's humiliation,* spoken of in Articles 3 and 4 of the Apostles' Creed. They are (1) His birth; (2) His sufferings; (3) His death; (4) His burial; (5) His descent into hell.

By Jesus' "humiliation" is meant his coming from heaven to live in this wicked world and be under the guilt of sin and to suffer its awful consequences. From heaven's glory Jesus went down deeper and deeper into the wrath of God, until at last He suffered the full torment of hell itself.

Questions 35 and 36 explain Article 3 of the Creed, namely, the virgin birth of Jesus: how it happened and why. Matthew 1 and 2 and Luke 1 and 2 tell the story of our Lord's virgin birth in Bethlehem.

The human nature (body and soul) of Jesus was conceived in the womb of Mary by the Holy Spirit. From Mary, then, Jesus received a true human nature and was made like us in every way, except that He had no sin. We learned back in question 16 why Jesus must have a true human nature. Review that question.

Modernists deny the virgin birth of Jesus and say, rather, that Joseph was the flesh-and-blood father of Jesus. But if Jesus had a sinful human father, He, too, would have been born with a sinful nature and so could not be our savior. After Jesus' birth, *then* Mary and Joseph had natural children of their own (John 7:3; Acts 1:14), though the Roman Catholics deny this.

Why is it important that our Lord is "the true seed of David," as the answer states. Does Psalm 132:11 give a clue?

Questions on Number 35

1. The Apostles' Creed, in Articles _____ and _____,
    tells of the _____ steps of Christ's humiliation.

2. What is meant by Jesus' humiliation? _____
    _____

3. Christ was conceived (*check one*):
    ☐ a. by Joseph and Mary
    ☐ b. within Mary by the power of the Holy Spirit
    ☐ c. by Mary alone.

4. When the Son of God became a man, He ceased to be the true and
    eternal God. ☐ True ☐ False

5. Through a miracle by the Holy Spirit within Mary, Jesus
    "took upon _____
    the _____ nature _____."

6. Which Gospels tell us of the conception and birth of Jesus?
    _____

7. What do Modernist ministers teach about the begetting of Jesus, that
    is, who Jesus' father was? _____

8. Why is it necessary that Jesus was conceived by the Holy Spirit and
    born of the Virgin Mary? _____

9. If Mary was of the royal line of David, to what office did her Son
    have a right? _____
    _____

10. Write out Luke 1:35. _____
    _____
    _____
    _____
    _____

❦ *Benefits of Christ's Incarnation*

Q36. What benefit do you receive from the holy conception and birth of Christ?

That He is our Mediator, and with His innocence and perfect holiness covers, in the sight of God, my sin, wherein I was conceived.

Here we learn the *purpose* of Jesus' being conceived in the virgin Mary by the Holy Spirit. It was in order that He might have a perfect human nature. This holy conception brought the Son of God and His *sinless human nature* into a perfect union. The God-Man, Jesus, was thus able to be our Substitute and Mediator, our Savior.

If Jesus had been conceived by Joseph and Mary, He would have been just another human person, corrupted by Adam's sin and deserving of hell. But because He was conceived by the Holy Spirit, He is a Divine Person with a sinless human nature and thus able to be our perfect Savior. His righteousness is imputed to us and our sins are imputed to Him.

To reject the supernatural conception and the virgin birth of Jesus Christ, as the Modernists do, is to reject the sinless Son of God, Who alone can save us from our sin.

The truth of the *incarnation* (God entering human nature) *is* of basic importance not only for our individual salvation but also for human freedom. Here is the explanation: No human institution may now claim to be a god over men's lives, such as godless governments do. Christ alone is both God and man. All human authority comes from Christ and must be obedient to His law. This truth when applied will *limit* all governments and thus protect human freedom. Christ, not man, is the only link between man and God—and no human government may make that claim!

Questions on Number 36

1. In question 36 we learn the _____
    of Jesus' being divinely conceived and born of a virgin.

2. Check the most correct answer:
    ☐ a. The conception of Jesus (made a baby in Mary) was a miracle.
    ☐ b. The birth of Jesus was a miracle.
    ☐ c. Both the conception and birth of Jesus were miracles.

3. In what way was Jesus Christ *not* like us? (see Hebrews 4:15)

4. In what way was Jesus Christ *like* us? _____

_____

5. If Jesus had been begotten by Joseph, He would not have been able to be our Mediator. Why not? _____

_____

_____

6. The human nature of Jesus and the person of the Son of God came from Mary. ☐ True ☐ False

7. Do you think it was important that God chose Joseph to be Jesus' *legal* father? (see Matthew 1:20; Luke 1:27; Luke 2:4) _____

_____

_____

8. What connection, if any, does Isaiah 7:14 have with the birth of Christ? _____

_____

9. How does the Incarnation of our Lord Jesus Christ have a bearing on human government? _____

_____

_____

10. Write out Galatians 4:4–5. _____

_____

_____

_____

_____

_____

❦ *The Sufferings of Christ*

Q37. What do you understand by the word "suffered"?

That all the time He lived on earth, but especially at the end of His life, He bore, in body and soul, the wrath of God against the sin of the whole human race; in order that by His suffering, as the only atoning sacrifice, He might redeem our body and soul from everlasting damnation, and obtain for us the grace of God, righteousness, and eternal life.

Questions 37, 38, and 39 explain the second stage of our Lord's humiliation, namely, His sufferings. With this question we also begin a study of the fourth article of the Apostles' Creed: "Suffered under Pontius Pilate, was crucified, dead and buried; He descended into hell." We shall be dealing with this fourth article of the Creed through question 44.

Our Lord Jesus Christ suffered! All of us know something about suffering. Some people know a great deal about physical suffering, as they lie on beds of pain for many years. Others experience intense mental anguish because of tragedy in their lives; some commit suicide because their suffering is so unbearable.

Our Savior's whole life on earth was spent suffering in His body, and especially in His soul. These sufferings grew greater as He came to the appointed hour of His sacrifice. His soul almost burst in the Garden of Gethsemane (Luke 22:39–46); and His body experienced indescribable torture as He was whipped and then hung on the cross to die with nails through His hands and feet. But Jesus' sufferings were unlike the sufferings of sinful people, who deserve to suffer.

Why did Jesus go through all this suffering: This question gives us the answer:

1. His sufferings were a punishment from God: "The *wrath of God*" was directed against the body and soul of Jesus Christ.

2. His sufferings were the punishment for *our sins,* not His own, because Jesus was sinless. God was punishing Jesus for the sins of all of His elect people. He took our sufferings and death.

The blessed *results* of Jesus' "atoning sacrifice" are:

1. Our complete redemption "from everlasting damnation."

2. The full purchase of "the grace of God, righteousness, and eternal life" for those for whom He died.

One expression in this question needs further explanation: "The whole human race." We have seen many times already in the Catechism that God intends to save only His Church, the elect, and therefore we must not think that Jesus' death is an atoning sacrifice for all men, elect and non-elect alike. "The whole human race" *means all kinds of people in every age.* The rest of the question is clear as to whom Jesus died for—"for us;" that is for those who actually receive the gift of grace, righteousness, and life, but for no others. They must suffer and die for their own sins.

The Arminian theology teaches a universal atonement for every human being, that is, that Christ died for every person. Why is this teaching wrong? What does 1 John 2:2 teach?

Questions on Number 37

1. In questions 37 through 39 we study the _____
    stage of our Lord's _____.

2. When in His life did Jesus suffer? _____
    _____
    _____

3. How did Jesus experience suffering when He was a small baby?
    (see Matthew 2:13-14) _____
    _____

4. What kind of sufferings did Jesus experience in Matthew 4:1-11?
    ☐ a. bodily suffering   ☐ b. spiritual suffering   ☐ c. both

5. Jesus' sufferings in His soul in the Garden of Gethsemane were so
    great that (see Luke 22:44) _____
    _____
    _____.

6. Our answer explains why Jesus' sufferings were extreme in both His
    body and soul. "He bore in _____
    and _____ the _____ of God."

7. What are the two results of Jesus' sufferings and sacrifice for us?
    a) _____
    b) _____

8. The phrase, the "whole human race, " means every human being
    who ever lived and who ever shall live. ☐ True ☐ False.
    ▶ *Explain:* _____
    _____

9. How do the Arminians explain 1 John 2:2? _____
    _____
    _____

    How do *you* explain it? _____
    _____

10. Write out 1 Peter 2:24. _____

_____

_____

_____

❦ *Christ Condemned under Pilate*

Q38. Why did He suffer "under Pontius Pilate" as judge?

That He, being innocent, might be condemned by the temporal judge, and thereby deliver us from the severe judgment of God, to which we were exposed.

The short Apostles' Creed gives the names of only two people besides God: Mary, who gave birth to Jesus, and Pontius Pilate, who sentenced Him to death. Why is this evil man mentioned? The reason is this: Pilate was the official judge who had charge of Jesus' trial when He was falsely accused by the Jews. Now Pilate was appointed by the Caesar (ruler) of Rome, and thus the authority of the world government and the authority of God Himself was behind Pilate's judgment.

First, Pilate, after hearing the false charges against Jesus, declared Him to be just and innocent (Luke 23:4, 14; John 19:4). By the authority of the government of the world Jesus was officially pronounced innocent. *That decision can never be reversed!* Jesus was, indeed, not guilty of any crime. But, secondly, Pilate also delivered Jesus over to the soldiers to be executed as a criminal (Luke 23:24-25). So that same world authority condemned Jesus to death as an innocent man!

All this is very meaningful! *Behind* these actions of the Roman world government stands the authority of God (see Romans 13:1-2). God was declaring, through Pilate, that Jesus was personally innocent! But God, also through Pilate, condemned Jesus to death because He was bearing the sins of God's people. Now Pilate did not know that Jesus was really being condemned by God the Judge, so Pilate's action in turning over the innocent Jesus for death was a wicked crime. In killing Jesus, the world, as represented by the Roman government, was condemning itself to death before God for killing the holy Son of God.

In Jesus' strange trial, the *church* was being saved from the Judgment of God by the innocent Jesus being condemned; and the *world* was being condemned for condemning Jesus!

Questions on Number 38

1. Who was Pontius Pilate? (Luke 3:1) _____

_____

2. What was the official verdict of Pilate as judge as to Jesus' guilt or
    innocence? _____

    _____

3. If Jesus was pronounced innocent, then what should Pilate have
    done as Jesus' judge? _____

    _____

4. Pilate condemned himself and the whole world when he executed an
    innocent man. ☐ True ☐ False

5. Behind Pilate's official actions stood the Judge of all men.
    Who is He? _____

6. It was necessary that Jesus die as a condemned criminal because God
    was executing Him for ☐ His own sins; ☐ our sins.

7. If Jesus had died by sickness, old age, or an accidental death, rather
    than as a condemned criminal, He could not "deliver us from the
    severe judgment of God to which we were exposed." ☐ True ☐ False
    ▶ *Explain:* _____

    _____

8. The trial of Jesus was the strangest trial man has ever seen.
    ☐ True ☐ False ▶ *Explain:* _____

    _____

    _____

9. How did our Lord suffer under Pontius Pilate? _____

    _____

    _____

10. Write out Acts 4:27–28. _____

    _____

    _____

    _____

🔥 The Crucifixion of Christ

Q39. Is there anything more in His having been "crucified" than if He had suffered some other death?

Yes, for thereby I am assured that He took upon Himself the curse which lay upon me, because the death of the cross was accursed of God.

This question further explains the idea presented in question 38, namely, that Christ's death had to be by official execution—crucifixion—and not an ordinary kind of death. Jesus died a horrible death by crucifixion, the Roman form of capital punishment.

Though Jesus died by Roman crucifixion (being nailed to a cross made of two pieces of wood), His execution was also an *Old Testament* curse. In Deuteronomy 21:22-23 we read how a criminal's dead body (the Jewish form of execution was stoning) was to be hung on a pole or tree as a shame, and to warn the others that this person died as a law-breaker and as one cursed of God.

So Jesus' body on the cross was an *object of shame,* showing that the curse of God was upon Him. Jesus took the full curse and punishment of God, which we deserved, upon Himself. And so, if Jesus had died by drowning in the Sea of Galilee or had died of food poisoning or of old age, or some other natural way, His death would not have been counted as *accursed of God, a punishment for sin* on behalf of you and me.

Note, also, that here we find God administering the death penalty to His Son. How foolish are those persons who argue that capital punishment is immoral and should be abolished. They cannot understand the justice of God and His hatred for human sin.

Questions on Number 39

1. The sufferings of Christ were greatly increased by His _____ under Pilate and His _____ on the cross.

2. How would you describe a crucifixion? _____
   _____

3. Crucifixion is the Jewish method of executing a criminal.
   ☐ True   ☐ False

4. It is not important *how* Christ died—the important thing is *that* He died. ☐ True   ☐ False

5. How does Christ's dead body hanging on the cross fit in with the Old Testament? (*Explain and give a reference*): _____

_____

_____

6. "I am _____ that He took _____

   the _____ which _____."

7. Behind Jesus' official execution by the Roman world government stood God the Judge, who was executing His Son for what reason?

_____

_____

8. Jesus became "accursed of God" for us because by nature we were under the curse of God and deserved physical and spiritual death.
   ☐ True   ☐ False

9. The death of Christ was: (Which one(s)?)
   ☐ a. shameful   ☐ d. personally deserved
   ☐ b. glorious   ☐ e. an execution
   ☐ c. substitutionary

10. Write out Galatians 3:13–14. _____

_____

_____

_____

_____

_____

_____

_____

_____

_____

❦ *The Death of Christ*

Q40. Why was it necessary for Christ to suffer "death"?

Because the justice and truth of God required that satisfaction for our sins could be made in no other way than by the death of the Son of God.

In this question, the *third* stage of Christ's humiliation—His death—is explained. Someone might ask, "Would not the terrible sufferings that our Savior endured on the cross be sufficient to satisfy God?

Why did Jesus have to actually *die?*" The answer is found in God's sentence against sin, which is found throughout the Bible: "The soul who sins shall *die*" (Ezekiel 18:4, 20). "The wages of sin is *death*" (Romans 6:23). Nothing less than death itself is what God's Law and justice require of the sinner (Genesis 2:17).

Therefore, Jesus, who was bearing our sins, must die. What an amazing thing! The sinless human nature of Jesus Christ—the only man who deserved to live—experienced physical death, which is the separation of the soul from the body, and spiritual death, which is the full out pouring of God's wrath for sin. Jesus cried out, "My God, My God, why have You forsaken Me?" (Matthew 27:46). In no other way could the full penalty of sin be paid for us than by the death of the Son of God. Think of it! And think of it often!

Questions on Number 40

1. Death was which stage of Christ's humiliation?_____
   _____

2. What were the other stages that we have studied so far?
   _____

3. What is physical death? _____
   _____

4. What is spiritual death? _____
   _____

5. Why did Jesus have to die as well as suffer?_____
   _____

6. Which nature of Christ died on the cross?
   ☐ a. human nature

☐ b. divine nature

☐ c. both human and divine natures

7. The spiritual death of Christ on the Cross is indicated in His cry,

"_____

_____."

8. Write out the answer to question 40. _____

_____

_____

_____

9. If Jesus came to earth to die for us, then those who put Him to death did a good deed. ☐ True ☐ False

10. Write out Philippians 2:8. _____

_____

_____

_____

🔥 *The Burial of Christ*

Q41. Why was He "buried"?

To show thereby that He was really dead.

In this very short question and answer we learn the *reason* for the burial of Christ (the fourth stage of His humiliation). The reason given here is that the burial *proves the death* of Christ. Only dead persons are buried.

Why is this proof so important? There have been theories invented by unbelievers that Jesus did not really die. One theory is that He merely became unconscious on the cross; another is that He only pretended to be dead. But the burial of Christ was permitted by the authorities only because He was really dead. A Roman soldier thrust his spear into the side of Jesus, and out came blood and water (John 19:33–34); He was dead.

Also, the burial of Christ resulted from the curse placed on the body by God. In condemning Adam, God said, "For dust you are, and to dust you shall return" (Genesis 3:19). Christ's body was subject to the corruption of the grave for three days, for us. Now, our burial in the cemetery, after our death, is sanctified by the burial of our Savior. Although our bodies will become corrupted and return back to earth, we know that Christ has gotten the victory over the corruption of the grave by His blessed resurrection. In Christ, the gloom is taken away from our graves. "Death is swallowed up in victory!" (1 Corinthians 15:54).

Questions on Number 41

1. There are two answers in the Catechism that are shorter than this one. They are: _____

2. The fourth stage, or step, of Christ's humiliation was His
_____.

3. The Catechism gives what reason for Christ's burial _____
_____

4. What precaution did the Roman authorities take to make sure that Christ was really dead (John 19:33–34)? _____
_____
_____

5. If Christ's body were not dead, would He have been buried?
☐ Yes ☐ No

6. Genesis 3:19 speaks of physical death and returning to the dust as God's _____ on man's body for his sin.

7. Do you think Christ's body began to decay during the three days it was in the tomb?_____
_____

8. What connection, if any, does Christ's burial have with our burial?
_____
_____

9. Is there any hope for the dead bodies in their graves? ☐ Yes ☐ No
▶ *Explain:* _____
_____

10. Write out Luke 23:52–53. _____
_____
_____

❧ Why Christians Die

Q42. Since then Christ died for us, why must we also die?

Our death is not a satisfaction for our sin, but only a dying to sin and an entering into eternal life.

Question 42 answers one of the most common questions asked by young Christians when they learn that Christ died in our place. The question is, "Since then Christ died for us, why must we also die?" The answer is in two parts: a negative reason and a positive reason:

1. **The believer's death is not a satisfaction for his sin.**

That means he does not die under the curse of God as a punishment for his sins. The wages of sin is death (Romans 6:23), but for the *Christian* these wages have been paid by our Substitute, Jesus Christ. Jesus' death was the satisfaction, the "wages, " for our sin. The Christian's death, then, is not a punishment for his sins because Jesus took the full punishment for all his sins. The *curse* associated with death has been removed from the Christian believer by the accursed death of our Savior: "Christ has redeemed us from the curse of the Law, having become a curse for us" (Galatians 3:13).

2. **The believer's death is the means by which his soul is ushered into heaven.**

This is the positive answer to the question. By physical death, the Christian is graciously and lovingly delivered from this sinful world and from his sinful nature to enter into eternal glory. The Bible clearly teaches that to be absent from the body is to be present with the Lord (2 Corinthians 5:6-8) and that to die is our gain (Philippians 1:21). We should never fear death as Christians because this experience has been changed from a curse into a blessing! How gracious of God that He does not permit us to live in these sinful bodies forever on earth. How horrible that would be!

It must be remembered, however, that not all Christians will die physically. There will be a generation still living on the earth when Christ returns. They will not see death. Perhaps you will be one of those who will be caught up in the air by Christ when He returns and will not experience death—see 1 Thessalonians 4:17!

Questions on Number 42

1. Have you ever wondered why you must die since you know from the Word of God that Jesus died for you? ☐ Yes ☐ No

2. How will you explain the matter to someone who may ask you why a believer dies? _____
   _____

3. How will you explain to him the statement "our death is not a satisfaction for our sin"? _____
   _____
   _____

4. How will you explain that when a Christian dies, it is actually a great blessing to him? _____
   _____
   _____

5. What does the phrase "dying to sin" mean? _____
   _____
   _____

6. What does the phrase "entering into eternal life" mean?
   _____
   _____

7. Is it true that you may not experience physical death? ☐ Yes ☐ No

8. What does 1 Thessalonians 4:16–17 teach about the last generation of Christians? _____
   _____
   _____

9. When does eternal life begin (see John 5:24)? _____
   _____

10. Write out Romans 14:7–8. _____
   _____
   _____
   _____

_____

_____

_____

❦ *Benefits of the Death of Christ*

Q43. What further benefit do we receive from the sacrifice and death of Christ on the cross?

That by His power our old man is with Him crucified, slain and buried; so that the evil lusts of the flesh may no more reign in us, but that we may offer ourselves unto Him a sacrifice of thanksgiving.

The death of Christ was an atoning sacrifice for our sins. By His precious death we are cleansed from all sin with a double cleansing:

1. We are cleansed from the *guilt* of our sins. This is our *justification*.

2. We are cleansed from the *power* of our sins. This is our *sanctification*.

Question 43 teaches us that when our Savior died on the cross for us, He purchased for us the gift of the Holy Spirit, Who breaks the power of sin in our hearts. This question is based on Romans 6:1–13. It is very important that we know that Jesus died not only to take away our guilt, but also to break the power of sinful lusts and desires. He died to make us holy, to purify our hearts by the power of the Holy Spirit.

The expression, "old man" refers to the power of sin in our hearts which we inherited from Adam. This "old man" in us was the ruling power of sin which controlled us before we were born again. But by Jesus' crucifixion, death, and burial for us, that power of sin in our hearts has been given the death blow by the Holy Spirit. The Bible speaks of our having been "co-crucified" with Christ (Romans 6:6; Gal. 2:20) and "co-buried" (Romans 6:4) and "co-raised" (Col. 3:1) with Him. In other words, our persons were in Christ when He was crucified, buried and raised. Therefore, we are given the resurrection power of Christ's Spirit to overcome the rule of sin and unbelief in our lives. Christians enjoy the benefit of sanctification by the Spirit of Christ!

Being born again by the Holy Spirit, we now have the desire and the power (though not perfectly yet) to offer ourselves to Christ in love and to live a holy life of thanksgiving and obedience. Are you as thankful for the gift of sanctification (holy desires) as for the gift of justification (forgiveness of sins and deliverance from hell)?

Questions on Number 43

1. Christ obtained for us by His death, burial, and resurrection many benefits, not forgiveness alone. ☐ True ☐ False

2. We are cleansed from sin in two ways. What are they?
   a) _____
   b) _____

3. Question 43 speaks of which kind of cleansing? _____

4. The "old man" is:
   ☐ a. Adam
   ☐ b. our earthly father
   ☐ c. our sinful natures received from Adam
   ☐ d. our age

5. From which passage of Scripture is Question 43 taken? _____

6. We are said to be "crucified with Christ (Romans 6:6). This means:
   ☐ a. we were physically with Christ when He died
   ☐ b. we were in Christ spiritually by election and imputation

7. It is possible for a person to be in Christ and have His Holy Spirit, and still have the lusts of the flesh rule in him. ☐ True ☐ False

8. The sin in our hearts—"the evil lusts"—is destroyed more and more as we (*check all that apply*):
   ☐ a. read the Bible prayerfully   ☐ c. join in sinful activities
   ☐ b. skip church   ☐ d. pray for Holy Spirit's help

9. What must we offer to God to show our thanks for the benefit of sanctification? Answer in the words of the Catechism:
   _____
   _____
   _____

10. Write out Galatians 2:20. _____
   _____
   _____

_____

_____

_____

_____

_____

❧ *Christ's Descent into Hell*

Q44. Why is it added: "He descended into hell"?

That in my greatest temptations I may be assured that Christ my Lord, by His inexpressible anguish, pains and terrors, which He suffered in His soul on the cross and before, has redeemed me from the anguish and torment of hell.

We come now to the *fifth* and final step in Christ's humiliation (we are still dealing with the fourth article of the Apostles' Creed). The Creed says, "He descended into hell" and this expression has been interpreted in different ways. The Roman Catholic Church takes it to mean that Christ literally went to hell to suffer for three days and then took the Old Testament believers, who had died, to heaven. The Lutherans say that Jesus' soul went to hell not to suffer but to proclaim His victory over His enemies. The Reformed view (the biblical view) is that Jesus' soul went *immediately to heaven after death*. Remember what Christ told the thief on the cross: "Today you will be with Me in Paradise (heaven)" (Luke 23:43). Also, He said to the Father: "Into Your hands I commit My spirit" (Luke 23:46).

What, then, does this article mean? The Catechism makes it clear: Jesus suffered hell in His soul on the cross and also before when He agonized in the Garden of Gethsemane. No one will ever suffer the torments of hell in his soul as Jesus did for us. When He cried out, "My God, My God, why have You forsaken Me?" He was crying out from the lowest depths of hell. He was experiencing the full, infinite wrath of God which no mere creature could have sustained. Try to imagine the scene: Our Lord was suffering all the hells due to all the people of God, and He did so in the space of six hours on the Cross!

At death, His suffering of hell was complete.

Questions on Number 44

1. Do you think that death came before or after hell in the case of Jesus? ☐ before ☐ after

2. "Hell" means the place and the sufferings of the damned.
   ☐ True   ☐ False

3. *When* did Jesus experience the "inexpressible anguish, pains, and terrors of hell"? _____

   _____

4. Jesus' body went to the tomb for three days, and His soul went to
   ☐ a. hell   ☐ b. Paradise   ☐ c. the grave   ☐ d. the Father

5. What is the Lutheran interpretation of the phrase, "He descended into hell"? _____

   _____

   _____

6. Check which of these Old Testament references predict Christ's suffering in hell.
   ☐ Psalm 18:5–6   ☐ Psalm 113:9   ☐ Psalm 116:3   ☐ Isaiah 55:1

7. Hell is the eternal and complete separation of the soul and body from God's life, light, and love.   ☐ True   ☐ False

8. The common expression, "hell on earth," is a truth based on Scripture.   ☐ True   ☐ False ▶ *Explain:* _____

   _____

   _____

9. What benefit do believers receive from Christ's experience of hell? Answer with the appropriate phrase from the Catechism.

   _____

   _____

10. Write out Matthew 27:46. _____

    _____

    _____

    _____

    _____

    _____

❧ *Benefit of Christ's Resurrection*

Q45. What benefit do we receive from the "resurrection" of Christ?

First, by His resurrection He has overcome death, that He might make us partakers of the righteousness which He has obtained for us by His death. Second, by His power we are also now raised up to a new life. Third, the resurrection of Christ is to us a sure pledge of our blessed resurrection.

We have studied the five stages of our Lord's humiliation—from His birth to His descent into hell (Articles 3 and 4 of the Apostles' Creed). Now we begin our study of the *four* steps of our Lord's *exaltation* (His being raised up and given glory). These four steps are: (1) His resurrection, (2) His ascension into heaven, (3) His rule in heaven, (4) His second coming to judge the world. These four subjects are found in Articles 5, 6 and 7 of the Creed.

In question 45 we learn the *fact* and the *meaning* of the resurrection of Christ.

The Fact of the Christ's Resurrection

The Bible emphasizes the fact that the body of Jesus literally arose from the dead after being dead for three days. Of course, His body was changed and given great glory and supernatural powers by the resurrection, even as our bodies will be gloriously changed. We know that Jesus' resurrection is a *fact* because of all the witnesses of *both* the empty tomb and of the risen Savior Himself. Even "doubting" Thomas was convinced that Jesus had risen from the dead (John 20:24-29). Jesus appeared about 14 different times to the disciples, and at one time there were 500 people present who saw Him (1 Corinthians 15:6). Many people, such as the Modernists, deny the bodily resurrection. They just refuse to believe what the Apostles have written. In other words, they are implying that Matthew, Mark, Luke, John, Paul, Peter and all the witnesses of the resurrection are liars.

The Meaning of Christ's Resurrection

The *meaning* of the resurrection is as equally important as the *fact* of the resurrection. The resurrection of Christ gives us three great benefits, as question 45 teaches us:

1. Christ's resurrection proves that He overcame the power of death and, therefore, the power of Satan and sin which caused Him to die. We are now declared righteous and freed from sin because of our Savior's death and resurrection (Romans. 4:25). He satisfied the justice of God and thus death could no longer hold Him—or us.

2. Christ's resurrection life is given to us now in our regeneration (new birth), so that our dead souls are made alive and united to Him by the Holy Spirit (Romans 6:4, 11).

3. Our Savior's glorious resurrection guarantees that our bodies will also be resurrected from the graves, because both our souls and our bodies are united to Christ forever (1 Corinthians 15:21–23).

Questions on Number 45

1. In review, what were the five steps of our Savior's humiliation?

    a) _____

    b) _____

    c) _____

    d) _____

    e) _____

2. What are the four steps of His glorious exaltation?

    a) _____

    b) _____

    c) _____

    d) _____

3. The Bible and the Catechism teach us both the _____ and the _____ of our Lord's resurrection.

4. What proofs do we have that Jesus really rose from the dead? Name at least three.

    a) _____

    b) _____

    c) _____

5. Comment on the theory that Jesus' *teachings* and *example* rose again and live on to inspire us, but that His body is not *literally* alive now.

    _____

    _____

    _____

    _____

    _____

6. The resurrected body of Jesus was no different from the resurrected body of Lazarus. ☐ True   ☐ False

7. How many benefits do we receive from the resurrection of Christ according to the Catechism? _____
    Name them (You may use your own words): _____

    _____

    _____

    _____

8. The resurrection proves that God was fully satisfied with the atoning sacrifice and death of His Son. ☐ True ☐ False

9. If Jesus had not arisen from the dead, we could still be forgiven and saved. ☐ True   ☐ False

10. Write out 1 Corinthians 15:22–23. _____

    _____

    _____

    _____

    _____

    _____

    _____

    _____

❦ *Christ's Ascension into Heaven*

Q46. What do you understand by the words: "He ascended into heaven"?

That Christ, in the sight of His disciples, was taken up from the earth into heaven, and continues there in our behalf until He shall come again to judge the living and the dead.

The second stage of Jesus' exaltation was His ascension into heaven, which took place from the Mount of Olives (Acts 1) *forty* days after His resurrection. The first part of Article 5 says, "He ascended into heaven;" and the Catechism explains this in questions 46, 47, 48, and 49. In this question, the *fact* of the ascension is especially emphasized. Our Lord's ascension into the air from the mount is an historical fact, witnessed by the Apostles (and perhaps others). The reasons Jesus had remained on earth for forty days after His resurrection were:

1. To prove in many ways to His disciples that He had arisen (Acts 1:2).

2. To give them final instructions for carrying on His work, which would not have made sense to them before.

These instructions were:

1. To wait in Jerusalem until He sent His Holy Spirit to them to empower them to be His witnesses (Acts 1:4, 8).

2. To go into all the world as witnesses of the Resurrection, preaching the Kingdom of God (Acts 1:4, 8).

3. To make disciples of all nations through baptism and teaching His Word (Matthew 28:19–20).

And so, when they were gathered on the Mount of Olives near Jerusalem, Jesus "lifted up His hands and blessed them," and "while He blessed them He was parted from them and carried up into heaven" (Luke 24:50–51). Jesus is now in heaven in His risen body, having received all authority in heaven and earth (Matthew 28:18). He shall come back again at the appointed time to resurrect the dead and judge all men.

Questions on Number 46

1. The second step in Jesus' exaltation is His _____

   _____

2. How many questions do we have on this second step? _____

3. How many days did Jesus stay on the earth after His resurrection?

   _____

4. Give two reasons why Jesus remained on the earth for a while.

   a) _____

   b) _____

5. Do Jesus' parting instructions to the disciples in Acts 1:8 apply to us today? ☐ Yes ☐ No

6. Do *you*, as well as the ministers, have the job of witnessing to people about the resurrected Christ and His gospel? ☐ Yes ☐ No

7. Jesus ascended from what place? _____

   _____

8. What did the disciples do after Jesus went up into the sky and into heaven? (See Luke 24:52) _____

    _____

9. In heaven right now, Jesus "continues _____
    behalf _____

    _____ and the dead."

10. Write out Acts 1:9. _____

    _____

    _____

    _____

    _____

❦ *Christ's Presence with Believers*

Q47. But is not Christ with us even unto the end of the world, as He has promised?

Christ is true man and true God. According to His human nature He is now not on earth, but according to His Godhead, majesty, grace, and Spirit, He is at no time absent from us.

This question and the next are given to explain the meaning of our Savior's words which He spoke to His disciples: "I am with you always, even to the end of the age" (Matthew 28:20). Of course, Jesus could not have meant His physical body as, obviously, that left the earth when He ascended, a short time later.

Our Lutheran friends insist that Jesus' human nature is still on the earth. They take these words of Christ literally. The reason for this is that they believe Jesus' body and blood are literally present in the Lord's Supper. To hold to this view of the Lord's Supper, they also teach that the human nature of Christ became Divine (God) and is now *everywhere present*. So Christ's flesh and blood are actually present in London and New York, etc., at the same time when the Supper is celebrated.

The biblical answer to these Lutheran doctrines about the glorified human nature of Christ is that the glorification of Christ did not change His humanity into Deity. Christ's glorified human nature is still human nature and therefore it cannot be everywhere present on earth or consumed in the eating of the Lord's Supper. Christ's human nature is located in heaven only and is not now on the earth. John 13:1; 16:7, 28; Acts 3:21 and many other texts prove this.

Christ is still with us, indeed, by His Godhead, majesty, grace, and Holy Spirit. The glory and grace of Jesus Christ are continuously revealed to believers by the Holy Spirit through the Scriptures. The Holy Spirit is the Savior's "Personal Representative" to His Church on earth and our *abiding Comforter* (John 14:16).

Questions on Number 47

1. Questions 47 and 48 are given to correct the teaching of _____ _____ who wrongly interpret the words of Christ, "I am with you always."

2. Jesus told His disciples that His human body would remain with us always, even unto the end of the age. ☐ True ☐ False

3. Jesus' body and blood are physically present wherever the Lord's Supper is observed. ☐ True ☐ False

4. Is it foolish for the Lutherans and Reformed to argue about such a "little thing" as where the physical body of Christ is located?
☐ Yes ☐ No ▶ *Explain:* _____
_____
_____

5. It is improper to say that Christ is with us now. ☐ True ☐ False
▶ *Explain:* _____
_____

6. Whom did Christ send to be His "Personal Representative" to believers? _____

7. Having the Holy Spirit and the Bible, which is the Word of Christ, the Church on earth now has the power to serve Christ and make disciples of all nations. (See Matthew 28:19–20) ☐ True ☐ False

8. The _____ nature of Christ is in heaven.
The _____ nature of Christ is everywhere.

9. The human nature of Christ, although glorified, is not Divine and is *located* in one place in heaven. ☐ True ☐ False

10. Write out Hebrews 4:14. _____
_____

_____

_____

_____

❧ Union of Christ's Deity and Humanity

Q48. But are not, in this way, the two natures in Christ separated from one another, if the manhood is not wherever the Godhead is?

Not at all, for since the Godhead is incomprehensible and everywhere present, it must follow that it is indeed beyond the bounds of the manhood which it has assumed, but is yet nonetheless in the same also, and remains personally united to it.

In the light of what was just explained, namely, that the human nature of Christ is located in *one* place in heaven, whereas His Divine nature is "everywhere present" (in all places at the same time), does this mean that the two natures are now separated? Perhaps the Lutherans will accuse us of having a human Savior in heaven who is separated from the Divine nature, since we do not believe the physical body of Jesus is present in the Lord's Supper. However, this is not the case. The Divine nature, being everywhere, is also in heaven and is still united to the human nature of Christ. In fact, the Divine nature remained united to the dead body of Jesus as it lay in the tomb and also to His soul in heaven those three days after His death. The two natures are personally united to each other forever.

The Reformed understanding of Scripture on this matter of the location of the two natures of Christ is the position that the early Church Fathers also took. For example, the famous Christian teacher Augustine (died 430) taught:

> With respect to His human form, it must not be imagined that He has been effused [spread about] everywhere. For we must be on our guard, that we do not conceive of the Divinity of His person in such a manner as to destroy the reality of His humanity ... Both God and man constitute one person, even one Christ Jesus, who is everywhere present with respect to His Divinity, but in heaven with respect to His humanity. This is the Confession of the Christian Church, according to the simple understanding of this article of the Christian faith" (quoted in Thelemann's *An Aid To the Heidelberg Catechism*, p. 183).

Thus we see that the Reformed interpretation of Scripture also has the support of the early Christian Church.

In this question let us be reminded that Christ is the true and living God, that He has all the attributes (characteristics) of God, for example, *omnipotence* (He has all power), *omniscience* (He knows all things), and *omnipresence* (He is everywhere at every moment). Let us also remember that our Savior never leaves us alone. Though all men should forsake us, the Lord is with us as our Helper, our Guide, our Lord, and our Savior by His Holy Spirit and Word. Let us remember this in days of loneliness and hardship and sorrow.

Questions on Number 48

1. This question and the previous one have to do with:
   - ☐ a. the matter of the location of the human body of Christ
   - ☐ b. whether Jesus is God or not
   - ☐ c. whether God is everywhere present or not.

2. The human nature is present wherever Christ's Godhead is.
   ☐ True ☐ False

3. What does it mean, "the Godhead is incomprehensible?" (Look up the word in a dictionary.) _____

   _____

   _____

4. The Divine nature of Jesus is the second person of the Trinity.
   ☐ True ☐ False

5. Name three characteristics of God that no mere creature could possess.
   a) _____
   b) _____
   c) _____

6. The Godhead of Jesus and the human nature were separated for a short time at His death. ☐ True ☐ False

7. Since the *physical* presence of Christ is not on the earth or in the Lord's Supper, we do *not* believe that Christ is with us now.
   ☐ True ☐ False

8. Name a famous Church Father who taught that the human nature of the Person of Christ is located in heaven and is therefore not now on earth. _____

9. Who should you trust even when your closest friends leave you?

    _____

10. Write out Matthew 28:20. _____

    _____

    _____

    _____

❧ *Benefits of Christ's Ascension*

Q49. What benefit do we receive from Christ's ascension into heaven?

First, that He is our Advocate in the presence of His Father in heaven. Second, that we have our flesh in heaven as a sure pledge, that He as the Head, will also take us, His members, up to Himself. Third, that He sends us His Spirit as an earnest, by whose power we seek those things which are above, where Christ sits at the right hand of God, and not things on earth.

This question teaches three wonderful benefits that we receive because our Savior ascended into heaven and was received by God the Father.

1. The ascended Christ is our "Advocate."

An "advocate" is one, such as a lawyer, who pleads for his friend before a judge. In Hebrews 7:25 we read that Jesus "always lives to make intercession for them." Christ represents His people before the Father, praying for us and ever pleading His sacrifice made on our behalf. 1 John 2:1 says: "If anyone sins, we have an Advocate with the Father, Jesus Christ the righteous."

The *merits* of Christ's sacrifice must be applied to us continuously. Our prayers, also, can go to the Father only through Christ, our Advocate. Let us never forget to pray in the Name of Jesus Christ and be thankful that we have an Advocate who is ever present at the right hand of God in heaven.

2. The ascended Christ is the sure Guarantee of our ascension.

Being united forever to Christ by His Spirit, we must join Him personally in heaven. The fact that our human nature is already there (in Christ) *proves* that our bodies must some day be taken to heaven also. Our souls will go first, and then our bodies will follow, after the resurrection. Christ's body in heaven must always remind us that we are going to heaven also and that heaven is a place for bodies as well as souls.

3. The ascended Christ sends His Spirit to His elect.

Christ sends His Spirit and gospel to convert and sanctify His chosen people. Those who were redeemed by the death of Christ are called by the Holy Spirit, who brings the gifts of regeneration, faith, repentance, and sanctification to us. The word "earnest" means a "down payment." The gift of the Spirit is the "down payment" and foretaste of our eternal salvation. The Spirit of Christ in us causes us to seek Christ and to grow more like Him while we live in this sinful world.

Questions on Number 49

1. What three benefits do we receive from the ascension of our Savior?

   a) _____

   _____

   b) _____

   _____

   c) _____

   _____

2. Why is our Lord called an advocate? _____

   _____

   _____

3. The merits of Christ's one sacrifice must be applied to us every day by our Advocate in heaven. ☐ True ☐ False

4. What does the Catechism mean by "we have our flesh in heaven"?

   _____

   _____

5. Our Savior's being in heaven is a pledge to us of what?

   _____

   _____

6. Who does Christ send back to earth to apply His saving benefits to all God's elect? _____

7. The Holy Spirit is an "earnest," which means that:
   ☐ a. this is one of His names
   ☐ b. He is a "down payment" on our eternal salvation
   ☐ c. He has also ascended into heaven

8. The Holy Spirit is given by Christ to all men who hear the gospel
   preached.   ☐ True   ☐ False ▶ *Explain:* _____

   _____

   _____

   _____

9. Match these:

Head	Advocate (*do not match with Advocate*)
Advocate	Sure pledge
Earnest	Down payment
Our flesh	Members
1 John 2:1	Lawyer

10. Write out Colossians 3:1. _____

    _____

    _____

    _____

❧ *The Session of Christ*

Q50. Why is it added: "And sitteth at the right hand of God"?

Because Christ ascended into heaven for this end, that He might there appear as the Head of His Church, by whom the Father governs all things.

The first part of the sixth article of the Apostles' Creed speaks of Christ ascending into heaven; the last part of this article says: "And sitteth at the right hand of God the Father."

We may say that the explanation given this phrase by the Catechism teaches us benefits additional to the three just explained in question 49. However, Christ's ascension and Christ's sitting at the right hand of God are distinct ideas and must be looked at separately.

In this *"sitting"* (session), Christ is seen as the victorious Lord, who was crowned by God as the *Mediator-King* and given power over all creation. He earned the right to govern all things by His victory over sin and the Devil on the cross. He shall rule until all His enemies are fully destroyed (1 Corinthians 15:25; Hebrews 2:8). The angels ascend into heaven and we, too, shall ascend into heaven, but only Jesus Christ will ever be seated at the Right Hand of God.

What does this "sitting" mean? In olden times a king or other great man would show honor to some person by having him *sit at his right hand*. We read that King Solomon showed honor to his mother by having her sit at the right hand of his throne (1 Kings 2:19). The mother of James and John asked Jesus whether her two sons might be seated at the right and left hand of Jesus' throne (Matthew 20:21). So Jesus has been exalted to the highest position by God. He shall continue to rule over all creation; and as Head of His Church, He *directs all things on earth* to the gathering of His chosen and redeemed people, the establishment of His kingdom, and the judgment of His enemies.

By "right hand of God," of course, we are not to think that God has a body with hands, or a literal throne made out of gold. God is a pure Spirit and does not sit down. But the Bible uses this expression to teach us that Jesus, in His human nature, has been given all authority by God.

Questions on Number 50

1. With our Savior sitting at the right hand of God, we have further benefits from Christ in heaven, along with the three benefits mentioned in question 49. ☐ True ☐ False

2. The *sitting* of Christ as the Mediator-King in heaven is not to be distinguished from His *ascension into heaven*. ☐ True ☐ False

3. Sitting at the right hand of a king was a practice in olden times. It meant what? _____

   _____

   _____

   Give an example. _____

   _____

4. As our King in heaven, Christ has power: (*check all that apply*)
   ☐ a. over some matters on earth   ☐ d. over all men and angels
   ☐ b. over His Church only   ☐ e. over sin, death, and hell
   ☐ c. over the angels only

5. *How* does Christ govern His Church? (see Q31c for the answer).
   "By _____."

6. We believe that Christ has much power, but many things on earth such as war, crime, modernism, and incurable diseases are beyond His power to control. ☐ True   ☐ False

7. Christ is seated at the right hand of God because God actually has hands. ☐ True   ☐ False

8. Read 1 Corinthians 15:24–28 and answer the following:
   a) Christ must reign (rule) until all enemies are put _____
   _____ (v. 25).
   b) The last enemy that shall be destroyed is _____ (v. 26).
   c) When all things are finally subdued (made obedient), Christ will turn over His Kingdom to Whom? _____ (v. 24)
   d) The Son is subject to the Father that "God _____
   _____ all." (v. 28)

9. Christ governs His Church by His Word and Spirit and He governs all things by His "eternal _____
   _____." (see Q26.)

10. Write out Hebrews 10:12. _____
    _____
    _____
    _____
    _____
    _____

❦ *Benefits of Christ's Headship*

Q51. What does this glory of Christ, our Head, profit us?

First, that by His Holy Spirit He pours out heavenly gifts upon us, His members; then, that by His power He defends and preserves us against all enemies.

In this question we learn of two further benefits that we receive from the glorified Christ Who is in heaven at the "right hand of God." One could argue, however, that these two benefits were already included in questions 49 and 50. Here they are specified in more detail.

1. By His Holy Spirit Christ bestows the heavenly gifts upon us.

This took place at Pentecost originally (Acts 2), when the disciples were all filled with the Holy Spirit. But it is also true that every Christian has received the gift of the Holy Spirit sent to him by Jesus Christ. What are the "heavenly gifts" given to us by the Spirit? They include all the spiritual desires and abilities which we have: true faith, sorrow for sin, love for Christ, humility, the desire to obey God, peace and contentment in Christ, plus many other things. Galatians 5:22–23 gives a listing of some of the spiritual gifts that the chosen people of God receive from Christ through the Holy Spirit.

Note carefully that Christ must be given all the credit for any good thing found in ourselves. Our faith, love, devotion and obedience are produced in us by the Spirit of Christ.

2. Christ in heaven "defends and preserves us against all enemies."

Our enemies, of course, are our sinful nature, the evil world about us, and the Devil who goes about as a roaring lion seeking to destroy us (1 Pet. 5:8). Despite the fierceness of these foes, we know that our Lord in heaven will give us the grace and strength to remain true to Him even though we be killed by our enemies. Because Jesus is in control of all things, we know that all things work together for good to those who love God and are called according to His purpose (Romans 8:28).

Christ is not idle in heaven! His glorious work of saving His people goes on night and day, year in and year out.

Questions on Number 51

1. The death of Jesus on the cross is all that is necessary for us. He does not need to do anything for us now in heaven. ☐ True ☐ False

2. Jesus sends the _____ who is the third _____ of the Trinity, to bring spiritual gifts to us.

3. The Holy Spirit of Christ was first given to the disciples on what day? In what chapter of the Bible is this recorded? _____

4. Name some of the "heavenly gifts" which Christ gives us:

   _____

   What Bible passage gives us a list of them? _____

5. The gifts of the Holy Spirit are given to:
    ☐ a. all people   ☐ c. all the people for whom Christ died
    ☐ b. some Christians

6. Believers in Christ should be proud of themselves for having true
    faith because many others do not have such faith in Christ.
    ☐ True ☐ False ▶ *Explain:* _____
    _____

7. Satan was glad when Jesus left this earth, because Jesus, being now in
    heaven, cannot hinder Satan from doing his evil deeds.
    ☐ True ☐ False

8. From what enemies in particular does Jesus defend and preserve us?
    a) _____
    b) _____
    c) _____

9. Because Jesus Christ sits at the Right Hand of God, *all things* must
    work together for the good of the people of God. ☐ True ☐ False

10. Write out Acts 2:33. _____
    _____
    _____
    _____

❦ *The Return of Jesus Christ*

Q52. What comfort is it to you that Christ "shall come to judge the living and the dead"?

That in all my sorrows and persecutions, I, with uplifted head, look for the very One, who offered Himself for me to the judgment of God, and removed all curse from me, to come as Judge from heaven, who shall cast all His and my enemies into everlasting condemnation, but shall take me with all His chosen ones to Himself into heavenly joy and glory.

Question 52 explains the seventh article of the Apostles' Creed, which says, "From thence (heaven) He shall come to judge the living and the dead." The second coming of Christ is the fourth and final stage of our

Lord's exaltation. Do you still remember them? They are as follows: His Resurrection, Ascension, Session at God's Right Hand, and Second Coming.

The New Testament has much to say about the Second Coming of Christ from heaven, but very few people have any hope in it! Most people celebrate Christmas and the birth of Christ, but very few look forward expectantly to His coming again. The reason we know this is that they are not busy serving the Lord. 1 John 3:3 says, "Everyone who has this hope (of our Lord's Return) in Him purifies himself, just as He is pure." Christ is coming. Will He find you doing those things which please Him if He comes before you die?

When is the Lord coming back? This no one knows; all we know is that He is coming back when all things are ready.

Pre-millennialism

Many Christians today believe in "Pre-millennialism." We often hear this teaching on the radio and TV and in "Fundamentalist" churches. According to this theory, the end of the world will take place in several stages:

1. Christ will appear in the sky and cause all believers, the living and the dead, to arise to meet Him in the air. Then He will take them to heaven. The Pre-millennialists call this the "rapture" of the Church. Some say it will be a "secret rapture" as the rest of the world will not see it take place.

2. For seven more years the world will continue on with only unbelievers on the earth (Not all pre-millennialists believe this, however).

3. Then after the seven years, Christ will come back again to earth, kill His enemies, convert the Jewish nation, and set up a kingdom on earth (the so-called "millennium") for 1000 years with Jerusalem being the capitol city of the world. Apparently Jesus will have a capitol building or palace and a real throne on which to sit! Some pre-millennialists think that Jesus will have a new Temple built in Jerusalem.

4. After the millennium period is over, there will be one last revolt against Christ, who will then kill His enemies, raise the wicked dead, judge them, and cast them into hell, along with the Devil and his demons. *Below is a diagram of the Pre-millennialist view of the future.*

The Heidelberg Catechism rightly *rejects* this theory of Pre-millennialism. The Bible teaches, instead, that the gospel will be preached to the nations (Matthew 24:14; 28:18–20; Luke 24:47; Acts 1:8) and the Kingdom of God will be progressively established through the conversion of the elect Gentiles and Jews (Acts 15:14–18; Romans 11; 1 Corinthians 15:25). This entire period, the New Testament age, is

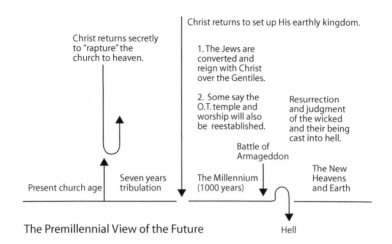

The Premillennial View of the Future

the "millennium" (the "1000 years" of Revelation 20:1-9, a symbolical number for a long period of time); it will be terminated by the Second Coming of Christ from heaven to raise the dead, judge all men and establish the new heavens and new earth.

The measure of success of the conversion of the world is debated by Reformed students.

Post-millennialism

Some (called Post-millennialists) think that the nations will be converted to Christianity prior to the second coming of Christ. They use such texts as Genesis 12:2-3; 17:4-6; Psalm 2:8-9; 18:43-45; 22:27-28; 72:8-19; 86:9; 110; Isaiah 2:1-4; 9:6-7; 11:4-9; Daniel 2:35, 44; 7:13-14; Malachi 1:11; Matthew 13:31-33; 28:18-20; Revelation 11:15; 15:3-4; 19:11-16.

A-millennialism

Others (called A-millennialists) think that there will be a growing anti-Christ system throughout the world that will all but destroy what remains of the church, except for the sudden intervention of Christ from heaven. They use such texts as Matthew 24:21-31; Luke 17:26-30; 18:8; 2 Thessalonians 2:3-4; Revelation 13.

In any case, at His second coming Christ will:

1. Raise all the bodies of all the dead both of the righteous and the unrighteous (John 5:28-29; Acts 24:15);

2. Judge all men, separating the "sheep" from the "goats" Matthew 25:31-46);

3. Make a new heavens and earth for His saints (2 Peter 3:13);

4. Cast the wicked into hell forever (Revelation 20:15).

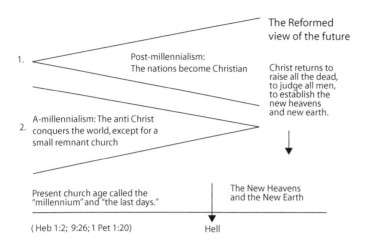

(Heb 1:2; 9:26; 1 Pet 1:20)

Will any Christians Be Lost in the Judgment?

The question arises, "Will there be any Christians who fail to pass the Judgment and be damned?" The answer is that no true Christians will fail on that terrible and wonderful Day, because Christ has already taken their judgment for them on the cross. All the curse was removed from "His chosen ones" when He offered Himself for us to the Judgment ("tribunal") of God on the cross.

However, we shall be examined as professing Christians, and those who lack the fruits of the Spirit will be exposed as false Christians ("goats") and shall be cast into hell along with those who were never in the visible church at all. It is essential, therefore, that we take the Judgment seriously and live accordingly. How awful it would be to deceive oneself and land in hell!

Questions on Number 52

1. To have an "uplifted head" means that: (*check one*)

    ☐ a. we are members of the Reformed Church.

    ☐ b. we serve the Lord when it is convenient for us.

    ☐ c. we put Christ *first* and eagerly long for Him to return for us.

    ☐ d. we doubt whether Christ will return in our lifetime.

2. Many so-called Christians show that they do not really believe Christ is coming because they are not busy preparing for Him by serving Him diligently. ☐ True ☐ False

3. For true Christians, their sins were already judged by God when Christ offered Himself for them on the cross. ☐ True ☐ False

4. As Christians who truly trust in Christ for salvation and are obeying Him, it is possible that we may still go to hell because of the Judgment to come. ☐ True ☐ False

5. Pre-millennialists believe there will be a "millennium" on earth. What do they mean by this? _____

    _____

    _____

    Is it true? ☐ Yes ☐ No

6. At Christ's return, what will happen to all the dead bodies? _____

    _____

    _____

7. The Judgment of the wicked will take place just ☐ *before* ☐ *after* their resurrection.

8. The souls of the wicked dead will have one more opportunity to be saved before the final Judgment. ☐ True ☐ False

9. Do you think it is fair for God to cast unbelievers into everlasting condemnation, when, after all, nobody is perfect? ☐ Yes ☐ No
    ▶ *Explain:* _____

    _____

    _____

10. Write out 2 Peter 3:14. _____

    _____

    _____

    _____

    _____

✹ *God the Holy Spirit*

Q53. What do you believe concerning the "Holy Ghost"?

First, that He is co-eternal God with the Father and the Son. Second, that He is also given unto me: by true faith makes me a partaker of Christ and all His benefits, comforts me, and shall abide with me forever.

We have now completed the explanation of Articles 2 through 7 of the Apostles' Creed which deal with God the Son and our Redemption (Questions 29-52 in the Catechism). Article 8 of the Creed speaks of God the Holy Spirit and our Sanctification. No doubt we are to consider that the remainder of the Apostles' Creed (8-12) comes under the subject of the Holy Spirit, just as Articles 2-7 come under the subject of Jesus Christ our Lord.

Question 53 gives a brief explanation of Article 8: "I believe in the Holy Spirit." Two things are here said concerning the blessed third Person of the Holy Trinity.

1. He is co-eternal God with the Father and the Son.

Re-read question 25 again and the Study Helps for that question. We should never speak of the Holy Spirit as an "It" (the King James translation does this in Romans 8:16), any more than we would refer to the Father or the Son as an "It." The Spirit is a Person—the Living God, having all the qualities and perfections of Divine Personality.

2. The Holy Spirit is our Sanctifier (see Q24 again).

This means that the Holy Spirit works *in* us and *applies to us personally* the benefits of redemption which Christ purchased for us on the cross.

It should be of interest to us, who are Reformed, to review a little history at this point. In the years 1618-1619, a Reformed synod was held in the city of Dordt, in the land of Holland, to study this very subject of the power of the grace of the Holy Spirit. This "Synod of Dordt" had to make a judgment on the teachings of a certain theological professor by the name of James Arminius (1516-1609). (His name was mentioned in our discussion of question 30.)

Arminius and his followers had been teaching in the Reformed Churches of Holland that God's grace and Holy Spirit are given equally to all who hear the gospel of Christ, and that it is a person's own will that determines if he will accept the grace of God or not. In other words, "Arminianism" teaches that God's grace is general and the Holy Spirit does only so much for all men. It is man who must decide whether he will cooperate with and use the grace that is given equally to all men. Salvation, then, is the product of the Holy Spirit's limited power plus the will-power of the sinner, say the Arminians.

Our Reformed Fathers condemned this teaching of Arminius, and other teachings of his, and taught, instead, the biblical truth of *irresistible grace*. They found that Scripture teaches a particular call and particular grace for the elect sinner only; and that the Holy Spirit of Christ comes with almighty power into the heart and will of the elect to regenerate them and turn their wills to Christ and His gospel. The Spirit "makes me a partaker of Christ and all His benefits" by irresistible, gracious power.

Here are a few of the many scripture references that teach irresistible grace: The examples of Saul of Tarsus and of Lydia of Philippi (Acts 9:1–6; 16:14); John 6:37; Acts 13:48; Romans 8:29–30; Ephesians 2:1, 5–10; Philippians 2:13.

The Five Points

The Synod of Dordt composed five biblical statements, or "canons," which condemned five errors of the Arminians. This document is known as the *Canons of Dordt* and should be studied by all persons who want to know the truth about

1. *Total Depravity*

2. *Unconditional Election*

3. *Limited Atonement*

4. *Irresistible Grace*

5. *Perseverance of the Saints*

These five doctrines have been nick-named the "Five Points of Calvinism," though John Calvin himself was not present at the Synod of Dordt (He died 55 years earlier). The theology of the "Five Points of Calvinism" is the theology of the sovereign, free grace of God. The theology of Arminianism, which most professed evangelical Christians hold to today, is really humanistic as it bases salvation on the supposed "free-will" of man.

Getting back to question 53, we are taught that the Holy Spirit is given personally to each elect believer. The Spirit unites us to Christ by the bond of true faith, and causes us to partake in all His saving benefits. These benefits include the fruits of the Spirit which are listed in Galatians 5:22–23.

Are you a Christian? Then you have the Holy Spirit of Christ: "If anyone does not have the Spirit of Christ, he is not His" (Romans 8:9). If you are a Christian believer, then the Holy Spirit is sanctifying you and causing you to live a holy Christian life. "Do not grieve the Holy Spirit of God" (Ephesians 4:30).

Questions on Number 53

1. Questions 29–52 instructed us about God the _____.

2. Question 53 deals with God the _____.

3. The Son of God is more important than the Holy Spirit. That is why the Apostles' Creed has more articles on the Son. ☐ True ☐ False

4. The Holy Spirit is "co-Father and the Son." This means what? (in your own words) _____

_____

_____

5. Where does our "true faith" come from according to this question?

_____

_____

6. Check the *wrong* answers among the following:
   ☐ a. The Holy Spirit makes us partakers of Christ.
   ☐ b. The Holy Spirit is an "It" (impersonal).
   ☐ c. "Holy Spirit" is a better translation than "Holy Ghost."
   ☐ d. Question 25 speaks of God as one Divine Person.

7. "Sanctification" is: ☐ the work of Christ for me on the cross ☐ the work of the Holy Spirit in my own heart ☐ neither.

8. The Holy Spirit, our Sanctifier, does three things for us, according to this question. Complete the following:
   a) "Makes me _____
   _____,"
   b) "_____ me,"
   c) "shall _____ forever."

9. The Synod of Dordt
   a) was held in the years _____.
   b) met to judge the teachings of _____.
   c) produced a document called _____

   _____.

10. The Synod of Dordt taught the biblical truth about these five doctrines:
    a) _____
    b) _____
    c) _____
    d) _____
    e) _____

11. If you have the Holy Spirit, you: (*check all that apply*)
    ☐ a. belong to Christ

☐ b. are living a perfect life

☐ c. will have Him forever

☐ d. can easily quench Him

☐ e. will persevere in the true faith until death

12. Write out 1 Corinthians 6:19. _____

_____

_____

_____

_____

_____

_____

_____

❦ *The Church of Jesus Christ*

Q54. What do you believe concerning the "Holy Catholic Church"?

That out of the whole human race, from the beginning to the end of the world, the Son of God, by His Spirit and Word, gathers, defends and preserves for Himself unto everlasting life a chosen communion in the unity of the true faith; and that I am and forever shall remain a living member of this communion.

In this question Article 9 of the Creed is explained. Some versions have, "I believe one Holy Christian Church;" others read, "I believe the Holy Catholic Church." The word "catholic" means universal, that is, that the Church of Jesus Christ is to be found in all parts of the world and in all ages. We are catholic but not *Roman* Catholic!

This article is speaking of the Church not as an organization or a denomination, but as it really is in God's eyes, a great Body of men and women and boys and girls who have been *chosen* by God, who have been *redeemed* by Christ, who are being *gathered* by the Spirit and the Word, and who will forever remain united to Christ. It is important that we belong to the Reformed Church, but it is far more important that we are members of *The One Body of Christ* by true faith!

Note the characteristics of the true Spiritual Church:

1. **It is one.** There is only one body of Christ from Adam to the last man.

2. **It is holy.** The elect of God are separated from sin to belong to the Lord.

3. **It is universal (catholic).** It includes all who have a true faith in Christ, regardless of race, age, or denominational affiliation.

It should be said that although there is only one true Church, and only one gospel, and only one Faith, there are *many church organizations* (over 300 in the United States). We call the One True Church the *Invisible Church, as* only God knows for sure who belong to it, whereas local church groups are called *visible churches,* as man can see who are in them.

The visible churches are never perfect and some have thrown away the gospel entirely. Some people belong to the invisible Church, but are not members of a local visible church. Many people belong to a visible church but are not true believers at all and are thus not in the invisible Church. We must be members of both, by faith in Christ and by confessing Christ.

The diagrams illustrate the relation between the Church as *invisible* and *visible*.

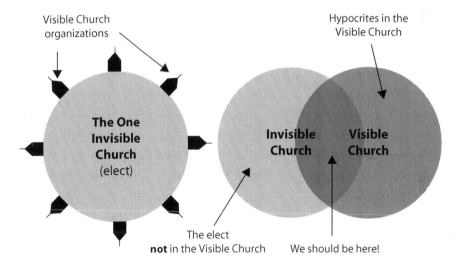

Questions on Number 54

1. God has many true, spiritual, invisible churches, chosen, redeemed and gathered. ☐ True ☐ False

2. Abraham did not belong to the same Church as the Apostle John. ☐ True ☐ False ▶ *Explain:* _____

3. Moses did not belong to the same Church as John Calvin.
    ☐ True   ☐ False ▶ *Explain:* _____

    _____

4. Match the following:

    A chosen communion   Gathers, defends, preserves

    His Spirit and   A living member of the same

    The Son of God   Elected by God

    I am   Word

5. Although there is only one invisible Church, there are many visible churches. ☐ True   ☐ False

6. It makes no difference which visible church you belong to just so you belong to Christ and are in His invisible Church. ☐ True   ☐ False

7. Draw a diagram showing the relationship of a visible church to the invisible Church.

8. Mark the spot where the believer should be in that diagram above.

9. Some visible churches have become Modernist and are not really a part of the true, universal Church at all. ☐ True   ☐ False

10. Write out Ephesians 4:4-5. _____

    _____

    _____

    _____

    _____

❧ The Communion of the Saints

Q55. What do you understand by the "communion of saints"?

First, that believers, one and all, as members of the Lord Jesus Christ, are partakers with Him in all His treasures and gifts; second, that each one must feel himself bound to use his gifts readily and cheerfully for the advantage and welfare of other members.

"The Communion of Saints" is part of the same Article 9 which speaks of the Church. The Church is a living body composed of those who are in Christ by the Holy Spirit. Being members of a living body, believers enjoy a spiritual relationship with one another. We all belong to the same spiritual family as the children of God. God is our common Father if we belong to Christ. We share the same spiritual desires and work for the same goals. We are all looking for our homeland, heaven.

This "togetherness" is called a communion or fellowship. But only the "saints" have it. The word "saint" simply means "a holy one," and refers to all true Christians. The Roman Catholics say that only certain famous people in their church are *made* saints, but the Bible says that all Christians *are* saints (see 1 Corinthians 1:2).

This question emphasizes two things:

1. That all believers partake of the treasures and gifts of Christ (spiritual abilities with which to serve Christ).

2. We are to use these gifts to bring blessing to our fellow Christians. Whether it is the gift of teaching, of music, of leadership, of making money, of bringing cheer and comfort to others, etc. that we have, we must use these gifts and talents to cheerfully serve Christ and our fellow saints.

The sin in our hearts works against this communion, seeking to make us hateful or bitter or envious or proud or independent or selfish toward others; but the Holy Spirit says: Seek to bring peace and maintain love among the people of God, overlooking their faults, ministering to their needs. Our happiness on this earth is dependent on our entering into true communion with the saints of God.

Questions on Number 55

1. Article 9 of the Creed also speaks of _____.

2. Communion or fellowship with other Christians is possible because Christians are all in fellowship with their common Lord and Savior. ☐ True ☐ False

3. "Saints" are special people and very few Christians ever reach that high honor of being a saint. ☐ True ☐ False

4. Each Christian "must _____ himself _____

    _____

    _____ of

    other members."

5. Some Christians are very talented, others have only average abilities to help others, and some have no gifts at all to help. ☐ True ☐ False

6. Name some "gifts" which Christians possess for the advantage and welfare of other members: _____

    _____

    _____

    _____

7. The communion of saints is experienced:
    ☐ a. in mutual helpfulness   ☐ e. in deeds of kindness
    ☐ b. in prayers for each other   ☐ f. in slandering others
    ☐ c. in forgetting and neglecting each other
    ☐ d. in supporting missions and the work of the church

8. Why do you think the word "cheerfully" is included in this answer, and how important is that for the communion of saints? _____

    _____

    _____

    _____

9. Gossip and petty criticism are not marks of brotherly love.
    ☐ True ☐ False

10. Write out Romans 12:5, 10. _____

    _____

    _____

_____

_____

_____

_____

_____

❦ God's Forgiveness of Sins

Q56. What do you believe concerning the "forgiveness of sins"?

That God, for the sake of Christ's satisfaction, will no more remember my sins, nor the sinful nature with which I have to struggle all my life long; but graciously imputes to me the righteousness of Christ, that I may nevermore come into condemnation.

We come now to Article 10 of the Apostles' Creed: "I believe in the forgiveness of sins." What a wonderful truth this is that our sins are forgiven! But what is sin? Questions 3 and 4 of the Catechism told us what sin is. Sin is the failure to keep God's perfect Law of love to God. The Law of God shows us our misery, namely, our guilt and our corruption by sin. Being guilty, we justly deserve condemnation and punishment. And this we shall surely receive—unless our sins are forgiven.

The Bible speaks over and over of forgiveness of sins by God. This is good news indeed! But just what does forgiveness mean? It simply means that the guilt of his sins is no more charged against the person who is forgiven. When you forgive a person, you no longer hold his sin or misdeed against him. If you *do* hold it against him, then you have not forgiven him. Here we are told that God "no more remembers our sins," that is, He no longer charges them against us. And *once* forgiven, we are *always* forgiven. We "never more come into condemnation."

Two kinds of sins are here mentioned:

1.   *Our individual acts of sins (thoughts, words, deed).*

2.   *Our sinful natures (our corrupt, depraved hearts).*

Our evil nature is itself hateful to God, and we deserve condemnation for even possessing such wicked hearts, But God *graciously* forgives our sinfulness and all the sins of which we are guilty.

How can God, who is righteous, forgive sins, without giving them their just punishment? The answer is, He cannot. He punished every sin and the guilt of our sinful natures in our Substitute, Jesus Christ. Only because Jesus Himself took our punishment can God forgive us. Here again we read of "Christ's satisfaction"—He alone satisfied God's Justice, and only He makes it possible for God to forgive us freely.

Who are forgiven? Not every one, but only those who truly *believe* on Christ and *confess* their sins and *ask* for forgiveness. Have you?

Questions on Number 56

1. The forgiveness of sins is stated in the _____
   article of the _____

2. The forgiveness of sins is ☐ important ☐ unimportant for us to know about.

3. What is sin? Give an explanation, using your own words if you wish.
   _____
   _____

4. What does forgiveness mean? _____
   _____
   _____

5. If you forgive a person, you:
   ☐ a. hold a grudge against him
   ☐ b. tell him that you hold nothing against him
   ☐ c. say sin is not really sin at all
   ☐ d. say you both had a misunderstanding

6. God forgives both the _____
   of sin and our sinful _____.

7. God can forgive us because He does not always punish sin.
   ☐ True   ☐ False

8. God forgave our sins by:
   ☐ a. forgetting them
   ☐ b. overlooking them
   ☐ c. demanding our personal punishment
   ☐ d. punishing our sins in Christ.

9. *Who* receives forgiveness of sins? _____
   _____

10. Write out Ephesians 1:7. _____

_____

_____

_____

_____

❧ *The Resurrection of the Body*

Q57. What comfort do you receive from the "resurrection of the body"?

That not only my soul after this life shall be immediately taken up to Christ its Head, but also that this my body, raised by the power of Christ, shall be reunited with my soul, and made like the glorious body of Christ.

This question explains Article 11 of the Apostles' Creed: "I believe in the resurrection of the body." We have already learned about this precious truth in questions 45 and 49; now we have a separate article on this subject.

The first thing that we must understand is that our souls at death are taken immediately to Christ in heaven. This is proved by Jesus' words to the thief on the cross (Luke 23:43), and by Stephen's prayer in Acts 7:59: "Lord Jesus, receive my spirit," and also by Philippians 1:23 and Revelation 6:9, 10. We reject as untrue the teaching of some religious groups, such as the Seventh Day Adventists, Jehovah's Witnesses and others, who say that the soul "sleeps" in the grave along with the body at death. One of the first books that the Reformer John Calvin wrote was against the error of "soul sleep." The title is *Psychopannychia*—which is the Greek word for soul sleep.

There is coming a great and glorious day, so the Bible teaches, when there will be the resurrection of all the dead bodies from the tombs and elsewhere. 1 Corinthians 15:51 tells us that this is a great mystery. It does not mean that every particle of the body that died will be restored, but there will be an essential identity of the body that died and the body that is raised. George Smith will not be raised as Bill Brown but as George Smith. The new body we receive will be like a new stalk of wheat that comes out of the seed that was planted (1 Corinthians 15:36-38): the seed and the stalk are different, but the one comes out of the other. We know that God's power is able to raise the dead bodies though we do not understand how He will do it, nor precisely what our new bodies will be like.

We can say three things for sure about the resurrection of our bodies:

1. It is a certainty, God promises it.

2. Our souls and bodies will be re-united, never more to be separated.

3. Our new bodies and perfect souls will be glorious, even like the glorious supernatural body of Christ after His resurrection (Philippians 3:21).

What about the bodies of unbelievers? They, too, will be resurrected, and their souls will also be re-united to their resurrected bodies; but they shall be cast back into hell to suffer God's punishment forever and ever. What a fearful day the resurrection of the lost will be (see Daniel 12:2)!

When will the resurrection take place? Turn to the lesson on Question 52 again and re-read how and when this age will come to its end.

Questions on Number 57

1. The subject of the resurrection of the body has not been mentioned before in the Catechism. ☐ True ☐ False

2. Would you like to have this inscription on *your* tombstone? "Here lie the body and soul of (your name)." ☐ Yes ☐ No
    ▶ *Explain:* _____
    _____
    _____

3. These groups teach wrongly about death: (*check all that apply*)
    ☐ a. Presbyterians   ☐ d. World Tomorrow
    ☐ b. Seventh Day Adventists   ☐ e. Calvinists
    ☐ c. Roman Catholics   ☐ f. Jehovah's Witnesses

4. The bodies which will be raised will be restored to the exact condition that they were in when they died. ☐ True ☐ False

5. The resurrected bodies will be so completely different that we will not recognize one another, and may not even recognize ourselves.
    ☐ True   ☐ False

6. Turn to 1 Corinthians 15, the greatest chapter on the resurrection in the New Testament, and using verses 42–44, match the following:

Sown in dishonor	Raised in power
Sown a natural body	Raised in incorruption
Sown in weakness	Raised in glory
Sown in corruption	Raised a spiritual body

7. 1 Corinthians 15:36–37 uses the illustration of *what* to show how the resurrection body comes out of the dead body? _____

_____

8. This we know for certain about our resurrection body:
   a) It will be "raised _____ of Christ."
   b) My body "shall be _____ soul."
   c) It will be "made _____ unto _____
   body _____."

9. The bodies of the wicked will also be resurrected. ☐ True ☐ False
   Prove it from Scripture: _____

_____

10. Write out John 6:40. _____

_____

_____

_____

_____

_____

_____

❧ *The Comfort of Everlasting Life*

Q58. What comfort do you receive from the article "life everlasting"?

That, inasmuch as I now feel in my heart the beginning of eternal joy, I shall after this life possess complete blessedness, such as eye has not seen, nor ear heard, neither has entered into the heart of man, therein to praise God forever.

We have now come to the twelfth and last article of the Apostles' Creed. The subject of this article is "life everlasting." The Bible speaks of eternal or everlasting life over and over again. In the Gospel of John alone the expression is repeated about 28 times! (See, for example, John 3:15, 16, 36; 6:27, 40, 47, 54, 68).

We usually think of everlasting life as that life which we will receive when we die and enter heaven. Question 42 might be interpreted that way. However, the emphasis is not so much on the length of that new life, but on the *nature* or quality of that new life. Eternal life is a life in fellowship with God through Christ and the Holy Spirit. That is the real meaning of eternal life. Jesus said in John 17:3: "This is eternal life, that they may know You, the only True God and Jesus Christ, Whom You have sent."

We see, then, that everlasting life is not something we have to wait for until after we die, but it is something we possess right now in this world if we have learned to know God and have entered into fellowship with Him through His Son, Jesus Christ. John 5:24 tells us that those who believe on Jesus Christ have (at the present time) everlasting life. Our Catechism here teaches this truth clearly as it speaks of our "*now* feeling in our heart the beginning of eternal joy."

Of course, this life in Christ is forever, and after our physical death (if we die), we shall enter into fellowship with God in a perfect way, as then we shall see Christ face to face (1 John 3:2; Revelation 22:4).

What will we do in heaven? The Bible does not say very much about this matter, as we would not be able to understand it anyway (it will be supernatural). We do know that we shall "possess perfect blessedness" (complete happiness and blessing) and that we shall "praise God forever" by serving Him in the tasks which He assigns us. The Bible tells us of a "new heavens and a new earth" (Isaiah 65:17; Revelation 21:1), which the Lord will make for us after the resurrection. What a wonderful future is ours because we have eternal life now! Do you feel in your heart this joy in Christ?

Questions on Number 58

1. What is the last article of the Apostles' Creed? _____

    _____

2. Eternal life is mentioned often in the Bible because we are able to understand what heaven will be like. ☐ True ☐ False

3. Name a book of the New Testament which refers to eternal life many times: _____ Give some references from that book.

    _____

4. "Eternal life" refers to the:
    ☐ a. length of life ☐ b. kind of life ☐ c. length and kind of life

5. It is correct to say that "eternal life" is fellowship with God through Christ, and that some people on the earth today actually have eternal life and will never die spiritually. ☐ True ☐ False

6. What is meant by the "complete bliss" that believers have in heaven?

    _____

    _____

    _____

7. The Catechism quotes part of a verse of Scripture in this answer (Q58). Give the Bible reference. _____

8. Unbelievers would be happy in heaven praising and serving Jesus Christ, though they refuse to do so now. ☐ True ☐ False

9. What is in store for us according to Revelation 21:1? _____

    _____

    _____

10. Write out Revelation 21:4. _____

    _____

    _____

    _____

    _____

    _____

❧ *The Blessing of a True Faith*

Q59. What does it help you now, that you believe all this?

That I am righteous in Christ before God, and an heir of eternal life.

This question provides a bridge or stepping-stone between the great truths of the gospel (the message of salvation), which we learned in the Apostles' Creed, and the great benefit of the gospel—justification by faith—which is taught in questions 59-64.

Remember that question 21 taught us the nature of true faith, and question 22 introduced the Apostles' Creed, which tells us what to believe (the content of faith). After the Creed was carefully explained in questions 23–58, we now have the question, "What does it help you now that you believe all this" (all the truth outlined in the Creed)? The answer is that we receive—through faith in the truth—the great benefit of righteousness and justification by grace alone. The order of the Catechism then is very clear and logical:

1. **The Nature of true faith:** a certain knowledge and a hearty trust. (Q21)

2. **The Content of true faith:** the Gospel as outlined in the Creed. (Q22–59)

3. **The Benefit of true faith:** Justification by grace, through faith alone. (Q60–64)

Here, the benefit of justification is stated briefly, to be explained in detail in the next five questions. We are "righteous in Christ before God," that is, we possess a righteousness (obedience to the Law of God), which is absolutely perfect in God's eyes. This righteousness is given to us by the grace of Christ and received by faith alone. Having this perfect righteousness, we are thus justified by God and made heirs of eternal life—it is ours as a right, never to be taken away. We are justified by God from all sin through the righteousness of Christ, our Redeemer, imputed to us.

Questions on Number 59

1. Question 59 serves as a _____ between the content of true faith and the benefit of true faith, which is _____

   _____

2. There is a definite connection between the Apostles' Creed and the doctrine of justification by faith. ☐ True ☐ False
   ▶ *Explain:* _____

   _____

   _____

3. Question 21 taught us the _____

   _____

   which is having a (1) _____
   and (2) _____

4. The Apostles' Creed gives us the content of true faith. This means:
   ☐ a. it tells us what must be known about Christ in order to be saved

☐ b. it was inspired by the Apostles

☐ c. it must be recited regularly if one is to be saved

5. A person can be saved by faith in Christ even if he has never heard of the Apostles' Creed. ☐ True ☐ False ▶ *Explain:* _____

_____

_____

_____

6. Match these statements:

Apostles' Creed   Knowing and trusting Christ

A benefit of faith   Content of true faith

The nature of true faith   Justification from all sin

7. Question 59 introduces us to the great truth of justification by faith apart from works. Whose righteousness is given to us by faith?

_____

8. "Righteousness" may be defined as perfect _____

to the _____ of God.

9. Being an "heir of eternal life" means what? _____

_____

_____

10. Write out Titus 3:7. _____

_____

_____

_____

_____

_____

❧ Justification Based on Imputed Righteousness

Q60. How are you righteous before God?

Only by true faith in Jesus Christ: that is, although my conscience accuses me, that I have grievously sinned against all the commandments of God, and have never kept any of them, and am still prone always to all evil; yet God, without any merit of mine, of mere grace, grants and imputes to me the perfect satisfaction, righteousness, and holiness of Christ, as if I had never committed nor had any sins, and had myself accomplished all the obedience which Christ has fulfilled for me; if only I accept such benefit with a believing heart.

In one sense, this question may be described as the *heart* of the Catechism. Everything has been leading up to this amazing and glorious truth of how we are righteous before God. Everything that follows is based on the wondrous fact that I am *now*—by faith in Christ—righteous in the sight of the holy God.

There is very much material packed into this answer. Let us see the main points:

1. We see the need of being perfectly righteous if we are to be accepted by the holy God. God the Law-giver must pronounce us to be perfect keepers of His perfect Law of love if we are to be approved by Him.

2. It is clearly *impossible* that we can be pronounced righteous and justified by God on the basis of our own personal performance. Even our own *consciences* accuse us that we have never kept any of God's commandments perfectly—and we never will in this life.

3. Notwithstanding our personal disobedience and guilt, we receive by *imputation* (something freely charged to our persons) the righteousness of Jesus Christ, Who did keep God's Law of love perfectly. When we receive this imputed righteousness of Christ by faith, God *justifies* us!

4. Only *believers* receive this imputed righteousness of Christ. We must personally put our full trust and confidence and hope in Jesus Christ—His life, death, and resurrection as the only means for our salvation. We are righteous before God and declared justified when we *believe* on Christ Jesus as our Lord. And since this faith in Christ is also a gift of God's grace, we can say assuredly that we are justified by grace alone. This was the great truth proclaimed to sin-burdened people by the Protestant Reformers. Do you also know this truth? And this blessing? Failure to trust in Christ is to remain in one's sins and under God's wrath.

Questions on Number 60

1. Do you think that this question might properly be called the "heart" of the Catechism? ☐ True ☐ False ▶ *Explain:* _____

_____

_____

_____

2. Why is the question "How can I be righteous before God?" an important question? _____

   _____

   _____

   _____

   _____

3. Everyone who calls himself a "Christian" is righteous before God.
   ☐ True ☐ False

4. A person who is indeed righteous before God:
   ☐ a. has Christ's righteousness alone
   ☐ b. has his own righteousness
   ☐ c. has Christ's righteousness *plus* his own righteousness

5. Being saved by grace means that we do not need to have perfect righteousness to present before God. He will take us without any righteousness. ☐ True ☐ False ▶ *Explain:* _____

   _____

6. What is meant by the following terms (consult the glossary):
   a)Imputation _____

   _____

   b) Righteousness _____

   _____

   c) Justification _____

   _____

7. If a person's conscience accuses him of being disobedient and a breaker of God's Law of love, he cannot be justified. ☐ True ☐ False

8. Justification is an act of:
   ☐ a. the church at confirmation
   ☐ b. of God the Judge
   ☐ c. of ourselves when we decide to be converted to Christ.

9. Justification includes "the perfect _____ , _____
   _____ , and _____ of _____
   _____ . . . and all the _____

which Christ _____."
(see Q&A 60)

10. Write out Romans 3:24, 26. _____

_____

_____

_____

_____

_____

_____

_____

❦ The Relation of Faith to Justification

Q61. Why do you say that you are righteous by faith only?

Not that I am acceptable to God on account of the worthiness
of my faith, but because only the satisfaction, righteousness and
holiness of Christ is my righteousness before God; and I can
receive the same and make it my own in no other way than by
faith only.

In question 60, we learned that we are justified by God, and freed from all
sin by the perfect righteousness (obedience) of Jesus Christ being imputed
to us. The Christian is a person who has had an "exchange" with Christ.
That is, Christ has taken the believer's sins on Himself (by imputation)
and has given to the Christian His own perfect righteousness. (Look up
2 Corinthians 5:21.)

Now in question 61 we see the *relation of faith to justification;* that
is, how a person receives the righteousness of Christ, and thus the
forgiveness of sins.

Only the person who truly believes on Christ is justified by God. It
is not all who hear about Christ who are saved, but only those who truly
believe. The Apostle said, "believe on the Lord Jesus Christ, and you will
be saved" (Acts 16:31). And again, "Therefore being justified by faith, we
have peace with God through our Lord Jesus Christ" (Romans 5:1).

But when we say we are saved (justified) by faith alone, we are not
saying that our faith itself merits or purchases our salvation, or makes
us acceptable to God. Today, we often hear it said that we just need
more faith and everything will be all right. But faith itself does not save
us; only Christ saves us. We don't have faith in "faith;" we have faith

in Christ! Faith has no merit; only Christ has merit, as this question plainly teaches.

Why is faith necessary then? Faith is the "hand" which reaches out and takes Christ. Faith is the "instrument" by which we receive Christ as our very own. No one is saved apart from exercising trust in Jesus Christ, though the merit is in Christ alone.

As we shall see in question 65, this faith in Christ is *created in us* by the Holy Spirit, using the written Word of God. Do *you* have faith in Jesus Christ as your own Savior? Are you confessing your faith?

Questions on Number 61

1. In question 61 we are told plainly the _____ _____ to justification.

2. This means that faith and salvation go together. ☐ True ☐ False

3. Since Christ alone can save a sinner, it makes no difference whether a sinner believes or does not believe the gospel. ☐ True ☐ False

4. Faith in Christ ☐ a. *merits* justification ☐ b. does *not* merit justification. ▶ *Explain:* _____

   _____

5. *What* is my righteousness, according to this question?

   _____

   _____

6. It makes no difference which religion you believe in the important thing is that you believe strongly and sincerely. ☐ True ☐ False
   ▶ *Explain:* _____

   _____

   _____

   _____

7. We might call "faith" the _____ through which Christ becomes ours personally.

8. God justifies us when we believe on Christ, because true faith has merit and worth in the sight of God. ☐ True ☐ False

9. Faith in Christ plus our church membership causes God to forgive us all our sins. ☐ True ☐ False

10. Write out Romans 3:28. _____

_____

_____

_____

_____

❧ *Works Cannot Merit Justification*

Q62. But why cannot our good works be the whole or part of our righteousness before God?

Because the righteousness which can stand before the judgment seat of God, must be perfect throughout and entirely conformable to the divine law, but even our best works in this life are all imperfect and defiled with sin.

Having seen that there is a definite relationship between faith and justification (faith being the "hand" that reaches out and receives Christ's righteousness for justification), we now are taught in questions 62-64 what the relation of good works is to justification.

Question 62 tells us that there is no merit in *works,* even as there is no merit in *faith.* Question 63 tells us that there are, however, "rewards" for good works. *Let us now consider good works and our justification.*

By nature, all men think in their hearts that they can somehow do something that will please God and help pay for their sins and buy a place in heaven for them after they die. All the religions of man teach that man can help save himself by doing things. Only Christianity, the true religion, teaches that man *cannot* help save himself by *doing* good deeds.

The reason our "good works" cannot be of any help in making us righteous and acceptable to God is that they are not *perfect* works, as God requires. A work, to be perfect, must be done with perfect love to God with no trace of sin in our hearts either toward God or toward man.

But as *we* have seen in the first part of the Catechism (re-read questions 5 and 8), the heart of man is so wicked that he cannot begin to obey God's holy Law with perfect love to God. Thus all our works are "imperfect and defiled with sin." Only one Person, Jesus Christ, God's Son, did perfect works in God's sight—and all of them were perfect and acceptable to God. The goodness and righteousness of Christ's works are given freely to us who simply believe on Him.

People who speak of their own good deeds and moral lives as giving them a ticket to heaven are fatally deceived. They are completely corrupted by "works" which are rotten in the sight of God. "There is none righteous, no not one" (Romans 3:10). We are justified, but *not* because of any so-called good works of our own.

Questions on Number 62

1. Questions 62–64 as a section tell us the relation of _____ _____ to our justification.

2. In question 62, we learn that our good works can be a part of our righteousness, but not the whole of it, since we need Christ also. ☐ True ☐ False

3. "Righteousness" is perfect obedience to God's holy Law from a pure heart. ☐ True ☐ False

4. We do not need righteousness at all, since God saves believers on the basis of grace only. ☐ True ☐ False ▶ *Explain:* _____

_____

_____

5. Check which of these works are "defiled with sin"?
   ☐ a. Lying to protect one's life   ☐ d. Reading our Bibles humbly
   ☐ b. Cheating a neighbor   ☐ e. Praying the Lord's Prayer
   ☐ c. Watching "dirty" movies   ☐ f. Joining a liberal church

6. What other questions in the Catechism teach that man's "good works" are not really righteous at all? _____

_____

7. All the religions of man, except Christianity, teach that man can help save himself by good works. ☐ True ☐ False

8. After we become Christians, we can do good works, but not perfect works. ☐ True ☐ False

9. Who did good works acceptable to God from a perfect heart of love?

_____

10. Write out Isaiah 64:6. _____

_____

_____

_____

_____

_____

❦ *God Rewards Good Works by Grace*

Q63. Do our good works merit nothing, even though it is God's will to reward them in this life and in that which is to come?

The reward comes not of merit, but of grace.

We are still continuing the discussion of the relation of our works to justification by faith. We saw in question 62 that good works do *not* possess any merit or worth in contributing to our righteousness before God.

1. God Rewards Those Who Do Good.

But now a problem arises which must be answered. Does not the Bible speak of God *rewarding* the good and obedient person and punishing the evil and disobedient person? It surely does. There are over 100 verses in the Bible that speak of rewards. Here are a few of them which teach that God rewards those who do good works by His grace; Psalm 19:11; Matthew 6:4; 19:29; 1 Corinthians 3:14; 1 Timothy 4:8; Hebrews 6:10 and Revelation 22:12. You should look at each of these references.

2. God Rewards Works Solely by Grace, not Merit.

If God gives rewards to those who do good, then it would seem that those good works really do have merit in them, and God *must* reward them. But this is not so! The *rewards* that God gives to those who obey Him are always on the basis of *grace,* not merit. God never *owes* man anything. The rewards of obedience are never earned.

3. All Good Works are Done by the Power of God.

No person can possibly do more good than he should do (Luke 17:10). Each person *owes* God perfect obedience as his natural duty. Further, all the good that we do—which is never enough—is done by the strength that God gives us (Philippians 2:13). So we can never claim that God *owes* us a reward. But God does, indeed, reward us, as we have seen. The rewards then must be given to us out of grace; God grants us blessing even though we can never merit it. Our salvation is all of grace, not of works, and that includes our rewards.

Questions on Number 63

1. Since our righteousness is received from Christ by faith, there are no such things as rewards for good works. ☐ True ☐ False

2. Give the Bible references to the following (*mentioned above*):
   a) "Shall reward you openly" _____
   b) "God is not unrighteous to forget your work" _____
   c) "In keeping of them there is great reward" _____

3. Men give rewards to others, but God never rewards sinful man.
   ☐ True ☐ False

4. Good works
   ☐ a. have merit before God
   ☐ b. are a fruit of faith
   ☐ c. are necessary for our righteousness before God
   ☐ d. are rewarded by God

5. If a person does what it was his duty to do, he can claim a special reward. ☐ True ☐ False

6. How does Luke 17:10 relate to our lesson? _____
   _____
   _____
   _____

7. Those who serve God with true faith in Jesus Christ may expect rewards
   ☐ a. at no time   ☐ c. in heaven only
   ☐ b. in this life only   ☐ d. in this life and in heaven

8. Which types of Christian service are rewarded, according to these verses?
   Matthew 10:42 _____
   Hebrews 11.6 _____
   James 1:12 _____
   1 Peter 5:1–4 _____
   Revelation 2:10 _____

9. If salvation is given to us by the _____
    of God, this means that we do not merit or deserve any part of our
    salvation. ☐ True ☐ False

10. Write out Revelation 22:12. _____

    _____

    _____

    _____

    _____

❦ The Necessity of Good Works

Q64. But does not this doctrine make men careless and profane?

No, for it is impossible that those who are implanted into Christ by true faith, should not bring forth fruits of thankfulness.

It might seem, after all that has been said about salvation being by grace alone and the righteousness of Christ being received by faith alone, that actually our works and personal conduct are not really important at all. Are good works necessary for the child of God?

1. Obedience to God's Commands is Necessary.

The Catechism gives us the truth of the Bible on this matter. Our obedience to God's commandments does not save us, *but* our obedience to God's commandments is necessary! We are not justified *by* our good works, but we are justified *in order to do* good works.

2. The Purpose of Salvation is to be Holy and do Good.

We have seen before in the Catechism that God saves us in order that we might live for Him and serve Him according to His holy Law (re-read questions 1 and 43). It is not only desirable that Christians live holy, obedient, thankful lives before their Savior—it is absolutely necessary. It is impossible for us not to bring forth fruits of thankfulness. The very purpose for our being saved is that we might be conformed to the holy image of Jesus Christ (Romans 8:29) and bring forth good works (Ephesians 2:10).

3. The Power to do Good Works is from the Holy Spirit.

Where does the believer receive the inner power to live a new, thankful life? We have received a new birth by the Holy Spirit (John 3:6-8; 1 John 3:9), and being born of God, *we are* given the power to obey God (though not perfectly yet).

4. Sanctification is Living a Life of Obedience.

In Romans 6:18, 22 we learn that we have been made the servants of God and that we are given the power to live holy lives in obedience to God's commandments. This is our *sanctification*, which is the fruit of our *justification* by faith in Christ. Is the Holy Spirit giving you the *desire* to *live as a* child of God? Each of us must ask himself that question often.

We have now concluded our study of the great biblical doctrine of justification by faith, which covered questions 59–64. We shall turn next to the Catechism's teaching on the holy sacraments, questions 65–82.

Questions on Number 64

1. Some people say that since they are not saved by works, they do not need to be concerned about doing good works. They are correct.
   ☐ True   ☐ False   ▶ *Explain:* _____

   _____

   _____

2. What does the word "profane" mean in this question? (*See your dictionary*) _____

   _____

   _____

3. We are justified by faith in Christ and given His Holy Spirit in order to "bring _____."

4. In Galatians 5:22–23 and Ephesians 5:9 we have a list of Christian "fruits." Name them.
   a) _____
   b) _____
   c) _____
   d) _____
   e) _____
   f) _____
   g) _____
   h) _____
   i) _____

j) _____

k) _____

l) _____

5. The "fruits of thankfulness" are our obedience to the Word of God, especially to the Ten Commandments. ☐ True ☐ False

6. The power in us to love God and serve Him comes from:
   ☐ a. our natural hearts
   ☐ b. our new birth
   ☐ c. seeing the good example of others
   ☐ d. the Holy Spirit

7. According to question 87, those who persist in disobeying God's Word will not be _____, even if they are members of the church.

8. According to question 114, the Christian:
   ☐ a. can keep the Law of God perfectly
   ☐ b. keeps the Law with earnest purpose
   ☐ c. lives according to *all* the commandments and not just some of them.

9. This question closes the section of the Catechism which teaches the doctrine of _____.
   This section covered questions _____ to _____.

10. Write out John 15:5. _____

   _____

   _____

   _____

   _____

   _____

   _____

🌿 *The Source of True Faith*

Q65. Since, then, we are made partakers of Christ and all His benefits by faith only, where does this faith come from?

The Holy Ghost works faith in our hearts by the preaching of the Holy Gospel, and confirms it by the use of the holy sacraments.

1. Why the Catechism discusses the Sacraments

With question 65 we begin a study of the sacraments. This will take us through question 82. Almost 20 questions are devoted to the two sacraments of Holy Baptism and the Lord's Supper. Why is there such a great emphasis on the sacraments when we had only one question on the Trinity (Question 25), only one question on the Church (Question 54), and no questions on the Bible itself? The reason is that when the Catechism was written (1563), these other doctrines were not disputed or questioned.

There was much controversy, however, over the sacraments. The Roman Catholics had their views of what the sacraments meant; the Lutherans had similar views; and the Anabaptists had still different views. The Reformed Church had yet another view, which, we believe, is the closest of all to the Scriptures.

2. The Holy Spirit produces faith by means of the Word of God.

Please note that this section of the Catechism begins by asking *where* does true faith come from. We have just seen in the previous section that salvation is received by faith in Christ apart from works. It is very important that we know where our faith in Christ comes from. Our faith comes either from ourselves or from God. If it comes from ourselves, we can thank ourselves for having it; but if it comes from God, we will thank God for giving it to us.

The Bible clearly teaches that saving faith is a special gift of God, given only to the elect (Ephesians 2:8; Titus 1:1). The Holy Spirit creates this faith into the hearts of the elect. How does He do it? By using the Word of God. Especially the *preaching* of the Word is used by the Spirit (Romans 10:14).

3. Faith has to be increased.

But after faith is created in the heart, it needs to be *strengthened* and *increased*. This is done by two means: first, by the continued preaching of the Word, and, second, by the use of the sacraments. Thus the Word of God is seen to be the *most important* means of grace for our faith. It is even more important than the sacraments; but the sacraments are important also, as we are about to see.

Questions on Number 65

1. Questions 65 to _____ explain the _____
    _____

2. The sacraments of Baptism and the Lord's Supper are more
    important than the preaching of the Word, and that is why we have
    so many questions on them. ☐ True ☐ False

3. The doctrines of the Trinity, the Church, and the nature of the Bible
    were not agreed upon by the Reformed and Lutheran churches.
    ☐ True ☐ False

4. Faith in Christ is a special gift from the Holy Spirit according to
    these Scriptures. _____
    _____
    _____

5. What connection is there between the strength of your faith and
    your attending the worship services? _____
    _____
    _____

6. What should be your attitude toward the preaching of the Bible? (*see
    Romans 10:17 for a hint*) _____
    _____
    _____

7. Faith in Christ is created when
    ☐ a. one is baptized
    ☐ b. the Lord's Supper is first observed
    ☐ c. any person reads the Bible
    ☐ d. the Holy Spirit plants the Word in our hearts

8. The sacraments are used by the Holy Spirit to do what for our faith?
    a) _____
    b) _____

9. With what churches do we disagree as to the meaning of the
    sacraments? _____

10. Write out Acts 20:32.

Meaning of the Sacraments

Q66. What are the sacraments?

The sacraments are visible holy signs and seals appointed by God for this end, that by their use He may the more fully declare and seal to us the promise of the Gospel, namely, that of free grace He grants us the forgiveness of sins and everlasting life for the sake of the one sacrifice of Christ accomplished on the cross.

The Purpose of the Sacraments

In questions 66 and 67, we learn the *purpose* of the sacraments: they point us to the sacrificial death of Jesus Christ and to what we receive from that death, namely, salvation.

Meaning of the Word "Sacrament"

Question 66 also *defines a* sacrament by showing the various elements or parts of it. But before considering these parts, let us see where the word "sacrament" comes from. You will not find the word in your English Bible. The Roman Catholics have it in their Latin translation of the Bible.

It comes from the Latin word, *"sacrare,"* which means sacred or holy. The word meant the *holy oath* that a Roman soldier took when he entered the army. Although the word is not in our Bible, it may be used, because the two ceremonies which the word designates *are* in the Bible: Baptism and the Lord's Supper.

Our question teaches us that a sacrament has four elements:

1. A Sacrament is visible.

Both Baptism and the Lord's Supper involve material substances which can be seen and felt. This is the external part of the sacrament. The spiritual part of the sacrament is the grace of God which accompanies the outward elements as they are used in faith.

2. A Sacrament is holy.

A sacrament is "appointed of God," not of man, and therefore it is holy and must be observed with reverence toward God. The common elements of water, bread and wine are *set apart* from ordinary usage to the service of God by the words of Christ's institution (cf. Exodus 29:33). The administration of the sacraments belongs only to the ordained ministers of the Word, and the sacraments are to be observed only in the worship of God, *never* privately.

3. A Sacrament is a sign.

Just as a road sign points travelers in a certain direction, so a sacrament points us to Christ. It teaches us, as an object lesson, the promise of the gospel. The Church Fathers called the sacrament "the visible sign of invisible grace."

4. A Sacrament is a seal or pledge.

A seal is a stamp or mark of authority. It carries with it the authority of the one who gives the seal. A sacrament is God's visible pledge that He will surely grant the promise of salvation to those who believe His gospel promise.

These terms, "sign" and "seal," come from Romans 4:11 where Paul spoke of the O.T. sacrament of circumcision as a sign and seal of the righteousness of God which Abraham received by faith in God's promises. The sacraments *"more fully* declare and seal to us the promise of the gospel." They are a great help to our faith in the Word of God.

The "promise of the gospel" is defined in the last part of the question, namely, forgiveness of sins and everlasting life through the work of Christ. We shall be reminded of this promise many times as we continue our study of these questions on the sacraments.

Questions on Number 66

1. If the word "sacrament" is not found in our Bible, we should not use it. ☐ True ☐ False

2. Where does the word "sacrament" come from, and what did it originally mean? _____

    _____

    _____

3. The *purpose* of the sacraments is to point us, in a special way, to what? _____

    _____

4. Name the four elements of a sacrament.

   a) _____

   b) _____

   c) _____

   d) _____

5. Who alone can appoint a sacrament for the Church? _____

6. Why are the sacraments called "signs"? _____

   _____

   _____

7. The sacraments are called *seals* because

   ☐ a. all who receive them surely are saved

   ☐ b. God pledges salvation to His people in them

   ☐ c. they are administered by the minister

8. The sacraments do not give more information about Christ, but they do strengthen our faith in Christ and help us know that we are saved. ☐ True ☐ False

9. The phrase "free grace" in this question emphasizes that salvation is completely unmerited and undeserved on our part. ☐ True ☐ False

10. Write out Romans 4:11a. _____

    _____

    _____

    _____

    _____

❧ *The Purpose of the Sacraments*

Q67. Are both the Word and the sacraments designed to direct our faith to the sacrifice of Christ on the cross as the only ground of our salvation?

Yes, truly, for the Holy Ghost teaches in the Gospel and assures us by the holy sacraments, that our whole salvation stands in the one sacrifice of Christ made for us on the cross.

Question 67 emphasizes that the Word and the sacraments work together in pointing us to Christ alone for our salvation. But the Word is primary, for without the presence of the Word, there would be no sacrament at all.

The differences between the gospel preached and the gospel presented in the sacrament may be stated as follows:

1. There is a difference in *approach:* the Word comes to us through the ear; the sacrament comes to us through the eye.

2. There is a difference in *effect:* the Word is used to create and strengthen faith in our hearts; the sacraments are used only to strengthen faith.

3. They differ in their *necessity:* the Word is absolutely essential to salvation; the sacraments are not absolutely essential.

Over against the Roman Catholic position which makes the sacraments primary, and the Word secondary, the Reformed Faith sees their proper relationship. We must not make too much of the sacraments, nor may we regard them as mere empty signs and ceremonies as do Baptist churches.

Again, we must see how the Catechism emphasizes the need of the Holy Spirit to bring Christ to us in the Word and the sacrament. Apart from the powerful work of the Spirit in our souls, the preaching of the Word and the partaking of the sacraments will do us no good. It is the Holy Spirit who causes us truly to trust in Christ and to feed on Him in the Word and the sacraments.

You have been baptized into Christ. The water teaches that your sins can be washed away only by the blood of Christ. Does your baptism *assure you* that you do belong to Christ? May the Holy Spirit give you that faith.

Questions on Number 67

1. This question corrects a wrong view of the importance of the
   sacraments by which church(es)? _____

   _____

2. The Word of God and the sacraments do not need to be used
   together. □ True □ False

3. Both the Word and the sacraments of Baptism and the Lord's Supper
   "direct _____

   _____ of Christ _____

   _____salvation"

   because our "whole _____

_____

_____ cross." (see Q67.)

4. What is the difference in *approach* between the Word and the sacraments? _____

_____

_____

5. The Word of God and the sacraments are both essential for salvation. ☐ True ☐ False

6. Why is it that some people hear the Word and use the sacraments, but still do not really have faith in Christ? _____

_____

_____

_____

7. Should a confirmed church member partake of the Lord's Supper every time it is given? ☐ Yes ☐ No ▶ *Explain:* _____

_____

_____

8. When a baby is baptized, do you believe that he, at that moment, has faith in Christ's one sacrifice? ☐ Yes ☐ No

9. Unbelievers who receive the sacraments receive
   ☐ a. the external sign only
   ☐ b. the signs and the grace of God
   ☐ c. the signs and greater condemnation.

10. Write out Mark 16:16. _____

_____

_____

_____

_____

_____

❧ The Number of Sacraments

Q68. How many Sacraments has Christ instituted in the New Testament?

Two: Holy Baptism and the Holy Supper.

1. There are Only Two Sacraments.

Having seen in questions 65–67 the *purpose* of the sacraments, we now learn in question 68 the *number* of sacraments that Christ instituted for His Church. There are *two*—no more, no less.

2. Roman Catholics Add Five Sacraments.

This may seem like an unnecessary question, but that is because we were not born in the Roman Catholic Church as were our Reformed fathers. The Roman Church added five more sacraments to the two that Christ gave in the New Testament. They added:

1. *Confirmation.* The grace of salvation is confirmed by the priest's laying on of hands;

2. *Penance.* The confession of sin before a priest and the performance of some act of suffering to atone for the sin;

3. *Holy Orders.* Ordination into the priesthood, whereby the priest receives the power to perform the mass (changing bread and wine into flesh and blood);

4. *Marriage.* Special grace is conferred by the priest to the ones being married;

5. *Extreme Unction.* An action by the priest in which he anoints with oil a person who is dying so that the person is strengthened for the final struggle with death.

In all of this, there is much superstition; and though these "sacraments" appear to be all right, they are only the inventions of men and, therefore, are to be condemned as not biblical. The Reformers returned to the truth of the Scriptures and rejected the five sacraments of Rome. We should thank God for those saints who returned us to the truth of the Bible.

3. The Bloody Sacraments of the Old Covenant are replaced by those of the New Covenant which are not bloody.

When we speak of only two sacraments, Baptism and the Lord's Supper, we must see that these are the *New* Testament sacraments which replace the two *Old* Testament sacraments of circumcision and the Passover. Baptism replaces circumcision, and the Supper replaces the

Passover. Both of the Old Testament sacraments were bloody; that is, they involved blood, and this pointed forward to the shedding of Christ's blood. The New Testament sacraments are not bloody, since the blood of Christ has already been shed once for all. Both the Old and the New Testament sacraments point to the death of Christ: circumcision and the Passover pointed *forward* to Christ's death; Baptism and the Supper point *backward* to Christ's death.

Questions on Number 68

1. Question 68 is not very important, since everyone knows what the two sacraments are. ☐ True ☐ False

2. The Roman Catholic Church practices how many "sacraments"? ___

3. If confirmation is *not a* sacrament, what is it? _____

   _____

   _____

4. The Roman Catholics call the Lord's Supper the _____

   _____

5. We have to call the adding of _____ (*how many?*) sacraments by Rome to the New Testament:
   ☐ a. mere superstition
   ☐ b. wicked inventions
   ☐ c. innocent mistakes

6. Can we say that any of the extra "sacraments" of Rome are proper Christian ceremonies but not sacraments? _____ If so, which ones? _____

   _____

7. Match the following Scriptures with the sacraments of the Old and New Testaments:

Matthew 28:1	Circumcision
Genesis 17:10–11	Lord's Supper
1 Cor. 11:23–25	Baptism
Exodus 12:43–50	Passover

8. The sacraments of the Old Testament were:

    a) _____

    b) _____

9. The sacraments of both the Old and New Testaments all point to what? _____

    _____

    _____

10. Write out 1 Corinthians 10:2–4. _____

    _____

    _____

    _____

    _____

    _____

    _____

    _____

    _____

    _____

❦ The Symbolism of Baptism

Q69. How is it signified and sealed to you in Holy Baptism that you have part in the one sacrifice of Christ on the cross?

Thus: that Christ instituted this outward washing with water and joined therewith this promise, that I am washed with His blood and Spirit from the pollution of my soul, that is, from all my sins, as certainly as I am washed outwardly with water, whereby commonly the filthiness of the body is taken away.

The first sacrament that we are to study is baptism, which is explained in questions 69–74. We should see at the beginning of this study that the Catechism asks the same questions about each of the two sacraments. Look at this chart to see how this works out:

	Baptism	Lord's Supper
The symbolism of	69	75
The essence of	70	76
The institution of	71	77

An error rejected	72	78; 80
The grace given in	73	79
The partakers of	74	81–82

The *symbolism* of baptism is explained in question 69. The sacraments consist of (1) an *outward sign* and (2) an *inward spiritual blessing*. The outward sign of baptism is the washing with water. The inward blessing is the washing away of sin by the blood and Spirit of Jesus Christ.

Water has many uses in our lives, and one of the most important is its cleansing quality. Daily, we use water to wash ourselves. Christ commands water baptism to point to the washing away of sin from our souls.

In the sacraments, we have more than a sign (the Baptists say that baptism is *only* a sign). We have also the promise of God "joined" to the sacrament. The grace of salvation is connected with the sacrament. Putting the last phrase first, we see this connection more clearly: "As certainly as I am washed with water ... I am washed with His blood and Spirit." Thus, baptism is an outward sign and seal of an inward blessing. To lack baptism is to lack the sign and seal of salvation. Do you thank God for the sign and seal of your spiritual cleansing?

Does this mean, then, that every baptized person is truly cleansed of his sins by the death of Christ and the regeneration of the Holy Spirit? No, the elect are not always cleansed at the time of baptism; but they will be cleansed before they die. The non-elect are never cleansed at all, even though they may have received the outward sign of baptism.

How much water is to be used in baptism? The Baptists say a tubful, so that the whole body can be *immersed*. Some churches practice *pouring*. We practice *sprinkling*. The washings in the Old Testament rituals were usually sprinklings (see Leviticus 16:15–16; Numbers 8:7; Ezekiel 36:25), and our washing by the blood of Christ is called a *sprinkling*—compare Hebrews 9:13–14 with 10:22. The *amount* of water is not the important thing in baptism. The important thing is the *meaning* of the water of baptism: it means a cleansing of the soul by the blood and Spirit of Jesus Christ.

Questions on Number 69

1. Question 69 speaks of the _____ of baptism just as question _____ speaks of the _____ of the Supper.

2. The Catechism follows a definite pattern in giving instruction.
   ☐ True ☐ False

3. A sacrament has two parts. What are they?

    a) _____

    b) _____

4. The washing with baptismal water points to what? _____

    _____

    _____

5. What are three ways of using water in baptism?

    a) _____

    b) _____

    c) _____

6. Give proof from the Bible that sprinkling is a proper form of baptism. _____

    _____

    _____

7. To all the elect, baptism has this promise of God joined to it: "That _____

    _____

    of my soul."

8. Baptism means the same thing for an infant as it does for an adult.
    ☐ True ☐ False ▶ *Explain:* _____

    _____

9. All baptized persons are truly saved by the death (blood) of Christ and regeneration by the Holy Spirit. ☐ True ☐ False

10. Write out 1 Peter 3:21. _____

    _____

    _____

    _____

    _____

    _____

❦ The Meaning of Baptism

Q70. What is it to be washed with the blood and Spirit of Christ?

It is to have the forgiveness of sins from God through grace, for the sake of Christ's blood, which He shed for us in His sacrifice on the cross; and also to be renewed by the Holy Spirit and sanctified to be members of Christ, so that we may more and more die unto sin and lead holy and unblameable lives.

Having seen in the previous question that the outward washing of water in baptism is a picture of an inward washing by the blood and Spirit of Christ, we now have that inward washing explained for us in greater detail. Question 70 gives us the *essence,* that is, the spiritual meaning of baptism.

The cleansing of salvation consists of two things: (1) cleansing by the blood of Christ and (2) cleansing by the Spirit of Christ. Just what is meant by this two-fold cleansing?

1. Cleansing by the blood of Christ

The "blood of Christ" *refers* to the death of Jesus Christ which, as we have seen many times in the Catechism, was a *sacrifice* in payment for our sins. His life was *substituted* for our lives, and his death was substituted for our deaths. The guilt of our sins was charged to Him, and God's curse fell on Him instead of on us. By His death, Christ merited life and salvation for us. Our sins (guilt) are washed away (forgiven) by the blood (sacrificial death) of the Savior.

2. Cleansing by the Spirit of Christ

However, we would never *personally* receive this cleansing by the blood except for the *second* step, which is cleansing by the "Spirit of Christ." The cleansing by the Holy Spirit is in two stages:

The first stage is the *renewal* of our heart, which is called the "new birth" and "regeneration" (John 3:3; Titus 3:5). Question 8 speaks of being "born again" and question 53 tells us that it is the Holy Spirit who gives us true faith and makes us a "partaker of Christ and all His benefits." The new birth takes place in an instant and is never repeated.

The second stage of the Spirit's cleansing is progressive *sanctification,* the continuous cleansing of the believer whereby we are empowered to "more and more die unto sin and lead holy and unblameable lives" (Ezekiel 36:25–27; 1 Peter 1:2). Notice that the Spirit's two-fold cleansing is based on the death of Christ.

Does your baptism teach you that your sins are forgiven by the death of Christ and that your heart is made new by the Spirit of Christ? Does your life show that you have had the double cleansing?

Questions on Number 70

1. In question 70 we are taught the _____
   _____
   _____
   _____

2. Baptism teaches us that we receive two cleansings, a cleansing of the body and a cleansing of the soul. ☐ True ☐ False

3. Both of our cleansings are connected with Christ. What are these?
   a) _____
   b) _____

4. What is referred to by the expression, the "blood of Christ"?
   _____
   _____
   _____
   _____

5. Name two things that Christ took upon Himself that rightfully belonged to us.
   a) _____
   b) _____

6. Cleansing by the Spirit of Christ refers to the cleansing of our corrupt hearts by the Holy Spirit. ☐ True ☐ False

7. Name the two stages of heart cleansing that a Christian receives from the Spirit of Christ, according to this question.
   a) _____
   b) _____

8. We may be forgiven:
   ☐ a. if we have the blood but not the Spirit of Christ
   ☐ b. if we have the Holy Spirit but not the blood of Christ
   ☐ c. only if we have both the death of Christ and the Holy Spirit
   ☐ d. none of these.

9. Match the following:

    blood of Christ   the condition of our souls

    regeneration   the essence of baptism

    corrupted   sacrificial death

    sanctification   the new birth

    Question 70   dying to sin and living in holiness

10. Write out Titus 3:5–6. _____

_____

_____

_____

_____

_____

_____

❦ *The Institution of Baptism*

Q71. Where has Christ promised that we are as certainly washed with His blood and Spirit as with the water of Baptism?

In the institution of Baptism, which says "Go ye therefore, and teach all nations, baptizing them in the name of the Father, and of the Son, and of the Holy Ghost." "He that believeth and is baptized shall be saved; but he that believeth not shall be damned." This promise is also repeated where Scripture calls Baptism the washing of regeneration and the washing away of sins.

In question 71 we have the *institution* of baptism, that is, the *Scriptural authority* and *command* for practicing baptism. As we have learned already, the sacraments are "appointed of God" (Question 66), especially by Jesus Christ. In this question we have four verses of Scripture quoted to prove that baptism is definitely commanded by God in the Bible.

1. Christ's Great Commission (Matthew 28:18–20)

This passage gives us the "Great Commission"—the instructions Christ gave to His Church just before He ascended into heaven. Here we learn that the Church is (a)to teach all nations (make converts of all races of men), (b) to baptize all who are converted to Christ into the Name of the Triune God (The Father, the Son, and the Holy Spirit), and (c) to continue to teach the baptized Christians all that Jesus commanded.

Though John the Baptist and the disciples of both John and Jesus practiced baptism, it is only in the Great Commission that we have Christian baptism in the Name of the Trinity commanded. This verse teaches us that baptism is really a sign and seal of the whole *covenant of grace* which the Triune God makes with us. Of course, *part* of the promise of the covenant is our cleansing by the blood and Spirit of Christ, which the Catechism especially stresses.

2. The Promise of Salvation (Mark 16:16)

This verse, also part of the "Great Commission," stresses the *promise* of salvation to the person who believes and is baptized. Note that baptism must be received by those who profess to believe on Christ. However, it is the absence of belief that results in damnation, not the absence of baptism. If a person refuses to be baptized, however, when he has the opportunity, then he has no true faith.

3. Spiritual Washing is Necessary (Titus 3:5)

This verse, which we have looked at before, says we are "saved through the washing of regeneration (new birth) and renewing of the Holy Spirit." The authors of the Catechism thought this verse referred to baptism. But water baptism is only indirectly involved. The verse is teaching the spiritual cleansing of the heart by the Holy Spirit through regeneration. It is not teaching regeneration by water baptism, and certainly the authors are not implying that, though their statement could be so interpreted. Calvin's comment on this verse is appropriate: "It is therefore the Spirit of God who regenerates us, and makes us new creatures; but because His grace is invisible and hidden, a visible symbol of it is beheld in baptism."

4. The Need for Cleansing of the Heart (Acts 22:16)

This verse, spoken by Ananias to the converted Paul, teaches the meaning of baptism: that it is a sign and seal of the cleansing of the heart. It is the "calling on the name of the Lord" that cleans, however, not the outward water, as the next question will teach us.

Perhaps you may think these verses teach that *only* older, converted people may be baptized. We shall see that this is not so when we study question 74.

Questions on Number 71

1. By the "institution" of baptism, we mean

☐ a. the practice of the church

☐ b. its Scriptural authority

☐ c. the water of baptism

2. In the four Bible verses quoted in this question, *water baptism* is definitely taught in each one. ☐ True ☐ False

3. Check the following *correct* statements:

☐ a. The Sermon on the Mount is also called the Great Commission.

☐ b. John the Baptist did not practice *Christian* baptism as we now have it.

☐ c. Baptism is a sign and seal of the Covenant of Grace.

☐ d. The Great Commission was given to the Church just before Christ died.

4. Baptism must be in *whose* name? _____

_____

5. This shows that it is really a sign and seal of the _____

_____ , of which our

spiritual cleansing is a part.

6. Mark 16:16 teaches that if a person is *not* baptized, he will be damned. ☐ True ☐ False ▶ *Explain:* _____

_____

_____

7. If a person says that he believes on Christ, but refuses to be baptized and join Christ's Church, what do you think of his faith?

_____

_____

8. The proper interpretation of Titus 3:5

☐ a. has nothing whatsoever to do with Christian baptism

☐ b. definitely speaks of water baptism

☐ c. speaks of the cleansing of the heart to which baptism also points

9. According to Acts 22:16, Ananias told Paul that all that he needed to do was to be baptized to have his sins washed away. ☐ True ☐ False

10. Mark 16:16 definitely teaches that only converted believers may be baptized, and not infants. ☐ True   ☐ False ▶ *Explain:* _____

_____

_____

_____

11. Write out Matthew 28:19. _____

_____

_____

_____

_____

_____

_____

❦ An Error Corrected

Q72. Is, then, the outward washing with water itself the washing away of sins?

No, for only the blood of Jesus Christ and the Holy Spirit cleanse us from all sin.

1. The Error of Roman Catholics and Lutherans

The Catechism in question 72 *rejects an error,* an error held by both the Roman Catholic and the Lutheran Churches. It is the false teaching that there is an *automatic* cleansing of the soul in the act of baptism. The Romanists actually teach that there is a spiritual cleansing power in the holy baptismal water, which works *if* the person baptized does not resist the grace of God.

The Lutheran teaching is not quite so extreme; it puts more emphasis on faith. But, still, Luther taught that the sacrament *had a holy power in itself.* He wrote thus in his Catechism: "Baptism works forgiveness of sins, delivers from death and the devil, and confers everlasting salvation on all who believe." Again he wrote: "Baptism is a gracious water of life, and a washing of regeneration" (*Luther's Small Catechism*).

2. The Reformed Teaching Stresses the Holy Spirit

The Reformed (Scriptural) teaching is that the cleansing of the soul is *only* by the blood of Christ (His death) and the Spirit of Christ in regeneration, and that this cleansing is *not tied to the act of water baptism.*

Rather, regeneration is given to the elect *before, during,* or *after* the act of baptism or *even apart from* baptism, depending on the purpose and operation of the Holy Spirit. There is no automatic saving power in the sacraments.

3. The Error of Baptismal Regeneration

In our time, there is another church denomination, calling itself "The Disciples of Christ" or "Church of Christ," which, like the Roman Church, also teaches baptismal regeneration. In other words, a person's sins are washed away when he obeys the command to be baptized.

But the truth is that our hearts are cleansed from the power of sin only by the Holy Spirit using the Word of God. And as we believe in Christ's death, the guilt and punishment of our sins are removed (read question 70 again). Water baptism is a sign and seal of a *spiritual* cleansing which may or may not take place when the water is applied to the body.

Questions on Number 72

1. Our Catechism, in this question, rejects an error taught by _____

   _____

   _____

2. It is not good Christian manners to mention the errors of other churches and that should, therefore, be avoided. ☐ True ☐ False

3. Check the churches that teach that baptism automatically washes away sins: ☐ Baptist ☐ Roman Catholic ☐ Presbyterian ☐ Reformed ☐ Lutheran ☐ Church of Christ

4. Both the Roman Catholic and the Lutheran Churches teach that when a baby is baptized, he experiences the new birth (regeneration). ☐ True ☐ False

5. The Holy Spirit can cleanse our hearts
   ☐ a. *before* ☐ b. *during* ☐ c. *after* the act of water baptism.

6. *Complete:* "Only _____
   _____ and the Holy _____
   _____ sin."

7. There is no connection whatsoever between regeneration and the act of baptism. ☐ True ☐ False ▶ *Explain:* _____

   _____

_____

_____

8. Which question explains more fully what is meant by the phrase, "cleansing by the blood and Spirit of Christ"? _____

9. Which comes first in your soul?
    ☐ cleansing by the Spirit of Christ
    ☐ cleansing by the blood of Christ
    ▶ *Explain:* _____

    _____

    _____

10. Write out Acts 10:44 and 47. _____

    _____

    _____

    _____

    _____

    _____

    _____

    _____

❦ The Value of Baptism

Q73. Why then does the Holy Ghost call Baptism the washing of regeneration and the washing away of sins?

God speaks thus with great cause, namely, not only to teach us thereby that just as the filthiness of the body is taken away by water, so our sins are taken away by the blood and Spirit of Christ; but much more, that by this divine pledge and token He may assure us that we are as really washed from our sins spiritually as our bodies are washed with water.

Having seen in question 72 that it is an error to think that our sins are actually washed away by the act of water baptism, the Catechism once again reminds us that we are not to belittle water baptism or think that it is unimportant.

1. Assurance is Connected to Holy Baptism.

Indeed, God has established a close spiritual connection between the sacrament of baptism and the washing of our souls by the blood and Spirit of Christ. This question is much like question 69. Both questions stress that God's "promise" and "pledge" and "token" of salvation are received in this sacrament.

Though baptism itself does not save us, yet the Holy Spirit uses our baptism to *assure* us that we are "really washed from our sins." So *close* is baptism to salvation that the Bible often speaks of the outward cleansing as if it were the inward cleansing. Acts 2:38 says: "Repent, and let every one of you be baptized in the name of Jesus Christ for the remission of sins." Acts 22:16 says: "Arise and be baptized, and wash away your sins, calling on the name of the Lord." 1 Peter 3:21 says: "There is also an antitype which now saves us—baptism (not the removal of the filth of the flesh, but the answer of a good conscience toward God), through the resurrection of Jesus Christ." Notice that it is always Christ, not water, that saves us; but the water is also commanded by our Savior as a sign and seal of His saving grace.

Thus, our baptism is necessary, as a sign, to teach us that only Christ can wash our sins away; and, as a seal, to *assure* us that our sins have, in fact, been washed away by Christ.

2. Baptism is a Christian Duty.

Water baptism, then, is a *biblical duty,* which, if neglected, involves a person in sinful disobedience to God. But we should also remember that Baptist Christians, who do not give this sacrament to their covenant children, are not *willfully disobeying* the Word of God, and therefore, are not to be condemned as unbelievers. It is their understanding, not their hearts, that is wrong, and we must not judge their hearts.

Should infants of believers also be baptized? Our next question will tell us the answer.

Questions on Number 73

1. Since the outward washing with water cannot possibly cleanse our souls, we may say that water baptism is not at all important.
   ☐ True ☐ False

2. What other question is much like question 73? _____
   What do they both stress? _____

   _____

   _____

3. Give three Bible references which show that the Holy Spirit (the Author of all Scripture) teaches a close spiritual connection between the outward washing with water and the inward washing of salvation.

    a) _____

    b) _____

    c) _____

4. Each of these verses (*given above*) tells who and what really washes away sins (*Quote the proper phrases*).

    a) _____

    _____

    b) _____

    _____

    c) _____

    _____

5. Peter calls baptism a "figure," which means that the water itself does not actually wash away sins. ☐ True ☐ False

6. The sacrament of baptism is said to "_____ us thereby" that "our sins are taken away." It is also said to be a "divine _____" and a "_____" to "assure us that we are really washed from our sins."

7. We have been taught in these questions on baptism that we are cleansed from sin by "the _____ and the _____ of Christ."

8. Baptism, being a command of God, "is a _____ which, if neglected, involves a person in _____ to God."

9. May we say that God will condemn all Baptists because they do not give their infants holy baptism? ☐ Yes ☐ No ▶ *Explain:* _____

    _____

    _____

10. Write out Ezekiel 36:25. _____

_____

_____

_____

_____

_____

❦ The Subjects of Baptism

Q74. Are infants also to be baptized?

Yes, for since they, as well as their parents, belong to the covenant and people of God, and through the blood of Christ both redemption from sin and the Holy Ghost, who works faith, are promised to them no less than to their parents, they are also by Baptism, as a sign of the covenant, to be ingrafted into the Christian Church, and distinguished from the children of unbelievers, as was done in the Old Testament by circumcision, in place of which in the New Testament Baptism is appointed.

We finish up the section on baptism with question 74. In this last question, we are told who are the *subjects of baptism.* This is a very important question, for it explains that *both* Christian parents and their infant children are to be given baptism, the sign and seal of salvation. This question corrects the error of the Baptist Churches, just as question 72 corrects the error of the Roman Catholic and Lutheran Churches regarding baptism.

There is much in this question that could be discussed, but we can consider only the main points briefly.

1. The Children of Believers were Circumcised in the Old Covenant.

First of all, the Catechism, following Scripture, teaches the baptism of infants on the *basis* of the "Covenant of Salvation" or the "Covenant of Grace," which is *the promise of God to save His elect people through Christ and His Spirit and to be their God and friend forever.*

This covenant is spoken of throughout the Bible. When God told Abraham about His covenant of salvation, He assured him that infants were also included in the covenant. We read of this in Genesis 17:1–9. Notice in verse 7 that God's covenant is "an everlasting covenant" though all the generations of believers that would live after Abraham.

Beginning with Abraham and continuing through the Old Testament, the sign and seal of the covenant was the sacrament of circumcision, given to the baby boys (see Genesis 17:10–14).

2. The Place of the Children of Believers in the New Covenant

In the New Testament, the covenant remains the same, although the sign and seal of it, as we have seen, is baptism, which replaces circumcision. The same covenant continues through the generations of believers who are still called the "children of Abraham" (Galatians 3:7, 29).

Also, the children of believers are still included in God's covenant, even as in the Old Testament. This is proved by Peter's sermon on the day of Pentecost, when he said; "The promise (covenant) is to you (who believe), *and to your children,* and to all who are afar off, as many as the Lord our God will call" (Acts 2:39). Our Savior showed that the covenant promise of salvation still belongs to children when He said that the infants are to be brought to Him, for they are also in the Kingdom of God (see Luke 18:15–16).

So, to the children of Christian believers, God *still* promises redemption through Christ, regeneration by the Holy Spirit, and the gift of faith. Having this promise of the covenant, such children, then, are entitled to its sign and seal, which is baptism. This covenant promise, it must be noted, is *only* for the children of believers; it is not for the children of unbelievers, who are still the children of the Devil.

3. Baptist Objections to Infant Baptism

In days to come, you will have discussions with Baptist Christians. You should know why they are against infant baptism, and how to answer them. Here are the Baptist objections to infant baptism and how we answer these objections from the Scriptures:

Objection 1: Infants are not capable of repenting, believing on Christ, and understanding baptism and therefore should not be baptized.

Answer: Neither did the infants in the Old Testament understand the meaning of circumcision but they were commanded to be circumcised. The covenant promise is given to infants not because they can understand it, but because they are included in God's covenant of grace.

Objection 2: There is no command in the Bible to baptize infants.

Answer: There is no need for such a command. The covenant continues as an everlasting covenant, and the children of believers are still included in it, as Peter said in Acts 2:39. The Baptists must show us from the Bible that God cancelled His covenant!

Objection 3: There are no examples of infant baptism in the Bible.

Answer: If this is true, it does not prove that the practice is wrong. The covenant includes the children, and they must be given the sign of the covenant. Besides, Acts 16:15, 33; 18:8 and 1 Corinthians 1:16 speak of family baptisms, which could have included infants.

Objection 4: Matthew 28:19 and Mark 16:16 place faith before baptism.

Answer: These Great Commission passages refer especially to the conversion of unbaptized heathen adults on the mission fields. Every non-Christian adult must first be converted before he can be baptized. But after adults become Christians and are baptized, the covenant of salvation requires that their children also be baptized.

The Baptists exclude their infants from baptism because they do not properly understand the covenant of the Old and New Testaments. We repeat, in conclusion, that we do not believe that every infant who is baptized is saved. Some infants are cleansed by the blood and Spirit of Christ *before* they are baptized and some after. Some are never cleansed if they are not God's elect. But all infants, *born of Christian parents within the church,* are to be baptized because of God's command.

Questions on Number 74

1. Question 74 tells us who are the _____ of _____ and we learn that the _____ are in error on this point.

2. The Catechism shows that the basis for infant baptism is:
   - ☐ a. the innocency of children
   - ☐ b. an example of infant baptism in the New Testament
   - ☐ c. the Covenant of Grace
   - ☐ d. that children also need to be saved.

3. What is the "Covenant of Grace" or "Covenant of Salvation"?

   _____

   _____

   _____

   _____

   _____

4. The Covenant of Salvation that God made with _____ in Genesis chapter _____ continued through the Old Testament and continues now in the _____.

5. The sign and seal of the Covenant in the Old Testament was

   _____.

   In the New Testament, it is _____.

6. The promise of God made to children, according to question 74, includes:

   a)"Redemption _____

   _____ Christ."

   b) "The Holy _____ faith."

   Whose infants are to be baptized? _____

7. Check the verses which show that children of believers are included in the Covenant of Salvation:

   ☐ Genesis 17:10   ☐ Genesis 26:12

   ☐ Joel 2:16   ☐ Matthew 19:14

   ☐ John 7:1   ☐ Acts 2:39

   ☐ 1 Corinthians 7:14

8. The Covenant of Salvation: (*check all that apply*)

   ☐ a. continues through all generations

   ☐ b. is understood correctly by the Baptists

   ☐ c. was preached by Peter

   ☐ d. includes only those who repent and believe on Christ

   ☐ e. is the basis for infant baptism

9. How would you answer these Baptist arguments:

   a)There is no command in the N.T. to baptize babies. _____

   _____

   _____

   _____

   b) Babies cannot understand the Gospel of Christ and therefore should not be baptized. _____

   _____

   _____

   _____

   _____

10. Write out Genesis 17:7. _____

   _____

   _____

_____

_____

_____

 The Symbolism of the Lord's Supper

Q75. How is it signified and sealed to you in the Holy Supper that you partake of the one sacrifice of Christ on the cross and all His benefits?

Thus: that Christ has commanded me and all believers to eat of this broken bread and to drink of this cup in remembrance of Him, and has joined therewith these promises: first, that His body was offered and broken on the cross for me and His blood shed for me, as certainly as I see with my eyes the bread of the Lord broken for me and the cup communicated to me; and further, that with His crucified body and shed blood He Himself feeds and nourishes my soul to everlasting life, as certainly as I receive from the hand of the minister and taste with my mouth the bread and cup of the Lord, which are given me as certain tokens of the body and blood of Christ.

Questions 75 through 82 deal with the second sacrament instituted by our Savior, the Lord's Supper. The same pattern will be followed as with the section on baptism (refer to question 69 again for the chart). This question asks the same question with reference to the supper as question 69 did with reference to baptism, namely, its *symbolism*.

1. The Two Elements: Bread and Wine

In the Lord's Supper (also called "Holy Communion" and "the Lord's Table") we have *two* elements: bread and wine. These were very common articles of food in Bible times and, of course, bread is still one of our main foods. Christ chose *food* to be the symbol of a holy sacrament.

Why did Christ choose food? Because just as food is necessary for the continued life of our physical bodies, so His body and blood are necessary for the spiritual life of our souls. The bread and wine remind us of Christ's body and blood. Bread must be *broken* (they did not cut it with a knife in those days) in order to eat it; and Christ's body must be broken to pay for our sins. (Please note that the bones of Christ were not broken (see John 19:31–36), but His body and soul were separated by death, and in this sense His body was "broken" for us.) Wine is red and resembles blood; also it is a stimulant for the faint and weary.

2. Meaning of the Lord's Supper

In this question we see that the Lord's Supper teaches us two things: (1) what Christ *once* did and (2) what He *continues* to do. His body and blood were once offered on the Cross. And the righteousness and spiritual life that He purchased for us by His precious death are continuously "communicated" or given to us by the Holy Spirit. We need food constantly and we need the life of Christ and His grace constantly or our spiritual life would cease.

Thus, the broken bread and the poured wine remind us of what Christ did on the Cross; and as we see the bread and wine, and as we *partake* of them, we are assured that "He Himself feeds and nourishes my soul to everlasting life." Note that twice the word "certainly" is used. The outward elements of this sacrament *certainly* point us to our union with Christ. Christ has joined His promise of spiritual nourishment to the Lord's Supper, just as He joined the promise of spiritual cleansing to baptism.

Questions on Number 75

1. Question 75 teaches the _____of the Lord's Supper, just as question _____ taught the same about baptism.

2. Give the various names for this sacrament. _____
    _____
    _____

3. Who should take the Lord's Supper, according to this answer?
    _____
    _____

4. We may say that the Lord's Supper is a "food sacrament." Why?
    _____
    _____

5. The bread and wine teach us two things about the work of Christ. They are:

    a) _____
    _____

    b) _____
    _____

6. In speaking of Christ's "broken body," we are referring to:
   ☐ a. His horrible bone fractures
   ☐ b. the separation of His soul and body at death

7. The death of Christ provides continuous righteousness and spiritual life to believers. ☐ True ☐ False

8. The promises God gives to us in the Lord's Supper are: (*Check the correct answer(s)*):
   ☐ a. that all who partake are certainly true believers.
   ☐ b. that Christ's body was once offered for the salvation of all true believers.
   ☐ c. that Christ continues to feed our souls by the benefits of His death.
   ☐ d. that all who see and taste the bread and wine truly belong to Christ.

9. The food elements of the Supper are appropriate because Christ is the Real Food for our souls. ☐ True ☐ False

10. Write out Luke 22:19–20. _____

_____

_____

_____

_____

_____

_____

❧ The Meaning of the Lord's Supper

Q76. What does it mean to eat the crucified body and drink the shed blood of Christ?

It means not only to embrace with a believing heart all the sufferings and death of Christ, and thereby to obtain the forgiveness of sins and life eternal, but moreover, also, to be so united more and more to His sacred body by the Holy Spirit, who dwells both in Christ and in us, that, although He is in heaven and we on earth, we are nevertheless flesh of His flesh and bone of His bone, and live and are governed forever by one Spirit, as members of the same body are governed by one soul.

This question explains the *essence,* or spiritual meaning, of the Supper. Just as question 70 explained that spiritual cleansing is accomplished by the blood and Spirit of Christ, so here we learn what is the spiritual eating and drinking of Christ.

1. Communion with Christ in the Supper

To an unbeliever, it must sound very strange and even repulsive to hear about eating human flesh and drinking human blood. In the early days of Christianity, the Christians were charged by their enemies with practicing cannibalism! But, of course, the Lord's Supper is a *spiritual* feeding on Christ, not a literal, physical eating and drinking of Him.

We are here taught that we feed on Christ by faith—we "embrace Christ with a believing heart." As the preceding question also indicated, there are especially two things about Christ that we believe as we take the Supper:

a.   We believe in His atoning sacrifice on the Cross—"the sufferings and death of Christ"—for forgiveness and life.

b.   We believe that we are united spiritually to Christ's body by the Holy Spirit, so that Christ's resurrection life flows from Him to our souls. Christ is our Head and we are members of His Body, the Church. We are as close to Christ as the flesh and bones of His own physical body!

2. True Faith is Strengthened in the Lord's Supper.

In eating the Lord's Supper, our faith in Christ's sacrifice on earth and our union with His person in heaven is strengthened. As we eat, we are assured that we belong to Him and that nothing will ever separate us from His righteousness, His life and His love.

In the Lord's Supper our faith is very active. We meditate deeply on what Christ means to us. This is a difference between baptism and the Lord's Supper. Baptism is a sign and seal of God's joining us to Himself while we are *passive* and perhaps even *unconscious* of what He is doing. We have nothing to do with our new birth.

But in the Lord's Supper, our souls are very *active* and *conscious.* We see, we taste, we eat—our souls feed on and enjoy Christ. Also, since we are joined to God only once, we can be baptized only once; but we must *continuously* feed on Christ every day—and so we must take the Lord's Supper all our lives. We should remember that our communion with Christ through the Lord's Supper is not for only a few brief moments, but the blessing of it lasts until we take it again.

Questions on Number 76

1. In question 76, we learn what is the _____

    _____ of the Lord's Supper, that is, what is

    really meant by feeding on Christ.

2. We must admit that we are Christian cannibals because we eat the

    flesh and drink the blood of Jesus Christ. ☐ True ☐ False

    ▶ *Explain:* _____

    _____

    _____

3. Look up John 6:53–58, and answer the following:

    a) By eating and drinking Christ, we receive what? (vs. 54)

    _____

    b) As believers eat and drink Christ, they _____ in Him

    and He _____ in them (vs. 56).

    c) Christ is the living _____ from heaven

    the Israelites ate the _____ and are dead(vs. 49, 58).

    d) By eating Christ, our souls shall live forever, and our bodies shall

    be _____ on the last day (vs. 54).

4. In eating Christ by faith, we believe two things especially about Him.

    a) _____

    _____

    b) _____

    _____

5. Christians are united so closely to Christ that the Bible says what

    about them? (*see Ephesians 5:30*): _____

    _____

6. The resurrection life of Christ continuously flows to believers souls

    by the Holy Spirit. ☐ True ☐ False

7. If unbelievers take the Lord's Supper, they receive only the physical

    elements of bread and wine, but they do not feed on Christ.

    ☐ True ☐ False

8. If all believers are united to Christ's body, they are also spiritually
   united to each other. ☐ True ☐ False

9. The difference between baptism and the Lord's Supper is that
   baptism is a sign of God's grace given while *passive*, whereas the
   Lord's Supper is a sign of God's grace is given while very *active*.
   ☐ True ☐ False

10. Write out 1 Corinthians 10:16. _____

    _____

    _____

    _____

    _____

    _____

    _____

❦ The Institution of the Supper

**Q77. Where has Christ promised that He will thus feed and
nourish believers with His body and blood as certainly as they
eat of this broken bread and drink of this cup?**

In the institution of the Supper, which says: "The Lord Jesus the
same night in which He was betrayed took bread: and when He
had given thanks, He brake it, and said, Take eat: this is my body,
which is broken for you: this do in remembrance of me. After
the same manner also He took the cup, when He had supped,
saying, This cup is the new testament in my blood: this do ye, as
oft as ye drink it, in remembrance of me. For as often as ye eat
this bread, and drink this cup, ye do show the Lord's death till
He come." And this promise is also repeated by the Apostle Paul,
where he says: "The cup of blessing which we bless, is it not the
communion of the blood of Christ? The bread which we break, is
it not the communion of the body of Christ? Because there is one
bread, so we being many are one body, for we are all partakers of
that one bread."

In question 77 *the institution of the Lord's Supper* is stated; that is, the
Scriptural authority that this is really a sacrament given by Christ.
This question is similar to question 71 which showed the *institution* of
baptism. (We must have *biblical authority* for the sacraments if they are
to be anything more than mere human ceremonies.)

Three Gospels (Matthew, Mark, and Luke) and 1 Corinthians 11:23–25 speak of the institution of the Supper. The promise of spiritually feeding on Christ's death and His Person is stated in these passages. An additional passage, 1 Corinthians 10:16–17 is also quoted in the Catechism under the heading: "And this promise is also repeated ..." (Note that this same phrase is also used in the last part of question 71, which is evidently intended to show, in both cases, that the sacraments as instituted by Christ were re-affirmed by the Apostle Paul).

Let us consider some further matters about the observance of the Holy Supper:

1. The Lord's Supper was *instituted* or appointed by Christ in connection with the Passover celebration.

After the Passover meal has been eaten, Jesus used the unleavened bread and the wine of the Passover table to institute this new sacrament. It is really the *continuation* of the Passover sacrament, except that in the Supper we look back and "remember" Christ's death, whereas in the Old Testament, the Passover sacrament pointed forward to Christ's death. Another difference: the Passover was a bloody sacrament, whereas the Lord's Supper is not, since the blood has already been shed once for all.

2. The Lord's Supper is *commanded* by Christ for all believers.

"This do" means that those who believe in Christ must feed on Him in the Lord's Supper. To neglect it is a great sin against Christ and His atoning death.

3. The Lord's Supper is to be *observed often* in the Church.

"For as often as you eat ... and drink" (1 Corinthians 11:25). There is no set number of times per year given in Scripture for this observance. Some churches observe it once a month; others once every three months; and some three times per year. The frequency must be determined by the local church rulers for the best order and edification of the congregation.

4. This sacrament, as is baptism, is a *church* ordinance.

It is to be observed in the *congregation* in connection with the preaching of the Word. Christ had His disciples gathered together when He instituted the Supper. It is not to be administered privately, though it may be given in a private home so long as the elders of the church govern the celebration.

5. There is a spiritual fellowship in the Supper *with the other believers* who also partake of it.

This is clearly taught in 1 Corinthians 10:17, which really reads as follows: "Since it is one bread (loaf), we the many (partakers) *are one body,* for we are all partakers of that one Bread (Christ)." At the

Communion table we commune with one another in Christ, the Living Bread, by eating of the *one* loaf.

Questions on Number 77

1. In question 77, we have the biblical authority for the Lord's Supper. It is indeed a _____ appointed by Christ.

2. Matthew, Luke, and John all tell of the giving of the Lord's Supper.
   ☐ True   ☐ False

3. The Lord's Supper is really a continuation of *what* Old Testament celebration? _____

4. What proof is there that all believers are commanded to take the Holy Supper each time it is given? _____

   _____

   _____

   _____

   _____

5. The Bible tells us to observe the Lord's Supper four times per year.
   ☐ True   ☐ False ▶ *Explain:* _____

   _____

   _____

6. Since Christ gave the Lord's Supper to the Apostles gathered together, we may say that the Supper (*check one*):
   ☐ a. is only for the Apostles
   ☐ b. may be given privately by the minister whenever he feels like it
   ☐ c. must be given only to the church gathered under the preaching of the Word

7. What do you think of the practice of private communion in some churches, such as permitting a confirmation class to take Communion privately while the congregation looks on? _____

   _____

   _____

   _____

   _____

8. Match the following:

Institution of the sacraments   Forbidden by Scripture

Old Testament Passover Feast   To neglect it is to sin

Private Communion service   Communion of believers

"This do in remembrance of Me"   Questions 71 and 77

One Bread   Continued in the Lord's Supper

9. The "One bread" of the Communion Service teaches us that all believers who partake of Christ the Living Bread are communing:
   - ☐ a. with Christ only
   - ☐ b. with fellow Christians only
   - ☐ c. with both Christ and other Christians

10. Write out Matthew 26:26–27. _____

_____

_____

_____

_____

_____

_____

_____

❧ *An Error Rejected*

Q78. Do, then, the bread and the wine become the real body and blood of Christ?

No, but as the water in Baptism is not changed into the blood of Christ, nor becomes the washing away of sins itself, being only the divine token and assurance thereof, so also in the Lord's Supper the sacred bread does not become the body of Christ itself, though agreeably to the nature and usage of sacraments it is called the body of Christ.

1. The Romanist Error of Transubstantiation

In question 78, we have an *error rejected,* an error of the Roman Catholic Church. (This question is the counterpart of question 72, which rejected an error concerning baptism.) The Roman Church in A.D. 1215 adopted the teaching that the bread and wine of the Supper are literally changed into the physical body and blood of Christ. This change is called "transubstantiation" (from the Latin *trans* = across; *substantia* = substance; the substance goes across to another substance.) Question 80, which also deals with this Roman error of transubstantiation, was added to the Catechism later, as we shall see.

The false teaching of transubstantiation, that the bread and wine are miraculously changed into the real body and blood of Christ, is so fantastic that you may wonder how anyone could have gotten such an idea. This false doctrine comes from a wrong interpretation of a little phrase spoken by the Lord at the Supper. He said in Matthew 26:26, 28: "This *is* My body" (referring to the bread) and "this *is* My blood of the new covenant" (referring to the wine). But Jesus did not mean that He was holding a piece of His own flesh in His hand or a cup of His own blood! Rather, the little verb "is" means *represents.* The bread and wine *represent* His body and blood.

Can we prove this? Yes, for when Jesus said, "I am the door" (John 10:7) and when He said "I am the true vine" (John 15:1), He did not mean He was a literal door or a literal vine. He could not have been *both* at the same time anyway! Rather, He *represented* a door and a vine.

But not only does the Roman doctrine twist Scripture, it is contrary to our sense. It is non-sense. How can a piece of *bread* which looks like bread, feels like bread, tastes like bread, and *is* bread according to chemical analysis, be really human flesh? This is not *faith;* it is mere superstition. The miracles that Christ performed were *real* miracles. When He changed the water to wine (John 2:6–11), that was true transubstantiation! And no one had any doubts about it.

Why does this question speak of the bread only and not of the wine? Because in the Roman Catholic "Supper" (they call it "mass") only the bread is given to the people; and since flesh has blood in it, the people get the "blood" also when they eat the "flesh" (bread). Of course, this is just more wicked human reasoning.

2. The Lutheran Error of Consubstantiation

The Lutheran doctrine is not much better. Luther taught *consubstantiation* (*con* = with). That is, the physical flesh and blood of Christ are *with* the bread and wine, though they have not actually changed. This, too, contradicts Scripture and our common sense. Christ's physical body in heaven is one; it is not shredded into millions of pieces and scattered over the Communion tables of all churches in all ages! The body of Christ is not spiritual, but physical, and it cannot be eaten physically.

We feed on Christ's body in the sense that we receive the saving blessings of His death and His resurrection by faith, through the working of the Holy Spirit in our hearts (as the next question will teach).

Questions on Number 78

1. Like question 72, this question rejects an _____ held by the _____ Church.

2. The false teaching of _____ was officially accepted by that Church in what year? _____

3. What does the term "transubstantiation" mean, and how does it refer to the Lord's Supper? _____

    _____

    _____

    _____

4. How would *you* interpret the words of Jesus, "This is My body"?

    _____

    _____

    _____

    Give Scriptural proof: _____

5. The "miracle" of the Roman Catholic mass is a weak and defective miracle, for the bread, after it is supposedly changed to "flesh," still

    _____

    _____

6. If the people do not drink the wine in the Roman Catholic mass how do they think they are getting the blood of Christ? _____

    _____

    _____

7. The Lutheran doctrine of the Supper is described as
    ☐ a. transubstantiation ☐ b. consubstantiation.

8. The Lutherans think they eat the physical body and drink the physical blood of Jesus Christ in the Holy Supper. ☐ True ☐ False

9. The physical body of Christ cannot be present in the Lord's Supper
    because _____

    _____

    _____

10. Write out John 6:35. _____

    _____

    _____

    _____

    _____

❦ *The Assurance Given in the Supper*

Q79. Why then does Christ call the bread His body, and the cup His blood, or the new testament in His blood, and the Apostle Paul, the communion of the body and the blood of Christ?

Christ speaks thus with great cause, namely, not only to teach us thereby, that like as the bread and wine sustain this temporal life, so also His crucified body and shed blood are the true meat and drink of our souls unto life eternal; but much more, by this visible sign and pledge to assure us that we are as really partakers of His true body and blood by the working of the Holy Ghost, as we receive by the mouth of the body these holy tokens in remembrance of Him; and that all His sufferings and obedience are as certainly our own, as if we ourselves had suffered and done all in our own person.

Having seen that there is no physical eating of the body nor drinking of the blood of Christ in the Lord's Supper, we now learn just what is received when we eat the bread and drink the wine. As in question 73, which taught that *the grace of assurance* is given in the sacrament of baptism, so we learn here that *the grace of assurance* is also given to the believer when he properly partakes of the Lord's Supper. God assures the believer that the body and blood of Christ—His death—are truly for *his* salvation.

We must be familiar with "sacramental language." By this is meant that the *outward sign* is often called the spiritual blessing itself. The baptismal water is called a "washing away of sins" (Acts 22:16), and the bread and wine are called the "body" and "blood" of Christ. That is because the promise of grace is joined to the outward elements when they are properly received. This is what a sacrament is: an outward sign that the Holy Spirit uses to convey the spiritual grace of the things signified. Neither baptism nor the Lord's Supper are mere empty observances. God gives His grace through them. We must emphasize, however, that the sacraments are not *converting ordinances;* but they do strengthen and confirm the grace that is already present or will be present (in the case of infant baptism).

In this question, both the *sign* and *seal* aspects of the Supper are again emphasized (they were also emphasized in question 75). First, we are *taught* that "His crucified body and shed blood are the true meat and drink of our souls unto life eternal." Second, the blessings of Christ's obedience and death are sealed to us by the Holy Spirit as we take the bread and wine in faith. That is, our hearts are *assured,* increasingly, that we really do belong to Christ.

We see, then, how very important it is that we properly understand the purpose and meaning of the Lord's Supper, and that we regard it as one of the greatest spiritual privileges that God has given us. Do not rest content until you have received permission to go to the Lord's Blessed Table!

Questions on Number 79

1. Question 79 teaches us that the _____

   _____ is given when the Lord's Supper is properly

   taken.

2. It is correct to say that in the Lord's Supper we have a remembrance of Christ, but that we receive nothing from Christ. ☐ True ☐ False

3. "Sacramental language" means: (*Check the right answer[s]*):

   ☐ a. the outward signs are not the real sacrament.

   ☐ b. the outward signs are themselves *called* the things they point to.

   ☐ c. the outward elements are changed into another substance.

4. It is never proper to call the sacramental bread and wine the body and blood of Christ. ☐ True ☐ False

5. A sacrament is a "converting ordinance" that is, it can bring spiritual life to a person who may be spiritually dead when he receives the sacrament. ☐ True ☐ False

   ▶ *Explain:* _____

_____

_____

6. The Lord's Supper is both a sign and a seal. As a *sign*, it teaches us
   that "His _____ body and _____ _____
   are the _____ _____ and _____
   of our souls _____."
   As a *seal*, it "assures us that we are ... really _____
   of His true _____ and _____
   by the working of _____ ."

7. Do unbelievers receive nothing at all except a little bread and wine if
   they partake of the Lord's Supper? (*See 1 Corinthians 11:29*)

   _____

8. If *you* are now a believer, do you think you should take the
   Lord's Supper *before* you make public confession of your faith at
   Confirmation? ☐ Yes ☐ No ▶ *Explain:* _____

   _____

   _____

9. As you are learning more about the blessing of Holy Communion,
   are you also becoming more desirous of partaking of it?
   ☐ Yes ☐ No

10. Write out 1 Corinthians 5:8. _____

   _____

   _____

   _____

   _____

   _____

❧ *The Lord's Supper versus the Popish Mass*

Q80. What difference is there between the Lord's Supper and the Pope's Mass?

The Lord's Supper testifies to us that we have full forgiveness of all our sins by the one sacrifice of Jesus Christ, which He Himself once accomplished on the cross; and that by the Holy Ghost we are ingrafted into Christ, who, with His true body, is now in heaven at the right hand of the Father, and is there to be worshiped. But the Mass teaches that the living and the dead do not have forgiveness of sins through the sufferings of Christ, unless Christ is still daily offered for them by the priests, and that Christ is bodily under the form of bread and wine, and is therefore to be worshiped in them. And thus the Mass at bottom is nothing else than a denial of the one sacrifice and suffering of Jesus Christ, and an accursed idolatry.

As we check our chart given with question 69, we see that the error rejected relating to baptism is condemned with *one* question (Question 72), but that there are *two* questions condemning the Roman Catholic error of the Lord's Supper (Questions 78 and 80). Question 80 looks out of place according to the pattern that the Catechism has followed in explaining the sacraments.

The reason for this is that question 80 was not part of the Catechism as it was originally written. It was inserted later by order of Elector Frederick III to further condemn the Roman Catholic Mass. He felt question 78 was not strong enough in denouncing the wickedness of the Mass.

Why does the Roman Catholic Church call the Lord's Supper the "Mass"? This word comes from the Latin *missa,* which means "to dismiss." In the early days of Christianity, those who could not partake of the Lord's Supper were dismissed after the sermon and before the Supper. Thus, the term for dismissing part of the congregation from the supper became the word used for the Supper itself! Actually, it means that they have dismissed the Lord's Supper!

The first part of the answer gives the Scriptural meaning of the Lord's Supper, which we have considered in the previous questions. The second part of the answer speaks of two very wicked errors associated with the Romish Mass. We shall consider the second part of the answer.

1. The Mass pretends to offer up Christ again.

The Mass pretends to be a *new* sacrifice of Christ each time it is performed. A Roman Catholic Catechism says that "the mass is the same sacrifice as the sacrifice on the cross" (Baltimore Catechism #931). Thus the Roman Catholic does not believe that Jesus *died* for him, but that Jesus *dies* for him continuously. This makes the "death" of Christ nothing. Then there is no real death that once and for all paid for sin. If Christ has not finished dying after 2000 years, how can we be sure that He will *ever* finish dying? Thus, neither those who died in Jesus, nor those who now believe in Him, can be saved by a *finished* sacrifice. The Bible teaches just the opposite, however, for Jesus said, "It is finished"

(John 19:30) and Hebrews 9:26, 28 and 10:12 teach that Christ was *once* offered to bear away the sins of many. The Roman Catholic usually trusts in the Church, the priest and the wafer, but not in the one sacrifice of Christ on the cross!

2. Romanism teaches that the host is to be worshiped.

The Roman Church teaches that since Christ is really present in the bread and wine when transubstantiation takes place, He must be "adored" (worshiped) in them. Therefore, when the priest holds up the wafer and cup (the host), all are to bow and worship those elements. This involves the worshipers in idolatry—the worship of an idol. The Catechism is not too strong, therefore, in condemning the mass as a "denial of the sacrifice of Christ and an accursed idolatry." This judgment is the same as Luther's who spoke of the "mass of the papacy as the greatest and most monstrous abomination" and "the extreme of all papal idolatries" (*Smalkald Articles*, Part 2, Art. 2).

And do you know that there are some Protestants who believe that the Roman Catholic Church is all right! Their ignorance is very great and tragic.

Questions on Number 80

1. How do we account for the fact that question 80 seems to be out of place when we look at the pattern of questions that the Catechism has followed up until now? _____

   _____

   _____

   _____

2. Do you think that question 80 is too strong in condemning the Roman Mass? ☐ Yes ☐ No ▶ *Explain:* _____

   _____

   _____

   _____

3. The word "mass" came from a (*check one*)
   ☐ a. New Testament verse
   ☐ b. Greek word meaning "supper"
   ☐ c. Latin word meaning "to dismiss"

4. The two chief errors of the Mass according to this question are:
   a) "Christ is still _____

   _____ priests," which is "nothing else than _____

_____ of Jesus Christ."

b) "Christ is bodily _____

_____

_____

_____ in them," which is "an accursed

_____ ."

5. If Christ keeps dying in the Mass, then we are not saved by the *one death* of Christ. ☐ True ☐ False

6. The Scriptures teach that Christ's body is where? _____

_____

7. The Roman Catholics teach that Christ's body is where? _____

_____

8. It is all right for a Protestant to attend a Roman Catholic Church once in a while and worship with the others. ☐ True ☐ False

▶ *Explain:* _____

_____

9. If the Mass is "an accursed idolatry," what will happen to those who practice it? (See Ephesians 5:5–6) _____

_____

10. Write out Hebrews 10:12, 14. _____

_____

_____

_____

_____

_____

_____

❦ *The Partakers of the Supper*

Q81. Who are to come to the table of the Lord?

Those who are displeased with themselves for their sins, yet trust that these are forgiven them, and that their remaining infirmity is covered by the suffering and death of Christ; who also desire more and more to strengthen their faith and to amend their life. But the impenitent and hypocrites eat and drink judgment to themselves.

In questions 81 and 82 we learn *who* are to partake of the Lord's Supper. These questions correspond to question 74, which explained *who* the subjects of baptism are.

The Supper of the Lord is a *holy* supper, and only those who are accepted by Christ may partake of it with His blessing. Those not accepted by Christ partake to their condemnation (1 Corinthians 11:29). This question tells us the *personal qualifications* that a Christian must have to partake in a worthy manner. In the next question, we learn of the *church qualifications* that a person must also have to come to Holy Communion.

In partaking of the Supper, as of the Passover in the Old Testament, a person must be aware of the significance of the celebration; and only those persons who have come to years of understanding and have been properly instructed may partake of it. In the Supper, our faith must *feed* on Christ, and we must *remember* His death. Thus, children must first be instructed in the gospel before they may come to the Lord's Table. And this is why you are studying your Bible and Catechism now!

Before a Christian takes the Lord's Supper, he must examine himself anew (1 Corinthians 11:28). There are *three parts* to this self-examination, as outlined in question 81. Before he partakes, the believer must seriously ask himself about his *sins*, his *Savior*, and his *service* (which you recognize as the outline of the Catechism itself).

1. **My Sin.** Am I really sorry that I am a sinner? Am I displeased with myself because of my corrupt nature and my many transgressions of God's Law? Do I recognize that I do not love God or my fellow Christians and neighbors as I ought? Do I confess all these sins to God with a broken spirit?

2. **My Savior.** Am I trusting only in the death of Christ for the covering of my sins? Have I really confessed all my sins and depravity to Christ for forgiveness? Do I recognize that He, being the Son of God, is the only One who can save me and give me everlasting life?

3. **My Service.** Do I sincerely desire to live a more holy life for Christ?

Do I want a stronger faith and a more godly walk? Do I have a heartfelt desire to be *perfect* in obedience to God's will (Matthew 5:48)?

If anyone feels that he cannot sincerely answer these three kinds of questions properly, he is not spiritually fit to come to the Lord's Table. He should repent before God and pray for God's grace so that he may answer them satisfactorily. It is far better for an unprepared person not to eat and drink of the Lord than for him to do so just to be seen of men and then to meet with Christ's anger! The impenitent (unrepentant) and hypocrites (insincere) eat and drink to their own condemnation. Beware!

Questions on Number 81

1. In questions _____ and _____ we learn who may _____ of the Lord's Supper. The first one tells of the _____ qualifications necessary, the second one tells of the _____ qualifications necessary.

2. God calls (*which?*) to Holy Communion.
   ☐ a. all men   ☐ b. all baptized Christians
   ☐ c. all confessing believers

3. As with the _____ celebration of the Old Testament, only instructed believers may partake of this sacrament.
   ☐ True   ☐ False

4. 1 Corinthians 11:28 teaches that before a Christian partakes of the Lord's Supper, he should _____

   _____

   _____

5. Our Catechism speaks of _____ (*how many*) parts to one's personal self-examination. Should a Christian examine his heart and his faith only when it is time to take the Lord's Supper, or should he do so all the time? _____

   _____

6. Before coming to the Lord's Table, each one must ask himself questions about:
   a)his _____

b) his _____

c) his _____.

7. Should a young person be confirmed and permitted to go to the Lord's Supper because he is of a certain age (say, fourteen) or because he understands and believes the gospel sufficiently?

   ☐ Yes ☐ No

8. God requires partakers of Holy Communion to (*which one(s)?*)

   ☐ a. be perfect

   ☐ b. be sincerely sorry for their sins

   ☐ c. trust in their goodness

   ☐ d. respect Christ for being a great teacher only

   ☐ e. desire to live a more godly and obedient life

9. Those who do not make sincere examination of their hearts and lives should not eat the Lord's Supper because they will eat to their own _____ (1 Corinthians 11:28).

10. Write out 1 Corinthians 11:27–28. _____

   _____

   _____

   _____

   _____

   _____

   _____

❧ Qualifications for the Lord's Supper

Q82. Are they, then, also to be admitted to this Supper who show themselves by their confession and life to be unbelieving and ungodly?

No, for thereby the covenant of God is profaned and His wrath provoked against the whole congregation; therefore, the Christian Church is bound, according to the order of Christ and His Apostles, to exclude such persons by the Office of the Keys until they amend their lives.

In this question we learn of the *church qualifications* that every Christian must meet in order to partake of Holy Communion. The Reformed Church has always insisted that only those Christians who are in good standing in the church may partake of Communion. The Supper is to be guarded by the elders of the church so that only church members who confess the gospel properly and who live a godly life may partake.

Two evil results occur if unqualified people partake at the Lord's Table: (1) the covenant is profaned and God's wrath is provoked against the whole congregation, and, (2) The person who eats, being unqualified, eats condemnation to himself.

There are three views on the question of who may be permitted to partake of the Supper.

1. Open Communion

This view means that the sacrament is open for all who wish to partake. There are no restrictions. Each person may be asked to judge his own heart, but the elders do not judge the belief or the lives of those who come. Consequently, Modernists and adulterers, for example, may eat and drink with true Christians, if they so desire, while our own covenant children (unconfirmed) are kept back! But this is clearly wrong, as Jesus never gave the Supper to the world, but to His own disciples. And the Apostle Paul told the church to "put away from yourselves the evil person" (1 Corinthians 5:13) and to "withdraw from every brother who walks disorderly" (2 Thess. 3:6). This sacrament is only for confessing believers, and the elders must restrict the Table to them alone.

2. Closed Communion

This view is that only the members of one's own church or denomination may partake. This view assumes that all other churches are *false* churches and all members of those other churches are not true Christians. This is certainly not true, however, and it would be wrong to exclude true Christians from the Supper who may be members of another orthodox denomination.

3. Restricted Communion

This is the proper view, and the view that we must hold, namely, that the elders are responsible to admit only true Christians, as judged by their doctrine and life, to partake. Christians from other churches may also partake if they are found to (1) confess the truth of the gospel properly and (2) if they belong to a Bible-believing church and are in good standing in their own church. This necessitates an inquiry by the elders when such non-members request to join in the Communion Service.

In this manner, no true believers will be excluded, yet the wicked and unbelieving will not be allowed to profane the table and harm themselves and the church. Our elders need to be very much concerned about this matter, so that the Supper will be a Supper of blessing, not a table of judgment!

Questions on Number 82

1. In question 82, we learn that more is required of a person than that he examine his own heart; he must also be examined as to his

   _____ and his _____

   _____ by the elders of the church.

2. For the elders to admit a person to, or exclude him from, the Supper means that they must know something about that person.
   ☐ True ☐ False

3. What does the verb "to profane" mean? _____

   _____

   _____

   _____

4. If the sacraments are signs and seals of God's Covenant of salvation, then whom only must the church permit to take of the signs and seals of the Covenant? _____

   _____

   _____

   _____

   _____

5. The story of Achan and his theft of the gold and the garment (Joshua 7) proves that one man's sin can bring God's anger against the whole congregation. ☐ True ☐ False

6. It is ☐ kind ☐ unkind to a Modernist or a wicked person to deny him the Lord's Supper if he desires it.

7. Check which verses prove that the officers of the church have the authority to keep from the sacraments those people not entitled to them.
   ☐ a. Matthew 16:19   ☐ d. 1 Corinthians 5:13
   ☐ b. Galatians 1:21   ☐ e. 2 Thessalonians 3:14.
   ☐ c. John 20:23

8. Match the following:

"Open Communion"   Only confessing believers may partake

"Restricted Communion"   The elders of the church

"Closed Communion"   Anyone may partake of the Supper

Keys of the Kingdom   Only our own members are permitted

9. What form of Communion should we practice to guard the Lord's Table properly and yet not bar other true Christians from other churches from partaking? _____

_____

10. Write out Psalm 50:16–17. _____

_____

_____

_____

_____

_____

_____

❧ The Keys of the Kingdom

Q83. What is the Office of the Keys?

The preaching of the Holy Gospel and Christian discipline; by these two the kingdom of heaven is opened to believers and shut against unbelievers.

We have learned that the church, through its ordained officers called *elders*, has the duty to guard the Lord's Table from being profaned by persons who are either unbelieving (erring in doctrine) or ungodly (erring in morals). We are now led into the subject of *church authority* or the "office of the keys" in questions 83, 84 and 85.

Question 83 tells us that there are two "keys" to open and close the doors of God's Kingdom (which means the church visible and invisible, see question 54). This expression comes from our Savior's instructions in Matthew 16:19 and Revelations 1:18; 3:7–8. The keys are (1) official *church preaching* and (2) official *church discipline*, which are both under the authority of the elders.

As the keys are used, people are either admitted into the church or locked outside. This seems like too much power for mere men to have and, therefore, many Protestants reject the teaching of the "keys" of church authority. But this is the teaching of none other than Jesus Christ, and so we must pay careful attention to it.

As we consider the office of the keys, we must first understand the *government* of the church as taught in the New Testament. There are mainly *three* types of church government being practiced by churches today. They are:

1. The Hierarchical System

The system of superintendents, bishops, archbishops, popes, etc., who are superior to the lower clergy. This system of government is practiced by the Roman, Episcopalian, Methodist and Evangelical United Brethren churches, for example.

2. The Congregational System

The local congregation has the supreme power over itself—the whole membership must vote on the admission and dismission of members and other church matters. No elders or officers from other churches may exercise any authority over the local congregation. This form is practiced by Baptists, Congregationalists, and other "independent" churches. Some independent churches are not strictly congregational in government, as they are ruled by elders.

3. The Presbyterian or Reformed System

This system of church government:

a. Recognizes Christ as the Head of the Church (Ephesians 5:23).

b. Recognizes the office of *elder* ("bishop" or "presbyter") as the ruling office. The elders are chosen by the people, but they rule by the authority of Christ alone (Acts 20:17, 28; 1 Corinthians 12:28; Hebrews 13:17).

c. Recognizes that all elders (the pastors are elders, also) are equal in authority and that there must be at least two in each congregation, including the pastor (Acts 14:23; 1 Peter 5:1).

d. Recognizes the authority of other elders in other congregations when they meet in session called classes or presbyteries (Acts 15:22; 1 Timothy 4:14).

e. Recognizes the right of appeal from the local church court to higher church courts (Acts 15).

Only this Reformed (Presbyterian) system of church government recognizes all these biblical principles; hence, we can say that our system is the truest to Scripture.

So to the elders (teaching and ruling)—not to the people—are committed the office of the keys. It is very important that we give proper respect and obedience to these men in our churches who are ordained by God to the office of elder.

Questions on Number 83

1. The church has the duty to guard the Lord's Table from unqualified persons, because to the church Christ has given

   "the _____ of the _____."

2. The "office of the keys" is explained for us in questions _____.

3. As keys are used to lock and unlock doors, so the elders have authority from Jesus Christ to admit persons and to put persons out of the _____

   which means the church of Christ.

4. What are the two keys of the Kingdom?

   a) _____

   b) _____

5. Quote some Bible references which prove that the church has been given keys from Christ. _____

   _____

6. To properly understand the teaching of the keys and church authority, we must also know what the New Testament teaches about church government. ☐ True ☐ False

7. Name the three systems of church government that the various Christian churches use today:

   a) _____

   b) _____

   c) _____

8. According to the Bible, Christ is the _____ _____ of the church, and He gives officers called _____ to rule over the churches. These officers are _____ in authority and together they use the authority of the _____ of the Kingdom.

9. When they meet in a broader group, called a _____, they can rule over all the congregations represented.

This is the _____ or Reformed system of church

_____ , and it is the system taught in the

_____ .

10. It makes no difference which form of government a church has, just
    so long as Christ is preached as Savior in the church.
    ☐ True ☐ False ▶ *Explain:* _____

    _____

11. Write out Matthew 16:19. _____

    _____

    _____

    _____

    _____

    _____

    _____

❦ *The Key of Preaching*

Q84. How is the kingdom of heaven opened and shut by the preaching of the Holy Gospel?

In this way: that according to the command of Christ, it is proclaimed and openly witnessed to believers, one and all, that as often as they accept with true faith the promise of the Gospel, all their sins are really forgiven them of God for the sake of Christ's merits; and on the contrary, to all unbelievers and hypocrites, that the wrath of God and eternal condemnation abide on them so long as they are not converted. According to this testimony of the Gospel, God will judge men both in this life and in that which is to come.

Jesus said to Peter and the other Apostles (Matthew 16:19; 18:18) that whatsoever they bound on earth would be bound in heaven and whatsoever they loosed on earth would be loosed in heaven. This refers to the *pronouncement* that unrepentant sinners remain bound to their sins and to the *pronouncement* that repentant sinners are loosed from their sins. God alone forgives or condemns, but the church has the right to make the official declaration of who *is* and who is *not* forgiven. This is *the key of official church preaching* which is explained in question 84.

When a minister of the Word of God (who is called and ordained by Christ through the church) preaches the Word of God, he makes it known to all who hear that the door of the invisible Church (the Kingdom of God) is open wide to all who believe the gospel of Jesus Christ. All repentant believers are assured by the true preacher that their sins are forgiven and that they have eternal life. The preacher must declare, "Whoever calls on the name of the Lord shall be saved" (Romans 10:13) and that the gospel is the *power* of God to salvation for everyone who believes" (Romans 1:16).

Christ alone admits believers into His Kingdom, but He has His ministers declare this to the public. When a true preacher speaks the Word of God, it is Christ who speaks through him and opens the door of salvation to those who hunger and thirst after Him.

But the key of official church preaching also *closes* the door to many who hear the Word preached. The faithful minister must pronounce certain judgment on all who refuse to surrender to Jesus Christ. The wrath of God and eternal condemnation abide on unbelievers and hypocrites so long as they remain unconverted. The door to heaven is tightly shut against them, and this they must be told in no uncertain terms (John 3:36; Luke 13:3).

Whenever the gospel of Christ is officially proclaimed by a minister of Jesus Christ, a "loosing" and a "binding" take place: there is an opening and a shutting of the door of salvation. All who hear must be clearly informed as to which side of the door they are standing on. True preaching of the Word must clearly show both the marks of the Godly, regenerated, forgiven soul and the marks of the hypocrite who still loves sin and is under condemnation. How often do you pray for your pastor, that he will preach the Law and the gospel with great clarity and power, in the fear of God, so that saints may be comforted and sinners will tremble before the Sovereign Lord?

As the minister preaches the Word of God, he is a savor (smell) of death unto death to unbelievers and a savor of life unto life to believers (2 Corinthians 2:16).

Questions on Number 84

1. This question explains the first key of the Kingdom, which is

   _____

2. In whose name and by whose command does the preacher use this key? _____

3. As the minister preaches the Word of God, Christ opens the door of salvation to some persons and keeps it shut against others.
   ☐ True ☐ False

4. Is a minister using the key of preaching properly if he neglects to tell people how to be saved? ☐ Yes ☐ No

5. Is he using the key properly if he tells hypocrites that they will go to hell unless they repent? ☐ Yes ☐ No

6. A minister has no right to tell an unbeliever or hypocrite that he will be judged by God in *this* life. ☐ True ☐ False

7. In every sermon, we should hear words to the effect that whenever we "accept with _____ _____ the promise _____ _____ Gospel, all our sins _____ _____ _____ _____ (us) of God _____ _____ _____ _____ Christ's merits."

8. In using the key of preaching, the minister should judge the hearts of various individuals in the congregation. ☐ True ☐ False
    ▶ *Explain:* _____
    _____
    _____

9. The church building should be open to all persons on Sunday.
    ☐ True ☐ False

10. All persons who come should be told that they are in the Kingdom of God. ☐ True ☐ False

11. Why should all church members pray for the minister as he prepares and preaches his sermons? _____
    _____
    _____

12. Write out Acts 10:42–43. _____
    _____
    _____
    _____
    _____
    _____
    _____

❧ *The Key of Church Discipline*

Q85. How is the kingdom of heaven shut and opened by Christian discipline?

In this way: that, according to the command of Christ, if any under the Christian name show themselves unsound either in doctrine or in life, and after several brotherly admonitions do not turn from their errors or evil ways, they are complained of to the Church or to its proper officers; and, if they neglect to hear them also, are by them denied the holy sacraments and thereby excluded from the Christian communion, and by God Himself from the kingdom of Christ; and if they promise and show real amendment, they are again received as members of Christ and His Church.

Christ gave two keys to His church officers, the keys of preaching and church discipline. The second one is especially despised by many—if not most—churches today. But a biblically Reformed church will use *the key of official church discipline* as explained in the Catechism, question 85.

The key of church discipline must follow the preaching of the Word. As individuals are converted to Christ and brought into the Kingdom of heaven by the key of preaching, they must then be brought into the visible church, the local congregation, by the use of the second key. The elders must examine the confession and life of any professing convert and either open the door of church membership to him or keep it closed against him. In either case, it is done in the Name of and by the authority of Jesus Christ, the Head of the Church. Those who have been received into the church remain subject to the key of discipline in the hands of the elders. There is a *four-fold purpose* given for the two keys, as they are used together (they must never be separated), by the Word of God.

1.   They are used to bring into the church those who are outside and belong inside, by grace, though faith.

2.   They are used to cast out those who are inside and belong outside, because of disobedience and unbelief.

3.   They are used to keep outside those who belong outside because of their rebellion.

4.   They are used to keep inside those who are tempted to go outside but really belong inside because they are born again.

Many people are against the church disciplining its wayward members. They usually give reasons such as the following as to why nothing should be done about the ungodly in its membership:

1. Discipline offends people and therefore should be ignored.

Not only is the erring brother offended, when he is admonished, but his friends in the congregation will also be offended. The answer to this objection is that it is far better to offend men than to offend Christ. To imply that the key of discipline is harsh, unloving, and offensive is to charge Jesus Christ with these sins! The truth is that if Christian discipline is neglected, the soul of the sinner is being neglected, and he is being left to persist in and perhaps *die in* his stubbornness and sin. The *effect* of using the key of discipline in the church at Corinth was to bring a sinning church member to repentance (see 1 Corinthians 5:13; 2 Corinthians 2:6–8), and this result should certainly offend no one!

2. Discipline is wrong because this is judging a person's heart.

The answer to this pious-sounding argument is that it also is utterly false. Church discipline is never an attempt to judge a person's heart; rather, it is a judgment of a person's confession and life. If Christ tells the elders to use the key of discipline, they must obey Him and examine and judge the beliefs and behavior of the church members under their care. Matthew 7:16–20 does not contradict Matthew 7:1— "Judge not, that you be not judged."

Paul was not guilty of violating the Lord's words when he wrote 1 Corinthians 5:7; 1 Thessalonians 5:14; 2 Thessalonians 3:6, 14–15; 1 Timothy 5:20 and Titus 3:10. If it is wrong for the elders to make judgment and discipline the members inside the church, it is just as wrong for them to make judgment and admit members into the church in the first place. Of course, the deep motives of a person's heart can be known only to God, but his confession and life are known to the church and must be judged whether they are in accordance with the standards of Scripture.

3. The church should not be concerned about the private lives of its members.

The answer: The elders are held responsible by Christ to care for the soul of every member entrusted to them (Hebrews 13:17). The Scriptures do not make a hard and fast distinction between the private and public life of the church member. The elders must not be "nosey" and forever meddling in the private affairs of the members; but the elders are to be concerned about the spiritual well-being of every one of Christ's sheep, and this does necessitate personal contact and, perhaps, special inquiry on occasion. Regular family visitation is the biblical procedure for keeping up this contact (Acts 20:20). A private matter becomes a church matter when discipline does not succeed on the personal level (Matthew 18:17).

In question 85, we learn the procedure for church discipline. These instructions are based on Christ's instructions in Matthew 18:16–18.

Remember this Scriptural procedure; it is extremely important, though rarely followed:

a. Every church member has the duty to seek the recovery of an erring fellow member. If you have been offended, you are to go to the offender and speak to him personally about the sin in question (Galatians 6:1). If you have knowingly offended another person you are to go to him and ask his forgiveness.

b. If the sinning brother does not repent, then you must take with you two witnesses who shall hear both sides of the controversy.

c. If the sinning brother still refuses to confess his sin and repent of it, then the church elders must be called in and they shall make a judgment on the case.

d. The elders shall first *admonish* the sinner to repent. If he does not, then they must *suspend* him from church privileges, such as the sacraments and office-bearing. If he still refuses to repent of his sin, then, as a last resort, he must be *excommunicated*—cast out of the church altogether and regarded as a "heathen" (unbeliever).

The purpose of church discipline is to separate the Christian from his offending sins, not to remove the Christian from the church. However, if the key of discipline is resisted, then the sinner must be purged lest the whole body become corrupted and Christ's wrath come on the whole congregation (1 Corinthians 5:6–7).

All sin is accursed of God and must be righteously dealt with whenever it is manifested in the congregation. No public sin in the church may be ignored; and discipline must be used against such sin that is persisted in. Also, we must remember that upon repentance the worst of offenders must be forgiven and re-admitted. Christ promises forgiveness to every repentant sinner, and so must the church, His Body.

The congregation that is afraid to use the key of Christian discipline is no church of Christ. Is yours?

Questions on Number 85

1. The key of church discipline is

☐ a. overly used in the so-called Christian churches today

☐ b. rarely used in the so-called Christian churches today

☐ c. faithfully used in the so-called Christian churches today

2. A church which refuses to discipline its sinning members is

☐ a. overly concerned about their welfare

☐ b. is seeking to show the love and patience of Christ

☐ c. is living in disobedience to the Word of Christ and will suffer the evil consequences.

3. What relationship, if any, do the two keys have to each other?

_____

_____

_____

_____

_____

4. Name *one* of the four-fold purposes of the keys. _____

_____

_____

_____

5. What are three false objections against church discipline that are commonly given.

a) _____

_____

b) _____

_____

c) _____

_____

6. Quote a Bible verse in 2 Thessalonians which proves that the elders must discipline sinning church members. _____

_____

_____

_____

_____

7. The purpose of church discipline is
    ☐ a. to restore the sinner to Christ
    ☐ b. to embarrass people
    ☐ c. to keep the church pure for Christ
    ☐ d. to remove people from the church roll
    ☐ e. to keep people living in the fear of God

8. Match the following (look up Matthew 18:15–18):

First step of discipline   "Take with you one or two more."

Second step   "Let him be to you like a heathen."

Third step   "Go and tell him his fault ... alone."

Fourth step   "Tell it to the church (officers)"

9. It is proper to speak of another person's sin to others before you go to him in person and speak to him about it. ☐ True ☐ False

   ▶ *Explain:* _____

   _____

   _____

   _____

10. Write out James 5:20. _____

   _____

   _____

   _____

   _____

   _____

   _____

   _____

   _____

Part 3.
How I Should Be Thankful

❦ *The Purposes of Good Works*

Q86. Since, then, we are redeemed from our misery by grace through Christ, without any merit of ours, why should we do good works?

Because Christ, having redeemed us by His blood, also renews us by His Holy Spirit after His own image, that with our whole life we show ourselves thankful to God for His blessing, and that He be glorified through us; then also, that we ourselves may be assured of our faith by the fruits thereof; and by our godly walk win also others to Christ.

Having completed the second and longest part of the Catechism which deals with our Redemption (Questions 12–85), we now begin our study of the third and final part of the Catechism, which teaches us *Thankfulness* and *Service*.

How great is our debt to the Lord for giving us salvation! We show our gratitude to God for His mercies by presenting ourselves always to Him as His obedient servants. Jesus once said that a person who has been forgiven much will love much in return (see Luke 7:47). If you really have been redeemed from sin and hell by Christ, you will show your thankfulness by the way you live—you will live a converted and holy life; and you will pray, read God's Word every day, and seek to grow in God's grace and truth.

It is important to know also that Christian holiness (living a godly life) is possible only if we have personally experienced the new birth and conversion. Modernists tell people that they should live Christian lives, yet they deny the truths of Christian redemption which alone make it possible to live for Christ. Christian doctrine is the foundation of our Christian living. Unbelieving Modernists cannot live truly Christian lives.

In questions 86 through 91, we are taught the biblical doctrine of *good works*. We shall see:

1. *The Purposes of good works (Q86)*

2. *The Necessity of good works (Q87)*

3. *The Source of good works (Q88-90)*

4.   The Nature of good works (Q91)

Good works are those fruits and deeds which proceed from our regenerated hearts and are performed by our bodies, according to the will of God. They are acts of loving obedience to God which He helps us to do and which are pleasing to Him.

"Why should we do good works?" The answer is as follows: Because we are both *redeemed* by the blood (death) of Christ and *renewed* (born again) by His Holy Spirit. We are saved in order to do good works. We do not do good works in order to redeem or renew ourselves. These good works which redeemed Christians do have several *purposes*. They are these:

a.   That we may show ourselves thankful to God. How else could we show our thankfulness than by good works done in obedience to God?

b.   That God may be glorified in us. God's Name is honored when His creatures do what He says. The ungodly despise the Name of God by their evil works.

c.   That we may be assured of our faith and union with Christ. If we break God's commandments, we can have no assurance that we are the Lord's. "Now by this we know that we know Him, if we keep His commandments" (1 John 2:3). An obedient life and assurance of faith cannot be separated from each other.

d.   That we may win others to Christ. We can be effective witnesses and interest others in becoming Christians only as we show by our lives what true Christianity is.

Do people realize that *you* represent Jesus Christ and the Word of God by the way you live? Let us be "zealous for good works" (Titus 2:14) that these four *purposes* might be accomplished in our lives.

Questions on Number 86

1.   The three parts of the Catechism are these:

a) my _____

b) my _____

c) my _____

2.   Thankfulness and service to Christ are necessary on our part if He has really rescued us from the misery of sin and hell.

☐ True   ☐ False

3.   It is possible for a person to live a good Christian life and keep God's commandments even if he rejects what the Bible says about the

Virgin Birth of Christ and His resurrection from the dead.
☐ True ☐ False

4. Questions 86 through 91 teach us what? _____

    _____

5. According to this question, we should do good works:
    ☐ a. in order to redeem ourselves from misery
    ☐ b. to gain merit before God
    ☐ c. because we have been renewed by the Holy Spirit
    ☐ d. to show that we are better than others
    ☐ e. to win others to Christ

6. Good works are:
    ☐ a. fruits of thankfulness
    ☐ b. man's duty to his Creator
    ☐ c. useful, but not at all necessary

7. What is the connection between doing good works (*obedience to God's Word*) and knowing that we possess faith in Christ? _____

    _____

    _____

8. Because we are born again by the Holy Spirit after the _____
    of God, we must show ourselves thankful to Him "with our
    _____ life."

9. The reason that God saves us is that we may be His loyal, loving
    children who delight to do His will. ☐ True ☐ False

10. Write out Titus 3:8. _____

    _____

    _____

    _____

    _____

    _____

❦ The Necessity of Good Works

Q87. Can they, then, not be saved who do not turn to God from their unthankful, impenitent life?

By no means, for, as the Scripture says, no unchaste person, idolator, adulterer, thief, covetous man, drunkard, slanderer, robber, or the like shall inherit the kingdom of God.

When we speak of good works as being the fruits of thankfulness, we might get the idea that they are not really necessary even though very desirable. This is not true. A life of good works is *absolutely necessary* for the Christian, and the Bible warns us that all who walk in sin and commandment-breaking will *not* enter heaven, even though they profess to be Christians and are church members now.

A Christian who is not concerned about living a holy life is no Christian at all. If the Spirit of God is not sanctifying our lives, then we do not belong to Christ. Our "faith" is a false faith, not a true, living faith.

But having said that good works are essential for the Christian, we have not said that good works earn or merit salvation. The Roman Catholic Church teaches that good works do merit salvation, but this is damnable doctrine. The Bible teaches that we are saved in order to do good works (Titus 2:14); it does not teach that we do good works in order to earn salvation (Titus 3:5). There is a great difference between these two doctrines.

Thus, the Catechism is true to the Bible when it tells us that the commandment-breakers shall not "inherit the Kingdom of God." If the Spirit of God is not giving us a desire to live a holy life according to the will of God, then we do not have the Holy Spirit. Does this mean that we can attain to perfection in this life? No, it means we will pray and strive for perfection in this life and sincerely confess our sins when we fail.

This answer speaks of certain especially wicked sins following the Apostle Paul's listing of sins in 1 Corinthians 6:9–10; Galatians 5:19–21 and Ephesians 5:5–6. We should not conclude that it is indulgence in *these* sins only that will bring one into condemnation. The sin of "covetousness" includes *all* forms of sin, whether of the mind or the body. We must daily pray to the Lord for forgiveness of sins and strength to resist all temptation to sin.

Is the Spirit of Christ working in you to make you hunger and thirst after righteousness and obedience to God?

Questions on Number 87

1. Some people are not thankful when they receive gifts, and some true Christians do not show thankfulness for salvation.
    ☐ True   ☐ False

2. Living a life of sanctification (good works) is:
    ☐ a. *necessary*   ☐ b. *not necessary*   ☐ c. *useful, but not essential*
    for a person to go to heaven.

3. What does the Roman Catholic Church teach about good works and salvation? _____
    _____
    _____

4. Would you say that good works and Christian obedience *earn* for us salvation? or that they are the *fruits* of a renewed heart or both?
    _____
    _____

5. Check the verses that show that a life of obedience to God is necessary if one is saved.
    ☐ Matthew 5:19–20   ☐ Luke 16:20
    ☐ Romans 6:22   ☐ 1 Corinthians 6:9–10
    ☐ Galatians 1:1   ☐ Ephesians 2:10
    ☐ Titus 3:14

6. If a person does not love the laws of God, can he truthfully say that he loves Jesus Christ? _____

7. Which of the Ten Commandments do the following persons break:
    Idolater _____
    Adulterer _____
    Thief _____
    Covetous man _____
    Drunkard _____
    Slanderer _____
    Robber _____.

8. What does *impenitent* mean? _____

_____

9. Who must work in our hearts to make us hunger and thirst after the will of God? _____

10. Write out Revelation 22:14–15. _____

_____

_____

_____

_____

_____

_____

_____

❦ The Source of Good Works

Q88. In how many things does true repentance or conversion consist?

In two things: the dying of the old man, and the making alive of the new.

Having seen that good works are essential to Christian experience, we learn in questions 88, 89 and 90, the *source* of good works, that is, how we who are sinful can produce works that please God, Who is perfect.

The source or root of good works in the life of a Christian is a converted heart, which is indwelt by the Holy Spirit. So here the Catechism instructs us in the truth about the *conversion* of the heart.

There are false views of conversion in many churches today. For example, many churches hold "evangelistic meetings" or "revival meetings" in an effort to get people "converted." Usually, a so-called "Evangelist" is brought to town to preach "revival sermons." Quite often in such meetings, the preacher says very little about the Bible itself, but, rather, entertains the people with stories and music to stir them up. After the story-telling part of the "service," the preacher begs the unconverted people to come forward and pray with him. Those who come forward are counted as converts, and they are urged to join the church. Very often these so-called "converts" do not really understand the gospel of salvation because it was never explained to them; and after the revival meetings have ended, they soon lose their interest and return to their old ways. Often, these "back-sliders" are "reconverted" the next year when another "Evangelist" comes to town, and the same thing happens over again. This is false conversion because:

1. *The gospel is not clearly preached from the Scriptures.*

2. *The preacher tries to convert people by his own devices.*

3. *The sinner is told that he has the power to convert himself by an act of his free will.*

4. *Sinners are assured that they are converted just because they come forward to the "altar" and say a prayer.*

5. *True converts do not go back to the world again.*

When the Bible speaks about conversion, it refers to the work of God's Spirit in the heart of an elect person, by which his heart is given spiritual life and the power to believe the gospel and turn in faith to Christ and away from sin. No human emotional persuasion by an evangelist can do this work in a sinner's dead soul. No one can be converted by the will of man (John 1:13).

The New Testament speaks of our sinful nature as an "old man" (Romans 6:6; Ephesians 4:22; Colossians 3:9) because it is as *old as* Adam, from whom it came; and it is a "man" because sin is in every part of our soul. This "old man" or sinful nature has complete control over us until the Holy Spirit renews or regenerates our souls. Then we become a "new man" in Christ (see Ephesians 4:24 and Colossians 3:10). The new spiritual life brought to our hearts by the Spirit causes us to *turn* or convert *to* Christ and *away from* the "old man" as the truth of the gospel is understood.

The conversion of our souls has two parts:

1. **Repentance.** This word refers to our turning away from sin with godly sorrow by the power of the Holy Spirit—"the killing of the old man."

2. **Faith.** This refers to our trusting in Christ alone for forgiveness and salvation—"the making alive or quickening of the new man." We shall learn more of these two parts in the next two questions.

Questions on Number 88

1. Questions 88–91 explain the _____ of good works which believers do. It is the _____ heart.

2. Many churches hold "revival meetings" in order to get sinners converted. Give some reasons why many of these "converts" are not really converted to Christ.

a) _____

_____

b) _____

_____

c) _____

_____

3. All sinners have the power to convert themselves by their free will.
   ☐ True   ☐ False

4. True conversion is experienced only by the _____
   (1 Thess. 1:4) when their _____ hearts (Ephesians 2:1) are
   _____ (Ephesians 2:5) by the power of the Holy Spirit
   to turn to _____ from _____
   to serve the _____ and _____
   _____ (1 Thess. 1:9).

5. The unconverted person has an _____ _____
   in him. The converted person has both the " _____ _____ "
   and a " _____ _____ " in him.

6. What is meant by the word "conversion"? (*Look it up in the glossary*)

   _____

   _____

7. Conversion, according to Scripture (Acts 20:21) has two parts.
   a) _____
   b) _____

8. It is not necessary for you to be converted if you were born in the
   Reformed Church and were baptized as a child of the covenant.
   ☐ True   ☐ False

9. Check the verses that speak of conversion to God:
   ☐ Matthew 18:3   ☐ Isaiah 6:10   ☐ Luke 1:40
   ☐ Luke 22:32   ☐ Acts 3:19   ☐ 1 Corinthians 7:29
   ☐ James 5:19–20.

10. Write out Acts 20:21. _____

    _____

❦ *A Life of Repentance*

Q89. What is the dying of the old man?

Heartfelt sorrow for sin, causing us to hate and turn from it always more and more.

Questions 89 and 90 explain the two parts of conversion, which are *repentance* and *faith* or "the killing of the old man" and the "making alive of the new man." Remember that this discussion of conversion is to show us the source of our good works—a converted heart, regenerated by the Holy Spirit.

Repentance, or the killing of the old man of sin, is very necessary to the salvation of our souls. By nature, we are completely under the power of that sinful disposition which causes us to hate God and His Law and to love Satan and his ways. This power of sin must be broken in our hearts if we are to have fellowship with the Holy God. God does this for us by the work of His Holy Spirit.

When regeneration—the new birth—takes place, at that moment the heart begins to react against the power of sin; this is repentance. The three parts of true repentance are these:

1. *The knowledge of sin (Romans 3:20b)*

2. *Heartfelt sorrow and hatred for sin (2 Corinthians 7:10)*

3. *Turning from sin (Romans 8:13; Colossians 3:5-10)*

Some important truths about repentance are as follows:

1. **Repentance is a gift of God's grace.** "God ... granted repentance to life" (Acts 11:18). Christ the Exalted Prince "gives repentance to Israel and forgiveness of sins" (Acts 5:31).

2. **Repentance is a conscious experience in the mind of the child of God.** Our souls must daily rise up in holy horror and hatred against sin, because sin is directed against the Holy God, our Heavenly Father.

3. **Repentance must be complete.** All the parts of repentance must be present in our minds or we do not have true repentance. We must learn sin, and sorrow over our own sins. But we must do still more: We must turn away from them. To say we sorrow over our sins and yet deliberately live in them shows a false repentance.

4. **Repentance is a continuing experience.** The more we grow in grace and knowledge, the deeper our repentance becomes. That is why the Catechism speaks of turning from sin more and more. We never stop repenting and killing the old man of sin so long as we are living in these temporal and sinful bodies.

One note about this question. The word "dying" in our Catechism could be translated "killing," because we are active in killing the old man. We don't just sit back and watch him die by himself! We must seek God's grace each day to put to death our "old man" a little more, even though we cannot destroy it completely in this life. Our old nature will always have some power to fight against us in his service of Satan.

Questions on Number 89

1. Why does the Catechism teach the truth about conversion at this place? In other words, what does this truth have to do with the subject of good works? _____

   _____

2. The word _____ means the "killing of the old man."

3. Why is our sinful heart called the "old man"? (See explanation of question 88.) _____

   _____

   _____

4. It is not necessary that the power of sin in our hearts be broken as long as Jesus is our Lord and Savior. ☐ True ☐ False

   ▶ *Explain:* _____

   _____

5. The true Christian life is a struggle against _____.

6. Those "Christians" who are not concerned about this struggle ☐ *are* or ☐ *are not* living the converted life. (*check one*)

7. Name the three parts of true repentance:

   a) _____

   b) _____

   c) _____

8. Give four important truths about Christian repentance.

   a) _____

    b) _____

    c) _____

    d) _____

9. The experience of repentance (sorrowing over sin and turning from it) takes place
   - ☐ a. only when a sinner is first converted
   - ☐ b. only when we happen to commit a terrible sin
   - ☐ c. day by day in the true Christian's experience.

10. Killing the "old man" is
   - ☐ a. an easy matter
   - ☐ b. necessary if we are to be saved
   - ☐ c. completed finally when one reaches old age
   - ☐ d. done only by the help of the Word and the Spirit

11. Write out Romans 8:13 and Ephesians 4:22.

_____

_____

_____

_____

_____

_____

_____

_____

_____

_____

_____

❦ A Life of Joyful Obedience

Q90. What is the making alive of the new man?

Heartfelt joy in God through Christ, causing us to take delight in living according to the will of God in all good works.

The second part of conversion is *faith*, or the "making alive of the new man." The "new man" is the new spiritual life that we have received by regeneration or the new birth. This life is new because it comes to us with the new birth. It is called a "man" because this new life extends to our whole person; even our bodies will experience it at the resurrection. "If anyone is in Christ, he is a new creation" (2 Corinthians 5:17).

This "new man" or new life in Christ must be strengthened, day by day, by the means of grace: the Word, prayer, Sabbath worship, communion with the saints, and the sacraments. This strengthening of the new life in us is referred to as being "made alive."

The Apostle John calls the new life of the believer a "seed" (1 John 3:9). The seed of new spiritual life must grow by the water of the Word and Spirit and the sunshine of prayer and communion with God. Eventually the seed becomes a tree of the Lord's planting (see Isaiah 61:3; Psalm 1:3).

The Catechism speaks of two parts to this making alive of the new man:

1. "Heartfelt joy in God through Christ." Christ is the joy and delight of the believer. Note how sorrow for sin and joy in Christ go together. The more we sorrow for sin, the more we delight in Christ. As we learn of Christ, our "joy is full" (1 John 1:4).

2. "Taking delight in living according to the will of God in all good works." The new life is strengthened by our doing the will of God. We see that it works both ways. The new life produces good works, and the good works strengthen the new life! We shall see what those good works are in the next question.

These two diagrams show the spiritual difference between the unconverted (unregenerated) person and the converted (regenerated) person:

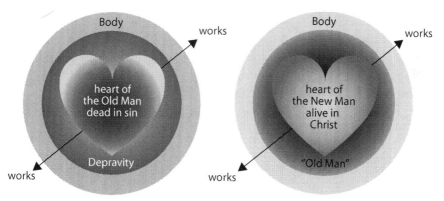

The **unregenerated** sinner   The **regenerated** sinner

1. The unregenerated sinner

The heart of the unregenerated unconverted person is completely controlled by the "old man" of sin, the Adamic nature. He cannot even think one God-honoring thought: Ephesians 2:1; 4:22.

All the *works* of the body, coming out of the evil heart, are only evil: Romans 6:19; 8:7–8; Galatians 5:19–21.

2. The regenerated Christian

a. The heart of the born again Christian has received the "new man" of spiritual life and righteousness through the new birth: John 3:3; Ephesians 4:24; Colossians 3:10; 1 John 3:9.

b. The "new man" of the Spirit now controls the Christian's heart, but the "old man" of sin is still present to fight and oppose the "new man": Romans 7:21; Galatians 5:6.

c. The *works* of the Christian's body and members are mostly good, because they proceed from the new man of the heart; but they are never perfect because they are all contaminated by the sin of the "old man": Romans 6:6, 12–14; 7:19.

d. The Christian is exhorted by the Word of God to continuously live after the new man and to put to death the old man by the power of the Holy Spirit.

Questions on Number 90

1. The second part of conversion is _____ , or the making alive of the new man.

2. What is meant by the term "new man"? _____

   _____

   _____

   _____

3. What is the difference between regeneration and conversion? (*See the glossary*) _____

   _____

   _____

   _____

4. Some people are new creatures in Christ, but the old man still dominates their hearts and lives. ☐ True   ☐ False (*See 2 Corinthians 5:17*).

5. What are the two parts of making alive the "new man"?

   a) _____

b) _____

_____

6. Name some ways by which we can strengthen the new life in our hearts.

_____

_____

_____

_____

7. Draw a diagram of the converted person and a diagram of the unconverted person. Which kind of "man" controls the hearts of each? What kind of deeds are produced by each?

8. Which activities will feed the new man, and which activities will feed the old man? (*Check "new" or "old" in front of each statement*)
   ☐ new ☐ old — Watching vulgar or suggestive programs on TV
   ☐ new ☐ old — Attending midweek Bible study
   ☐ new ☐ old — Listening to others tell dirty jokes
   ☐ new ☐ old — Praying daily to the Lord
   ☐ new ☐ old — Playing sports instead of attending church
   ☐ new ☐ old — Listening to evil gossip about fellow Christians

9. The converted person can produce only good works, and the unconverted person can produce only evil works. ☐ True ☐ False

10. Write out 1 John 2:5. _____

_____

_____

_____

_____

❧ *The Nature of Good Works*

Q91. What are good works?

Those only which proceed from true faith, and are done according to the Law of God, unto His glory, and not such as rest on our own opinion or the commandments of men.

Having seen that the source of good works is a converted heart in which the Holy Spirit lives, we now learn the *nature* of good works.

There are people who have a wrong idea of good works. For example, the Scribes and Pharisees in Jesus' day trusted in their so-called "good works" for salvation, rather than in Jesus. The Roman Catholic Church teaches that a person is justified by good works, rather than through faith in Christ alone (but see Titus 3:5). Most people think that even unbelievers do good works when they do such things as help their neighbors, donate blood, or drop money into an offering plate in a church.

But these are all false ideas about good works. The Bible teaches that for a work to be good in the sight of God, three things must be true of it: It must have a good *root,* a good *standard,* and a good *goal.*

1. The Root—true faith

Good works can only proceed from a true faith. Without faith in Christ, it is impossible to please God (Hebrews 11:6). God always looks at the attitude of the heart which lies behind all actions. In the case of the unbeliever, since he hates Christ, all his works are expressions of rebellion against Christ. Even his so-called good deeds to his fellowman are done from wrong motives.

2. The Standard—the law of God

Good works, in God's sight, are those done according to His holy Law. God alone sets the standard for goodness and this standard is His Law, which we shall study next. Some *wrong* standards for good works are the following:

a. "My conscience is my guide." The Bible says, however, that man's conscience is sinful (1 Timothy 4:2; Ephesians 4:18) and cannot give good directions.

b. "My church tells me what is right and wrong." The Bible teaches, however, that the commandments of man are often against the commandments of God (see Mark 7:7-9, 13). The Roman Catholic Church, for example, forbids marriage to the priests, and demands fasting during "Lent," and has many other laws contrary to Scripture.

Many Protestant churches have also invented their own commandments, such as total abstinence from alcoholic beverages, saying that all drinking, even of wine, is sinful. Others make the observance of certain "holy" days such as Christmas, Easter and Ascension Day to be binding laws. It is even possible for men to commit terrible crimes under the false conviction that they are serving God—see John 16:2. Being sincere is not enough; we must live according to God's standards alone.

3. The Goal—the glory of God

Good works are those that are directed to God's glory. The highest goal or end for man's life and activity is the glory of God. We are created to glorify Him alone; and if this is not man's intention when he does good, he is serving an idol.

Seeing what a good work is in the sight of God, we now understand that a non-Christian, an unconverted person, cannot possibly do a good work. When unbelievers do outwardly good deeds—such as helping their neighbors—they are still sinning, because they are not acting out of love to Christ and to the glory of God.

Questions on Number 91

1. In question 91, we learn the _____ of good works.

2. Many people have a wrong idea of good works. Give some examples:

   _____

   _____

   _____

3. For a human action to be good in the sight of God, what three things are necessary?

   a) _____

   b) _____

   c) _____

4. If an unbeliever gives a gift of $1,000 to a hospital, he is doing a good deed in the eyes of God. ☐ True ☐ False

5. What are two false standards of good works that people live by?

   a) _____

   b) _____

6. If a church teaches that drinking a can of beer is sinful, then it is sinful. ☐ True ☐ False

7. Every work, that is, every thought, word, and deed that a Christian does is good in the sight of God. ☐ True ☐ False

8. Look up Colossians 2:16–23 and answer the following:

   a) Which verse condemns man-made rules about meat, drink, and holy days? _____

   b) Which verse teaches that he who keeps man-made religious rules is "vainly puffed up by his fleshly mind"? _____

   c) Which verse condemns the commandments and doctrines of men? _____

   d) Man-made worship is called " _____ worship" (vs. 23).

9. If a person does good for man's sake, not for God's glory, he is serving an idol. ☐ True ☐ False

10. Write out 1 Corinthians 10:31. _____

    _____

    _____

    _____

    _____

❧ The Law of God

Q92. What is the Law of God?

God spake all these words, saying: I am the Lord thy God, which have brought thee out of the land of Egypt, out of the house of bondage.

First Commandment. Thou shalt have no other gods before me.

Second Commandment. Thou shalt not make unto thee any graven image, or any likeness of anything that is in heaven above, or that is in the earth beneath, or that is in the water under the earth:

thou shalt not bow down thyself to them, nor serve them: for I the Lord thy God am a jealous God, visiting the iniquity of the fathers upon the children unto the third and fourth generation of them that hate me; and shewing mercy unto thousands of them that love me, and keep my commandments.

Third Commandment. Thou shalt not take the name of the Lord thy God in vain; for the Lord will not hold him guiltless that taketh His name in vain.

Fourth Commandment. Remember the sabbath day, to keep it holy. Six days shalt thou labor, and do all thy work: but the seventh day is the sabbath of the Lord thy God: in it thou shalt not do any work, thou, nor thy son, nor thy daughter, thy manservant, nor thy maidservant, nor thy cattle, nor thy stranger that is within thy gates: for in six days the Lord made heaven and earth, the sea, and all that in them is, and rested the seventh day: wherefore the Lord blessed the sabbath day, and hallowed it.

Fifth Commandment. Honor thy father and thy mother that thy days may be long upon the land which the Lord thy God giveth thee.

Sixth Commandment. Thou shalt not kill.

Seventh Commandment. Thou shalt not commit adultery.

Eighth Commandment. Thou shalt not steal.

Ninth Commandment. Thou shalt not bear false witness against thy neighbor.

Tenth Commandment. Thou shalt not covet thy neighbor's house, thou shalt not covet thy neighbor's wife, nor his manservant, nor his maidservant, nor his ox, nor his ass, nor anything that is thy neighbor's.

We have now come the second time to the Law of God. The first time was at the beginning of the Catechism (Questions 3, 4, and 5), where the Law condemned us and drove us to Christ for redemption. Now that we have been graciously redeemed, Christ leads us back to the Law in order that we might live a life of Christian obedience and thankfulness to Him.

Questions 86–91 taught us the biblical doctrine of good works. We now enter into the explanation of the Ten Commandments (also called The Decalogue, which means the "Ten Words"), which is the standard or rule of good works. Notice the way that the Catechism has developed the subject of Christian thankfulness.

1. *The redeemed Christian must live in thankfulness.*

2. *To be thankful means to live a life of good works.*

3. *Good works are hearty, active obedience to the Law of God.*

So the subject of questions 92–115 is "The Law and Christian Thankfulness."

In questions 92 and 93, we have the Law introduced to us. We see its *content* in number 92 and its *divisions* in number 93. The giving of the Ten Commandments on Mt. Sinai (Exodus 19-20), about 1450 years before Christ, was one of the greatest of all God's acts to men. In importance, it is second only to the giving of Christ Himself. Ever after that event, the Ten Commandments have been rightly regarded as the basis of all goodness and morality, and the standard by which God tests and judges mankind. Let us consider some of the features of the Ten Commandments.

1. **The Ten Commandments are the permanent revelation of God's will.** Adam knew the will of God when he was created, and those who followed Adam also knew something of God's Law (Romans 2:14-15); but at Sinai God wrote it down permanently in tablets of stone as His unchangeable will for man so long as the world lasts. Some people say that Jesus came to do away with the Ten Commandments. But He said: "Do not think that I came to destroy the Law or the Prophets. I did not come to destroy but to fulfill (confirm)" (Matthew 5:17).

2. **The Ten Commandments are the moral Law of God for all men at all times.** God also gave other laws to Israel, the ceremonial and worship laws, but these laws were only temporary for Israel in the Old Testament. They were abolished when Christ came and fulfilled their meanings. The Ten Commandments, on the other hand, are moral and bind every man. They tell all men what duty we have, as humans, to God and to our fellow man. This law is the standard by which God will judge all men at the Judgment Day (Romans 3:19).

3. **The Ten Commandments give us the primary principles of morality.** All the moral teachings of the Bible, including the civil laws, are based on the Decalogue. The more we study all the Bible, the more we learn of the depth of meaning in each of the Ten Commandments. The Psalmist said, "Your commandment is exceedingly broad" (Psalm 119:96).

4. **The Ten Commandments have both a negative and a positive application.** By this is meant that not only do they forbid us from doing certain things when they say, "You shall not," but they intend for us to do the exact opposite, as our Catechism will show us. The commandments are kept only as they lead us to love God and our neighbor as ourselves. Love is the only acceptable way to keep the

law: "Therefore love is the fulfillment of the law" (Romans 13:10).

Questions on Number 92

1. The Catechism brings us to the Law twice. The *first* time, it is to teach us
    ☐ a. our goodness   ☐ b. our sin and misery   ☐ c. our thankfulness

2. The *second* time, it is to teach us
    ☐ a. our goodness
    ☐ b. how we are to live a life of thankfulness
    ☐ c. that we can't be perfect, so why even try?

3. Christian thankfulness, good works, serving God, obeying God's will—all these matters depend on our knowing and keeping the Decalogue.   ☐ True   ☐ False

4. In questions 92 and 93, we have the Law _____ .
    In question 92 we are told its _____ .

5. How important is the giving of the Law to the whole Bible story?
    _____
    _____

6. At Mount Sinai, God gave Israel the
    ☐ a. moral Law   ☐ b. Ten Commandments   ☐ c. Decalogue

7. State four important features of the Ten Commandments.
    a) _____
    b) _____
    c) _____
    d) _____

8. John 1:17 teaches that the Law of Moses was done away with when Christ came with His truth and grace.   ☐ True   ☐ False
    ▶ *Explain:* _____
    _____
    _____

9. Look up Romans 2:14–15 and 3:19 and answer the following:
    a) All mankind "show the _____ of the _____

written on their hearts."

b) All men, therefore, "do by nature the _____ Law."

c) Every man's conscience bears _____ to the Law of God.

d) Every man, therefore, is "under _____

that "all the _____ may be _____ before God."

10. People in heathen lands who have never heard of the Ten
Commandments will not be judged by them. ☐ True ☐ False

▶ *Explain:* _____

_____

11. Write out James 2:12. _____

_____

_____

_____

❧ *The Two Tables of the Law*

Q93. How are these Commandments divided?

Into two tables: the first of which teaches, in four commandments,
what duties we owe to God; the second, in six, what duties we
owe to our neighbor.

Continuing with the introduction to the Law of God, we see in this
question the division of the Ten Commandments. From Deuteronomy
6:5 and Leviticus 19:18, which are quoted by Christ in Matthew 22:37–
40, we learn that the Ten Commandments are divided into two main
sections.

The first section, which includes commandments one through four,
according to our Catechism, is called the "first and great commandment"
by Christ. These commandments teach us our duties to God, and they
can be summarized by "You shall love the Lord your God with all your
heart, with all your soul, and with all your mind."

The second division, commandments five through ten, teaches us
our duties to man; and Christ summed this section up as the "second"
great commandment—"You shall love your neighbor as yourself."
Further, Jesus said, "On these two commandments hang all the Law and
the Prophets" (Matthew 22:40), which means that the morality of the
whole Old Testament is based on the Ten Commandments.

Actually, the Bible does not say just where the dividing line is between the "first" and "second" Great Commandments. Some think that the fifth commandment belongs to the first section also; and they say this because the parents represent God to their children. Probably our division is the correct one, however.

There is also the question of the two tables of stone. We know that God wrote His law on two slabs of stone (Exodus 31:18; 32:15–16), but it is not clear whether the first four commands were on one and the second six on the other, or whether all ten were written on each tablet of stone.

Two more matters need to be mentioned concerning the divisions of the Law.

First, did you know that the Lutherans follow the Roman Church in combining the first two commandments into one, and then dividing the tenth commandment into two commandments in order to have ten commandments? This procedure is wrong because the first and second commandments do not speak of the same sin, as we shall see, and therefore should not be combined; whereas the entire tenth commandment is concerned with coveting, and it is wrong to divide it so as to make "You shall not covet your neighbor's wife" a separate commandment from the last part, "You shall not covet your neighbor's house ..."

The second matter has to do with the preface to the Law: "I am the Lord your God which have brought you out of the land of Egypt, out of the house of bondage." This statement is not part of the first commandment, but rather is the preface to the whole Law. It is very significant because it teaches that the God Who gives this Law to His people is:

1. **The Sovereign Lord.** He has all authority to give His Law to the creatures whom He has made. All men and angels must submit to the authority of their Creator.

2. **The Gracious Redeemer.** The Lord gives His Law to His redeemed people who were delivered out of bondage. Thus, a *double obligation* rested upon Israel and rests upon us also to obey God's Law: He is both our Creator *and* our Redeemer.

Questions on Number 93

1. This question tells us of the _____ of the Ten Commandments. We know there are _____ main divisions because _____ said so in Matthew _____

2. The Bible does *not* tell us clearly
   ☐ a. that there were two tables of stone

☐ b. that the first four commandments were on one table of stone
☐ c. that the division is between the 4th and 5th commandments

3. How did Jesus summarize the first section of the Law? _____

_____

_____

4. Unbelievers often keep the second part of the Law (our duties to man), even though they do not keep the first part (our duties to God). ☐ True ☐ False ▶ *Explain:* _____

_____

_____

5. The first commandment begins, "I am the Lord your God ...."
☐ True   ☐ False

6. How do the Roman and the Lutheran Churches arrange the first and tenth commandments? _____

_____

_____

7. Why is that arrangement wrong? _____

_____

_____

_____

8. The preface to the Law teaches us two things about God:
a) He is the _____
b) He is the _____

9. Like Israel, we have a double obligation to keep God's Law.
☐ True   ☐ False

10. Write out Deuteronomy 4:13. _____

_____

_____

_____

_____

🔥 First Commandment: God First

Q94. What does God require in the first Commandment?

That, on peril of my soul's salvation, I avoid and flee all idolatry, sorcery, enchantments, invocation of saints or other creatures; and that I rightly acknowledge the only true God, trust in Him alone, with all humility and patience expect all good from Him only, and love, fear and honor Him with my whole heart; so as rather to renounce all creatures than to do the least thing against His will.

The first four commandments teach us our duties to God:

1. *The first tells us our duty toward God's unique Being.*

2. *The second tells us our duty in God's Worship.*

3. *The third tells us our duty toward God's Name.*

4. *The fourth tells us our duty on God's Day.*

The First Commandment, "You shall have no other gods before Me" tells us Whom we are to serve and worship. There is one God only, and He is Three Persons: Father, Son, and Holy Spirit. This commandment is the foundation on which all the others depend. God is first, and He must be first in our hearts and lives. Although there is only one God, the sinful heart of man loves to invent false gods to take the place of the true God.

To have one or more false gods in one's heart is idolatry. All the heathen nations had false gods, and they made images of them. Modern American man has many false gods to serve also, such as family, money, pleasure, sex, fame, food, heroes, movie stars and countless others.

The first part of the answer tells us *what we must avoid* in order to love the true God: "Idolatry, sorcery, enchantments (soothsaying), invocation of saints or other creatures." The German Catechism includes "superstition" also in this list. These are the more obvious types of idolatry. The Westminster Larger Catechism lists no less than thirty-three violations of this commandment!

1. **Idolatry:** The giving of worship, love, and service to something other than the true God. We shall consider this further in the next question.

2. **Sorcery:** the use of magic and witchcraft by the power of evil spirits to gain benefits, rather than trusting in God alone.

3. **Enchantments (or Soothsayings):** Fortune-telling, astrology, and

prophecy by the power of evil spirits. This is Satan's substitute for God's Word.

4. **Superstition:** All forms of superstition, such as rabbits' feet, horseshoes, four-leaf clovers, lucky (and unlucky) numbers, charm bracelets, and ouija boards are denials of the one true God.

5. **Invocation of Saints:** Trusting in the so-called saints of the Roman Catholic Church—the main one being Mary—is to trust in a mere creature, rather than in the Almighty Creator, Who alone has all power and mercy.

6. **Trust in any other creature:** We are to use all lawful means to obtain good; but we are to trust in God alone, not in others or ourselves.

The second part of the answer gives us *positive directions* on how to love and serve the one true God properly.

1. **We must have the right knowledge of God.** This knowledge must come from the Bible. Only in Scripture can we learn of the true God and how *we* are to serve Him. Modernists, Jews, and other religious people talk of a "Supreme Being," but the True God is the Father, Son, and Holy Spirit of the Bible.

2. **We must trust in Him alone with all humility and patience.** We must believe that the true God is almighty, faithful, and true. He always keeps His promises. He will never leave us nor forsake us. We must submit to His will for our lives and humbly and patiently wait upon Him. We must trust Him and not complain or worry.

3. **We must expect all good from Him only.** The God of Scripture is the God of all goodness and blessing. He is the Fountain of Life. "Every good gift and every perfect gift is from above, and comes down from the Father of lights" (James 1:17). We must look to Him alone and not to any creature for life and happiness, both in this world and in the next world.

4. **We must love, fear, and glorify Him with our whole heart.** The love of God and the fear of God go together. To love Him is to desire to do His will; to fear Him is to reverence Him and respect His authority over us. Our whole heart must be taken up with God. We must drive away all idols that would seek to replace God in our hearts. He alone must reign supreme on the throne of our souls. We must always seek His glory above all other things. "For of Him and through Him and to Him are all things, to whom be glory forever. Amen" (Romans 11:36).

Are you willing to renounce (turn away from) all creatures, rather than do the least thing against His will? This is the first and basic requirement of the Christian religion.

Questions on Number 94

1. In the First Commandment, God admits that there really are "other living gods." ☐ True ☐ False

2. In the First Commandment, we learn of our duty toward _____.

3. The one true God is:
   ☐ a. the "Supreme Being" that the Jews and Modernists talk about
   ☐ b. Father, Son, and Holy Spirit
   ☐ c. the "Great White Father" that the Indians used to talk about

4. The Egyptians, Canaanites, Babylonians, Greeks, and Romans had many "gods," but all Americans today worship the one true God only. ☐ True ☐ False

5. It is correct to say that sorcery, enchantments, superstition, and trust in creatures are all forms of idolatry. ☐ True ☐ False

6. There is no harm in being superstitious about the number "13" or to trust in "good luck" charms, just so long as we believe on Jesus Christ alone for salvation. ☐ True ☐ False

7. Fortune-telling and other forms of prophecy are:
   ☐ a. all right if not taken too seriously
   ☐ b. the work of evil spirits
   ☐ c. a denial of the sufficiency of Scripture for our lives

8. Match the following:

Commandments 1, 2, 3, 4	33 violations of the First Commandment
sports, money, fame	fortune-telling
Westminster Larger Catechism	Father, Son, Holy Spirit
Satan's prophecy	our duties to God
The only true God	modern-day idols

9. State four things necessary in order for us to love and serve the one true God.
   a) _____

b) _____

c) _____

d) _____

10. What will happen to all idolaters, according to Revelation 22:14–15?

_____

11. Write out Deuteronomy 6:4, 14, 24.

_____

_____

_____

_____

_____

_____

_____

_____

_____

_____

❧ *Nature of Idolatry*

Q95. What is idolatry?

Idolatry is to conceive or have something else on which to place our trust instead of, or besides, the one true God who has revealed Himself in His Word.

In this second question on the First Commandment, we learn the true nature of idolatry: it is to conceive or devise something else on which to place our trust instead of, or besides, the one true God.

Idolatry takes many forms. The sinful human heart is a busy workshop producing new varieties and models of idols as substitutes for the true and living God!

Let us consider some of the different kinds of gods or idols in which men have put their trust. All idolatry may be placed in two main groups:

1. Gross idolatry, the worship of personal gods

The ancient peoples, and the non-Christian peoples of today, worship many gods and goddesses (belief in more than one god is called "polytheism"). The Egyptians had many gods (Sun god, River god, etc.)

but the God of Moses brought His wrath against the Egyptians and their gods by sending the Ten Plagues. The Canaanites had their gods also, such as Baal, Molech, Ashterah, Dagon. The Romans worshiped Fortuna, the goddess of chance; Bacchus, the god of wine; Jupiter, the protector god; Mars, the god of war, etc. The people of Lystra thought Barnabus and Paul were the Greek gods Zeus and Hermes (Jupiter and Mercury to the Romans)—Acts 14:11-13. The idols or statues which they made of the gods only represented the gods and goddesses whom they thought were real persons somewhere, having supernatural powers.

2. Mental idolatry, or the worship of the gods of human reasoning

Men, both ancient and modern, have devised various religious beliefs about themselves and the universe in which they live, attempting to explain things apart from the true and living God, the only Creator.

Atheism ("a" = no, "theism" = god) and **Materialism.** This system of belief says that there is no personal God or spirit, but only material things. Physical matter and energy are all that exist, and they are all that we can believe in. Communism, which is based on Atheism and Materialism, is a fanatical religion even though Communists claim to deny religion.

Pantheism. This word means "all-is-god" ("pan" = all; "theism" = god) and those who believe in pantheism say that god is everything and everything is god. Trees, birds, sun, men, and all things are all parts of god. To trust in such a "god," however, is to deny the true Creator God, Who is distinct and separate from all His creation.

Humanism. This is the popular religion of modern man and the real religion of many who call themselves Christians. Humanism is the worship of man: man's wisdom and power, man's good, man's freedom to do as he pleases, man's security as the highest goal. Everything must serve man; even "god" exists to serve man. Humanism is the religion behind most of modern "liberal" education, social and political action. Those who say that the civil government should become stronger in order to provide security and the good life to all the citizens are really making a god out of the government and trusting in political planners rather than in the True and Living God.

Worldliness. Non-Christians have all kinds of gods that they prefer to the God of the Bible. Some people put the getting of money first in their lives. Others live to become famous; others put their family first; and still others live only to enjoy pleasures of various kinds.

There is no end to the variety of idols that come from the assembly line of the sinful heart of man. But the true Christian puts God first and trusts only in Him.

Questions on Number 95

1. In question 95, we learn _____
   _____

2. What is idolatry? _____
   _____
   _____

3. Idolatry takes only one form—the making of a graven image of a god. ☐ True ☐ False

4. What are the two main types of idolatry?
   a) _____
   b) _____

5. When heathen people make idols, they really think that they are making an image of a live god. ☐ True ☐ False

6. According to 1 Corinthians 10:19-20, the gods behind idol worship are really _____

7. Since atheists do not believe in any god or religion, and since Communists are atheists, it is true that Communists do not have a religion or any idols. ☐ True ☐ False
   ▶ *Explain:* _____
   _____

8. Match the following:

   Humanism   The teaching that there is no God

   Pantheism   The putting of man in the place of God

   Atheism   Putting anything besides God first in our lives

   Worldliness   The teaching that everything is God

9. Many people today are trusting in the government to take care of them, rather than trusting in God, and this is idolatry.
   ☐ True ☐ False

10. Write out 1 John 5:21.
    _____

❦ Second Commandment: Worship

Q96. What does God require in the second Commandment?

That we in no way make any image of God, nor worship Him in any other way than He has commanded us in His Word.

The First Commandment told us *Whom* we are to worship; the one true God only. The Second Commandment tells us *how we* are to worship the true God, or *our duty in God's worship.* Thus, there are two different moral duties given to us in these two commandments; and it is a serious mistake to combine these two commandments into one as the Roman Catholics and Lutherans do.

The Second Commandment and the Fourth Commandment are the longest of all the commandments, showing their great importance in the sight of God.

God is a "jealous God." He is jealous of His own honor and glory. All sinful man's attempts to worship Him result in insulting God, because sinful man never thinks of God properly. Seeking to worship God by the use of images and other devices may seem helpful to man, but God abhors this kind of worship, as it takes away from His true glory. John 4:24 tells us that "God is Spirit and they that worship Him must worship in spirit (from the heart) and in truth (according to His directions)."

This commandment, then, condemns all worship which God has not authorized and prescribed in His Word. Let us see how this commandment has been broken by man:

1. Two men wanted to worship God. Each brought an offering. But God accepted the worship of Abel only, and rejected the worship of Cain (Genesis 4:3-4). Cain thought that he could worship God by his own methods, but he could not.

2. Nadab and Abihu "offered profane fire before the Lord"—a wrong kind of sacrifice—and God killed them (Numbers 3:4). King Saul was rejected by the Lord because He offered a sacrifice improperly (1 Samuel 13:9, 13).

3. Aaron and Jeroboam also broke this Second Commandment when they set up golden calves to "help" the people worship God (Exodus 32:1-5; 1 Kings 12:25-33). Jeroboam also instituted other ways to worship God; he appointed his own priests; he made his own houses of worship; and he set up his own feast days. He did not restrict himself to God's Word, but instituted a worship "which he had

devised of his own heart" (1 Kings 12:33).

In our day, there is a wrong view of worship that is very popular. That is the idea that the worship of God may include *whatever is not forbidden by the Word of God.* Hence, the Roman Catholics, Lutherans, and other Protestants make use of "altars," candles, holy days, fasting on Friday, crucifixes, rosaries, "signs of the Cross," holy water, special clothing for the minister, Christmas trees, movies, etc., etc., in their worship.

However, the true principle of worship, according to the Word of God, is that only what is commanded is right and what is not commanded is wrong. Any other principle destroys purity of worship. (*The three diagrams show the different views of worship.*)

Anything is permissible.	What is not forbidden is permissible.	Only what is commanded is permissible. (regulative principle)
Cain, Aaron, Jeroboam, Liberals	Roman Catholics, Greek Orthodox, Lutherans, Anglicans, Evangelicals	Reformed, Presbyterian

Questions on Number 96

1. The difference between the First and Second Commandments is:

    a) The First tells us _____

    b) The Second tells us _____

2. Those who combine the First and Second Commandments think only of idolatry and miss the point about *purity* of worship.
    ☐ True ☐ False

3. God is jealous of His honor and glory, so it makes no difference *how* men worship Him, just so they *do* worship Him. ☐ True ☐ False

4. Sinful man can never think rightly about God or worship Him correctly by himself. ☐ True ☐ False

5. Why can man never make a true image or likeness of God? (*Give a verse to prove your answer*) _____

_____

_____

6. Name some men in the Bible who tried to worship God by their own methods and who were punished for their attempts: _____

_____

7. Many churches today have a wrong principle of worship. What is it?

_____

_____

8. Diagram three views of worship.

9. What is the only true principle, or law, of worship, according to the Bible? _____

_____

_____

10. Write out Deuteronomy 12:32.

_____

_____

_____

_____

🔥 *Proper Use of Images*

Q97. May we not make any image at all?

God may not and cannot be imaged in any way; as for creatures, though they may indeed be imaged, yet God forbids the making or keeping of any likeness of them, either to worship them or to serve God by them.

Question 97 tells us that not only may no image of God be made, but that *no image of anything* may be used for the worship of God.

An image is any visible representation of some person or creature. Pictures and statues and photographs are all images. The question is not whether art is a proper activity. We believe that artistic talent is a gift from God and should be developed by man, especially by Christians.

However, art forms are not to be used as devices or helps in the worship of God. The reason for this is that worship is directed to God alone and God is a Spirit. He has no physical body. Therefore, He cannot be imaged or represented. He is invisible (1 Timothy 6:16), and He is everywhere (Jeremiah 23:24; 1 Kings 8:27). Any attempt to picture God is an insult to Him and is, rather, a degrading misrepresentation and a false picture. God will not be worshiped by false pictures.

Indeed, it must also be said that even mental pictures of God are also a violation of this commandment. We must always resist the temptation to imagine what God looks like, even though the Bible does use human terms in speaking of Him (These human descriptive terms used in reference to God are called anthropomorphisms—for example: God is said to have eyes, ears, mouth, hands, etc.).

If it is wrong to use images in the worship of God, we may ask why were pictures and images allowed in the Old Testament worship? You will remember that there were two golden angels standing on the mercy seat in the Holy of Holies (Exodus 25:18-20) and there were angels embroidered on the curtains of the tabernacle (Exodus 26:1, 31), and there were other images commanded by God in the Old Testament, such as the brass snake on the pole (Numbers 21:8-9).

The answer to this problem is two-fold. First, the images and pictures that God Himself commanded to be used were proper simply because God commanded them. Whatever God commands is right. Secondly, God never commanded that an image be made to represent *Him*.

The same two principles still hold for us:

1. **Whatever God commands us to use for His worship is not only proper but necessary.**

2. **We may never try to picture God Himself; Father, Son, or Holy Spirit.**

The punishment for breaking this commandment is not only for the violators, but for the children also, to the third and fourth generation. This means that they will be led into the same wicked paths that their parents walked, and they will suffer the awful consequences of breaking God's commandments also.

Questions on Number 97

1. Question 97 forbids the making of any pictures of any creatures.
   ☐ True ☐ False

2. The reason no pictures or images can be made of God is because of
   the kind of Person that He is.
   1 Timothy 6:16 tells us that He _____

   _____

   John 4:24 tells us that He is _____
   Jeremiah 23:24b tells us that He _____

3. A picture of God or an image to help us worship God is:
   ☐ a. degrading to God   ☐ c. misrepresenting God
   ☐ b. honoring to God   ☐ d. a lie
   (*check all that apply*)

4. Check the verses that speak against the use of images in God's
   worship:
   ☐ Exodus 32:8   ☐ Deuteronomy 4:15–16
   ☐ Deuteronomy 16:22   ☐ Psalm 54:2
   ☐ 2 Kings 18:4   ☐ Isaiah 53:1
   ☐ Habbakuk 2:18–19   ☐ Acts 17:29

5. When we pray, we must try to imagine what God looks like.
   ☐ True ☐ False ▶ *Explain:* _____

   _____

6. In either the Old or the New Testament there is no command of God
   to make *any* picture or image. ☐ True ☐ False

7. Numbers 21:8–9 tells us that God commanded Moses to make a
   _____ for the people to look at.

8. In 2 Kings 18:4 we read that Hezekiah broke this object to pieces
   because the people were doing what? _____

9. The Second Commandment gives what *warning* to its violators?

_____

_____

10. The Second Commandment gives what assurance to those who obey
it? _____

_____

11. Write out Isaiah 40:18 and 25.

_____

_____

_____

_____

_____

_____

_____

✸ The Importance of Preaching

Q98. But may not pictures be tolerated in churches as books for the people?

No, for we should not be wiser than God, who will not have His people taught by dumb idols, but by the lively preaching of His Word.

In this last question on the Second Commandment, we learn *why* no pictures (images) may be used in the worship of God. The reason that this question is put into the Catechism is because of the awful abuse of pictures in the Roman Catholic Church when the Catechism was written and to the present day.

One of the early Popes, Gregory, said that pictures were "lay-books" for those who could not read. He meant that a picture of Jesus could teach a great deal to an ignorant person who could neither read the Bible nor understand the Latin Church service. Thus, the Roman Catholic Church has long used pictures and statues and relics, rather than the Bible, to instruct its members.

The Reformers learned from the Bible that this was all wrong. The way to instruct people concerning Christ is to preach Christ to them from the Bible and to teach them to read the Bible for themselves. Those who depend on pictures to teach the gospel are trying to be wiser than

God. God has commanded that the gospel of Christ is to be preached by preachers, not pictured by painters! Pictures are silent idols. Preachers verbally and vocally *declare* the Word of God.

1. Religious Pictures

We may ask: Are any religious pictures permitted at any time for any purpose? It would seem that there is a place for illustrative artwork in teaching the truths of the Bible. We must know, for example, the geography of the land of Palestine. We must know the culture and customs of Bible times in order to understand many details of the Bible. For example, how would an Eskimo know what a lamb is if he were not shown a picture of one? So, pictures and illustrations can teach us these things and this is a proper use of the gift of art.

2. Pictures of Jesus Christ

Pictures of the Lord Jesus Christ are another matter, however. They are always sinful, even though most Protestants and even some Reformed people see nothing wrong with them. One Protestant pamphlet featuring a picture of "Jesus" on the front cover advises the possessor to "carry it wherever you go, in your billfold or purse. Place it where your eyes will rest upon it as you carry out your duties for the day." This is just plain idolatry and image worship of the Roman Catholic variety.

The reason that Christ may not be pictured is that He is God, and God may not be imaged. If it is objected that Christ is also true man, we reply that that is correct, but Christ's humanity cannot be separated from His Divine nature. Every so-called picture of Christ's human nature is not only a figment of the artist's imagination, but it is also an attempt to separate the two natures in Christ, and the result is a false Christ—an idol. Thus, the so-called pictures of Jesus are violations of the Second Commandment and they must never be found in our churches or in our homes.

Questions on Number 98

1. The reason for this special question in the Catechism is what?

2. What did Pope Gregory mean by pictures of Jesus being "laybooks"?

3. The way for unlearned (or illiterate) people to learn about Christ is:
   ☐ a. look at a religious picture book

  ☐ b. begin reading the Bible

  ☐ c. watch religious movies

  ☐ d. hear a preacher who preaches the Bible

4. The "living preaching" of the Word of God means:

  ☐ a. a preacher must shout and pound the pulpit once in awhile

  ☐ b. declaring the truth of Scripture

  ☐ c. attending the Passion Plays

5. We must say that all artwork is forbidden in helping us to understand life in ancient Israel. ☐ True ☐ False

6. Drawings of the Red Sea, a map of Judea, the temple of Solomon, a synagogue, a Galilean fishing boat are all forbidden by the Second Commandment. ☐ True ☐ False ▶ *Explain:* _____

  _____

  _____

7. Only Roman Catholics are guilty of violating the Second Commandment with pictures and statues of Jesus. ☐ True ☐ False

  ▶ *Explain:* _____

  _____

8. Check the answer(s) that explain why a picture of Christ is wrong:

  ☐ a. Christ is not a real man

  ☐ b. We do not know what Jesus looked like

  ☐ c. Jesus is God

  ☐ d. It separates His human and Divine natures

9. Pictures of Christ are forbidden in our churches, but they may be hung on our dining room walls for decoration. ☐ True ☐ False

  ▶ *Explain:* _____

  _____

10. Write out Romans 10:14.

  _____

  _____

  _____

❦ *Third Commandment: God's Name*

Q99. What is required in the third Commandment?

That we must not by cursing, or by false swearing, nor yet by unnecessary oaths, profane or abuse the name of God; nor even by our silence and connivance be partakers of these horrible sins in others; and in summary, that we use the holy name of God in no other way than with fear and reverence, so that He may be rightly confessed and worshiped by us, and be glorified in all our words and works.

Questions 99 through 102 explain the Third Commandment: "You shall not take the Name of the Lord your God in vain, for the Lord will not hold him guiltless that takes His Name in vain."

This commandment tells us our duty towards God's name. Taking God's name in vain is one of the most common sins of our day. Not only do crude, ignorant people use profanity, but we even hear it on the lips of public officials, entertainers, and other public figures; and we read it in books and magazines.

What is meant by the "name" of God?

God's name stands for His person. God reveals Himself not through pictures, but by His name—by all His names. When Adam named the animals (Genesis 2:19), he did so on the basis of their nature and character. In the Old Testament, men were often named on the basis of their character or activity, and thus their names described their persons. *Eve* means "mother of all living," *Noah* means "rest," *Abraham* means "father of a multitude," *Nabal* means "fool," *Elisha* means "God is salvation," etc. But if men in the Old Testament days had meaningful names, *God's* name means infinitely more.

Simply because His name is so full of meaning, it is an awful sin to use it lightly and in an irreverent way. God's name means His total revelation of Himself, especially by His various names or titles. Just as a flag represents a country, or a photograph represents a friend or relative, so God's name stands for all that God is. To step on the flag or spit on a person's photograph is to insult what or whom they represent; and to profane (despise or take lightly) the name of God is to blaspheme God Himself (Leviticus 24:11, 15).

God's *Name* is to be understood in two ways. It refers to:

1. The general Self-Revelation of God in nature

Psalm 8:1 says, "Oh Lord, our Lord, how excellent is Your name in all the earth!" All creation and providence reveal the name or person of God, and call us to worship and serve Him.

2. The specific Self-Revelation of God by particular names and titles used in Scripture

The Proper names of God. Such names as God, Jehovah, Lord, Father, Son, Lord Jesus Christ, Holy Spirit are the most common names of God that we find in Scripture. Note: Holy "Ghost" is a poor translation for the Holy Spirit.

The Descriptive titles of God. Such names as Almighty, Most High, Father of Mercies, The Holy One, Lord of Hosts, the Everlasting One, The Rock, etc. These titles reveal certain attributes and characteristics of God.

The word "name" in the Third Commandment refers especially to these names and titles of God, but also it applies to all the Self-Revelation of God in nature.

Man was created to cherish the name of God in his heart and to use it with reverence; but man the sinner hates God and His name and profanes it in various ways, as the Catechism teaches.

The main forms of profaning the name of God, according to question 99, are as follows:

1. Cursing

This means pronouncing a curse or asking God to pronounce a curse on something or someone. People often wickedly "damn" things; but only God has the authority to damn anyone. Cursing, therefore, is blaspheming God's name because a curse is pronounced apart from the authority of God.

2. False swearing or perjury

This refers to taking an oath, in the name of God, to tell the truth and then telling a lie in God's name instead. This is to call God a liar and to misuse His holy name.

3. Unnecessary oaths

An oath, or speaking in the name of God, is proper only on very solemn and sacred occasions. To use God's name lightly in connection with ordinary speech is to profane His name. Such expressions as "By God ..." or "By Christ ..." are examples of this sin. But there are many other disguised or "minced" oaths that even Christians speak in ignorance, such as "Golly" (God), "Gee" (Jesus), "Jeez" (Jesus) "darn" (damn), "Gosh" (God), "Oh Lordy," "Oh Heavens," etc. Jesus condemned all such false swearing in Matthew 5:34–37.

4. Being a conniver with others in profaning God's name

If we do not protest when others break this commandment, we are guilty also.

As Christians, we must abhor all such abuses of the holy name of our God and, as the Catechism says, even warn others who engage in such profanity and not remain silent.

Questions on Number 99

1. The Third Commandment tells us _____

   _____ and is explained by questions

   _____ in our Catechism.

2. In this answer, the first part tells us how we *are* to use God's name
   and the last part tells us how we are *not* to use God's name.
   ☐ True ☐ False

3. The "name" of God refers to:
   ☐ a. God's Person
   ☐ b. All His self-revelation in nature and in Scripture
   ☐ c. All His names and titles
   ☐ d. "The Lord your God" only

4. In the Old Testament, God's name had meaning, but people's names
   were never meaningful. ☐ True ☐ False

5. God's name refers to two things. They are:
   a) _____
   b) _____

6. List some of the proper names of God: _____

   _____

   _____

   _____

7. The Catechism says we are to use God's name with "fear and _____
   _____ so that He may be _____ _____
   and _____ by us, and be _____ _____
   in _____ our _____
   and _____ ."

8. The use of such expressions as "what the Devil," "oh golly," "gracious me," "in heaven's name," "go to hell" are violations of the Third Commandment. ☐ True ☐ False

9. What does "connivance" mean in this answer? _____

_____

_____

_____

10. Write out Leviticus 19:12.

_____

_____

_____

_____

❦ *The Seriousness of Profaning God's Name*

Q100. Is the profaning of God's name, by swearing and cursing, so grievous a sin that His wrath is kindled against those also who do not help as much as they can to hinder and forbid it?

Yes, truly, for no sin is greater and more provoking to God than the profaning of His name; wherefore He even commanded it to be punished with death.

In this question, we are told *our responsibility toward others who break the Third Commandment*. This is a further explanation of the warning given in the previous question against being a "partaker of these horrible sins in others."

It is rather frightening to realize that in order to keep this commandment it is not enough merely to keep our mouths shut and not utter profanity, but we have to open them and defend the name of God when others profane it. This is the positive application of the Third Commandment. As Christians, we are prophets (see Questions 31 and 32) and must "confess His name" to the world. A prophet cannot remain silent and still be a prophet. There are no silent prophets!

If we are ashamed to protest when others drag the name of God in the mud and speak irreverently of holy things, we betray Christ and become guilty of this sin also.

Cursing, using God's name in vain, and telling dirty jokes are great sins against the name of God. Even jokes about biblical subjects and the

"St. Peter" jokes, which Christians sometimes listen to and repeat, are a terrible offense against God. We must not encourage others in them, but rather reprove the tellers.

The practical problem arises: How are we to "hinder and forbid" this sin in others? This is a hard question to answer. But in some way we must show our disapproval when others in any way profane God's name. If we remain present and laugh when a dirty joke or story is told, we are guilty. If someone uses God's name in vain while talking to us and we do not show disapproval, we are guilty. On the other hand, if a person knows that we disapprove of his profanity and persists in using it just to annoy us, as sometimes happens, then we must try to ignore such a person as much as possible after telling him that God hates that sin.

As the Catechism reminds us, there is no greater sin than the profaning of God's name; and in the Old Testament it was punished with death. Those who are afraid or ashamed to defend the name of God when others profane it are also deserving of eternal death, unless they repent.

Questions on Number 100

1. In question 100 we are told _____
   _____
   _____

2. What connection does this question have with question 99? _____
   _____
   _____

3. We cannot remain silent when others defile God's name, because we are _____
   _____

4. If others think that they have the right to insult our God to us, we have more right to defend His name before them. ☐ True ☐ False

5. How would you handle the following situations:
   a) A friend begins telling a "St. Peter" joke to you. _____
   _____
   _____

   b) A guest in your home uses profanity when talking to you. _____
   _____
   _____

   c) A person with whom you must work likes to annoy you by

constantly taking God's name in vain. _____

_____

_____

6. What did God command the Israelites in the Old Testament to do
    when they heard profanity? (*See Leviticus 5:1, Proverbs 29:24*)

    _____

7. What is it that keeps us from doing our duty and speaking against
    this sin in others? (*See Proverbs 29:25*) _____

8. What was the punishment for blasphemy in the Old Testament?
    (*See Leviticus 24:15-16*) _____
    Do you think that was too severe? ☐ Yes ☐ No

9. How will God punish unrepentant blasphemers in eternity? _____

    _____

10. Do you think that the civil government should have laws against
    blasphemy and profanity? ☐ Yes ☐ No ▶ *Explain:* _____

    _____

    _____

    _____

11. Write out Ephesians 5:4, 11.

    _____

    _____

    _____

    _____

    _____

    _____

❧ Swearing Reverently by God's Name

Q101. But may we swear reverently by the name of God?

Yes, when the magistrate requires it, or when it may be needful
otherwise, to maintain and promote fidelity and truth to the glory
of God and our neighbor's good; for such an oath is grounded in

God's Word, and therefore was rightly used by the saints in the Old and New Testament.

In Questions 101 and 102, we are taught the lawful and proper use of oaths (swearing) in obedience to the Third Commandment. Question 101 tells *when* swearing an oath is lawful, and question 102 tells us the *nature* of an oath.

In the days of the Reformation, there were people who interpreted our Lord's words "do not swear at all" (Matthew 5:34) to mean that all oaths are forbidden. Even some churches today teach this. But Christ did not forbid all swearing, as other Scriptures prove. Indeed, the Old Testament commanded swearing on certain solemn occasions (Deuteronomy 10:20); and Christ came not to destroy the Old Testament but to fulfill it and magnify it. Moreover, He Himself swore an oath when commanded to do so by the High Priest—see Matthew 26:63-64.

Swearing an oath, as we have seen in question 99 and shall see in the next question, is speaking by the name of God—either to attest to a truth or to make a promise or vow. God's name is used to call down His curse on the one swearing if he deliberately speaks a lie. To swear, then, is the serious, religious act of calling upon God as Witness and Judge.

In this question we learn:

1. The Proper Occasion for Oaths

"When the magistrate requires it." On certain occasions the civil authorities can require a person to speak under oath in order to determine the truth of a matter (Exodus 22:10-11). At other times it is necessary to require persons to take an oath of faithfulness or sincerity (Ezra 10:5). Refusal to take an oath when the magistrate requires it is sin.

"When it may be needful otherwise." Another lawful occasion for speaking under oath is in a court of the church where the truth must be gotten from witnesses. Any other occasion for invoking the name of God on one's speech would also have to be solemn and sacred. The Apostle Paul did swear in the name of God in some of his New Testament writings. He did this in order to impress upon his readers that he was speaking the absolute truth before God (See Romans 1:9; 9:1; 2 Corinthians 1:23; 11:31; 12:19; Galatians 1:20; Philippians 1:8; 1 Thessalonians 2:5; 1 Timothy 2:7).

2. The Purpose of Oaths

The reason that oaths are commanded on certain occasions is "to maintain (confirm) fidelity (faithfulness) and truth to the glory of God and our neighbor's good." For determining truth in a court of law and to cause people to promise loyalty to their office, swearing is necessary. There is no higher motive for telling the truth or making a promise than the fear of God's wrath. A Christian society depends on men speaking truthfully and being faithful to their word. The oath is God's means for insuring that.

George Washington recognized the importance of the biblical oath to the well-being of the country when he declared: "Where is the security for property, for reputation, for life if the sense of religious obligation desert the oaths, which are the instruments of investigation in courts of justice?" He meant that our nation could only stand as it recognized the authority of God which it does in the oath to God.

How seriously are our courts and civil leaders taking the godly oath today? Is it having consequences?

Questions on Number 101

1. What do questions 101 and 102 explain for us? _____
    _____
    _____

2. Why do some people think that oaths are not lawful now? _____
    _____
    _____

3. Give proof from the Old Testament that oaths were lawful and
    proper then. _____
    _____
    _____
    _____

4. Give proof from the New Testament that oaths are lawful and proper
    now. _____
    _____
    _____
    _____

5. What did Jesus mean when He said, "do not swear at all" in
    Matthew 5:34? _____
    _____
    _____

6. Swearing by the name of God is lawful on what two occasions?
    a) _____
    b) _____

7. An oath may be used for
   - ☐ a. witnessing to a truth or fact
   - ☐ b. making a solemn promise
   - ☐ c. adding variety to our conversation

8. Check the occasions which are proper for swearing under oath:
   - ☐ a. When one is joking with friends.
   - ☐ b. When one is before a court of law.
   - ☐ c. When an elected official is inducted into office.
   - ☐ d. When a church member is called before a church court.
   - ☐ e. When a person is inducted into the armed forces.

9. According to our Catechism, what is the purpose of the oath?

   _____

   _____

10. Write out Deuteronomy 10:20.

    _____

    _____

    _____

    _____

❦ *Swearing by Other Creatures Prohibited*

Q102. May we swear by "the saints" or by any other creatures?

No, for a lawful oath is a calling upon God, that He, as the only searcher of hearts, may bear witness to the truth, and punish me if I swear falsely; which honor is due to no creature.

Oaths and Swearing

In this question, we learn more specifically the nature of an oath and how it is to be taken properly.

The question asks, "May we swear by the saints or by any other creatures?" The Roman Church permitted oaths in the name of the great "saints," because of their holiness and nearness to God. We often hear such swearing in the name of saints, especially by Irish Roman Catholics.

However, only God's name may be used in an oath and for the

following reasons:

1. God alone is the Author of all truth, and the Judge of all truth.

2. God alone searches the heart, and He alone can know if we speak the truth sincerely. No mere creature can do this. In taking an oath, we must say in our hearts with David: "There *is* not a word on my tongue, *But* behold, O Lord, You know it altogether" (Psalm 139:4).

3. God alone can punish the liar and oath-breaker with eternal destruction. Man may perjure (speak falsely) himself and never be discovered by men, but God knows all things, and He renders strict justice to all men. We must fear God's wrath against all lying.

4. God alone can bless the truth-speaker with His goodness. We may expect good from God as we swear in truth and sincerity by His holy name.

5. God alone must be given the glory when men swear to the truth in His name.

Therefore, only God's name may be invoked as an oath.

Making Vows

Closely associated with oaths are vows. A vow is similar to an oath in that it is a solemn promise made on a sacred occasion. The difference is this: an oath is a statement or promise made to men in God's name; a vow is a voluntary promise and obligation made directly to God, usually with the hope of receiving a special favor from Him (Genesis 28:20-22; Numbers 21:2; 1 Samuel 1:11; 2 Samuel 15:8).

"A vow may be either to *perform* (Genesis 28:20ff.) or *abstain from* (Psalm 132:2ff.) an act in return for God's favor (Numbers 21:1-3) or as an expression of zeal or devotion towards God (Psalm 22:25). It is no sin to vow or not to vow, but if made—Deuteronomy 23:23—a vow is as sacredly binding as an oath (Deuteronomy 23:21)" (*New Bible Dictionary*, p. 1313). The vow can be sinful as were the vows of the Jews about gifts "dedicated to God" (Mark 7:11). Paul's vow (Acts 18:18; 21:23) was a temporary Nazarite vow, a sincere and proper activity for a godly Jew. We make vows to God when we become communicant members of the church, when we get married, when we baptize our children and when men are ordained into the church offices. The idea of the vow is also present when we partake of Holy Communion.

Do all oaths and vows have to be kept, even if it means that we sin? The answer is NO. It is sinful to take an oath of promise or obligation to do something that is wrong—such as in the secret oaths that the Masonic Lodge requires of its members. But we are committing a second sin if we do not break such a promise. Herod sinned by not breaking his oath-promise to his step-daughter to kill John the Baptist (see Matthew

14:6–9). David did rightly by breaking his sinful oath to destroy Nabal and his household (1 Samuel 25:22, 32–34). Protestants who marry Roman Catholics and swear to train up their children in the Roman faith, sin by making such a vow and sin even further by keeping it.

This teaches us that we may never take an oath or a vow lightly. If we swear sinfully, we blaspheme the name of God. If we swear properly, we are bound before God to keep our word and vows. In the case of marriage, for example, only death can break the relationship which is created by the marriage vows.

Do men have to speak truthfully only when they take an oath? Of course not. We must speak the truth always. But because of man's proneness to speak lies, the oath is required in this sinful world. Do you think that the oath will be used in heaven?

Questions on Number 102

1. In this question, we learn the nature of an oath, that it is calling upon the Almighty God as our Witness. ☐ True ☐ False

2. Expressions such as "In heaven's name ...," "Holy Mary, look at that!," and "In the name of the saints ..." are wicked oaths.
   ☐ True ☐ False ▶ *Explain:* _____
   _____
   _____

3. Give five reasons why an oath must be solemnly taken in God's name:
   a) _____
   b) _____
   c) _____
   d) _____
   e) _____

4. What is the difference between an oath and a vow? _____
   _____
   _____
   _____

5. Name some occasions for the use of vows: _____
   _____
   _____

6. People should not be urged into taking church membership vows or marriage vows without their being fully informed as to what those vows require. ☐ True ☐ False ▶ *Explain:* _____

   _____

   _____

7. A promise made under oath must be kept under all circumstances. ☐ True ☐ False ▶ *Explain:* _____

   _____

   _____

8. Match the following:

   the only Searcher of hearts   Nabal

   Church membership and marriage   Matthew 14

   Herod's promise and oath   Masonic Lodge

   David's oath   Psalm 139:4

   unlawful oaths   vows to God

9. We are obligated to speak the truth only when we have taken an oath. ☐ True ☐ False

10. Write out 2 Corinthians 1:23.

    _____

    _____

    _____

    _____

🕭 *Fourth Commandment: Sabbath Rest*

Q103. What does God require in the fourth Commandment?

In the first place, God wills that the ministry of the Gospel and schools be maintained, and that I, especially on the day of rest, diligently attend church to learn the Word of God, to use the holy sacraments, to call publicly upon the Lord, and to give Christian alms. In the second place, that all the days of my life I rest from my evil works, allow the Lord to work in me by His Spirit, and thus begin in this life the everlasting Sabbath.

The Catechism devotes only one question to explaining the Fourth Commandment. This seems strange since the Fourth Commandment is the longest of the Ten Commandments. The Catechism devotes four questions to explaining the Third Commandment. Which other commandments are explained by only one question in the Catechism?

The sabbath commandment is very important, and it needs careful explanation. The first and main point of the commandment is this: "Remember the sabbath day, to keep it holy." The next part of the commandment tells how the sabbath is to be kept holy, and the last part tells why we are to keep the sabbath day. Catechism question 103 tells us first, how the sabbath is to be observed and then, second, the spiritual meaning of the sabbath.

The word "sabbath" means "rest."

There are various kinds of "rests" mentioned in the Old Testament. God Himself *rested* on the seventh day (Genesis 2:2-3) after finishing His six days of creative work. We next read of the sabbath in Exodus 16, where God instructed the Israelites to pick up a double portion of manna on the day before the sabbath, as there would be none given on the sabbath (16:22). Thus, the sabbath day was observed before God gave the Law on Mt. Sinai (Exocus 20).

The Fourth Commandment speaks of a *weekly* rest day, the seventh day in the Old Testament, which, incidentally, was a different day of the week each year. There was also a sabbath *year*—every seventh year (Leviticus 25:1-7; 20-22), in which the land was not to be worked. And every fiftieth year, the year after seven sabbath years (49 years), was called the "year of Jubilee" (Leviticus 25:8-12)—a year of rest and the release of slaves and cancellation of debts.

What does this "rest" idea or sabbath idea mean?

It first refers to God's rest, and then, secondly, to our rest.

1.   God rested from His works of creation, and Christ rested from His work of redemption when He arose from the dead. The weekly sabbath day reminds us of these two great works and rests of God.

2.   The sabbath day reminds us of our rest in Jesus Christ from our evil works of sin. The Catechism stresses this, does it not? Heaven is the final sabbath or rest of true believers according to Hebrews 4:1, 3, 9. The sabbath has already begun for us with the resurrection of the Savior from the dead. The weekly *Christian* sabbath day (the first day of the week) is God's constant reminder to us that we are not only His creatures, but also His redeemed children who have begun to enter into the eternal salvation-sabbath of Christ.

The Fourth Commandment then stands as a moral law for the church on earth to keep. The weekly sabbath day must be remembered and *kept*. The New Testament church does not keep the seventh day of the week, but, rather, the first day, for that was when Christ arose from the dead and entered into His rest from the curse of sin. The early Christians worshiped on Sunday, the first day of the week, after the resurrection (Acts 20:7; 1 Corinthians 16:2). The Seventh Day Adventists are wrong when they keep Saturday as their sabbath. It is as if the Savior had not yet died for them and risen again on the first day of the week!

How are we to keep the sabbath day?

First, it is a *day* we are to keep holy, not just a couple of hours on Sunday morning! The whole day is to be set aside from our weekly labors and cares. We should do no business, nor engage in any activity which prevents us from worshiping the Lord and being *restful*.

All church activities must be attended joyfully, and the other hours of the day are to be used to help develop our spiritual lives: reading the Bible and Christian books and periodicals, listening to Christian broadcasts, visiting others for Christian fellowship, especially the sick and the aged. The world is to be shut out and forgotten as much as possible! Read Isaiah 58:13-14: The Lord's Day is a day for us to "delight" in Him—and *our* "ways" and "words" are to be put aside.

Those who deliberately violate this commandment, will never enter into heavenly rest, but will be burdened with the concerns and pains of hell forevermore! God hates sabbath-breaking!

Questions on Number 103

1. The sabbath commandment belongs to which "table" of the Law of God? _____

2. What are the three parts of the Fourth Commandment?
   a) _____
   b) _____
   c) _____

3. Who would the "manservant" and "maidservant" and "cattle" and "stranger" refer to in our present-day circumstances? _____
   _____
   _____

4. The sabbath commandment was first given on Mt. Sinai when God gave His Law to Moses. ☐ True   ☐ False

5. We today are not obligated to obey the Fourth Commandment, but it is still a good policy to rest one day per week. ☐ True   ☐ False

6. What are the great "rests" or "sabbaths" of God Himself?

   a) _____

   b) _____

7. The Christian rests from what? _____

   _____

8. What does Hebrews 4 call heaven? _____

   _____

9. If we love our Savior and look forward to heaven, what kind of things will we do on Sunday? _____

   _____

   _____

10. What are the two places that we must certainly attend on the day of rest, according to the Catechism?

    a) _____

    b) _____

11. What is meant by "schools"? _____

    _____

12. Write out Isaiah 56:2.

    _____

    _____

    _____

    _____

    _____

    _____

❦ Fifth Commandment: Authority

Q104. What does God require in the fifth Commandment?

That I show all honor, love and faithfulness to my father and mother, and to all in authority over me, submit myself with due obedience to all their good instruction and correction, and also bear patiently with their infirmities, since it is God's will to govern us by their hand.

According to the common Reformed understanding (see Q93), the Fifth Commandment begins the second table of the Law—our duties to our neighbor in the fear of God. These six commandments of the second table may be titled as follows:

No. 5 — Our duty toward all lawful authority.

No. 6 — Our duty toward our neighbor's life.

No. 7 — Our duty toward our neighbor's marriage.

No. 8 — Our duty toward our neighbor's property.

No. 9 — Our duty toward our neighbor's name.

No. 10 — Our duty respecting God's providence.

The Fifth Commandment tells children to honor their parents and expect the blessing of a long and happy life. The Catechism correctly enlarges this to include "all in authority over me."

Behind this commandment is the truth that God has established various kinds of authority among men. All men are under authority of one kind or another. It is rebellion against God to try to be free from the authority of others. Yet, this is what thousands of people, young and old, are trying to do today. They say that they want "freedom."

Let us look at the various kinds of authority to which we must submit ourselves because God so orders it.

1. The Home

Authority begins for us in the home. God places parents over children. All children are to show "honor, love and faithfulness" to their parents. Ephesians 6:1-3 gives the New Testament interpretation of this commandment. God's promise of blessing to obedient children still stands! Disobedient children are wicked children who are preparing themselves for ungodly lives and eventually hell, if they do not repent.

2. The School

The school teacher takes the place of the parents and acts for the parents in so far as the formal education of the children is concerned. Children must be obedient to their teachers or expect punishment from their parents! The school is to be governed by the parents, not the government—as the children are given by God to the parents, not to the state. Under Communism, the state owns the children, and the schools must obey the state, not the parents. Are we getting close to Communism in our country?

3. The Church

God places believers under the authority of the church officers! We must obey our church rulers (Hebrews 13:17), because Christ stands behind them and rules us through them.

4. The Civil Government

Our government rulers, such as policemen, judges, governors, presidents, and congressmen, have received their authority from God—not from the people, as unbelievers think. And even though such officials may not be Christians themselves, still Christians must obey them. Romans 13:1-7 clearly teaches us our obligations to obey and honor our government leaders, because God has placed them in power, and they are His "ministers" (servants) (vs. 4).

5. The Employer

When we agree to work for others, then we owe obedience to them. Strikes and revolts by workers against their employers are a revolt against God—see 1 Peter 2:18.

6. The Aged

Leviticus 19:32 says: "You shall rise before the gray headed and honor the presence of an old man, and fear your God: I am the Lord." We must give respect to older persons. How often this is lacking today!

The main reason that we must honor and obey these superiors is not that they are stronger or wiser than we, but rather, *because God has placed them over us.* The church elders must obey the traffic-officer on the city streets and the Christian traffic-officer must obey the church elders when they administer the Laws of God. We are all under the authority of God in various ways.

The Catechism points out that our rulers do have "infirmities," as no man is perfect. But the infirmities of our rulers must never be used as an excuse to disobey them or show them disrespect.

There is one very important qualification and restriction upon our obedience to men. That is, when any man or group of men demand of us that we obey them contrary to God's will, we must disobey. Daniel had to disobey the king's orders, and the Apostles refused to obey the Sanhedrin when ordered to cease preaching the gospel. In such cases, we can only say with Peter: "We ought to obey God rather than men" (Acts 5:29 and 4:17-20), even if it means imprisonment or death for us. The blessing of God is on those children and adults who obey God's authority in society.

Questions on Number 104

1. According to common Reformed understanding, the second table of the Law begins with the _____ Commandment. This second table deals with what? _____

2. The Fifth Commandment reads thus: _____

    _____

    _____

    _____

    _____

3. The Fifth Commandment does not have reference to any authority
    except the authority of parents. ☐ True ☐ False

    ▶ *Explain:* _____

    _____

    _____

    _____

4. All lawful authority, which we must obey, comes from God, but
    Christians do not have to obey non-Christian rulers.

    ☐ True ☐ False

    ▶ *Explain:* _____

    _____

    _____

    _____

5. Name five realms of society where God's authority must be respected
    and obeyed:

    a) _____

    b) _____

    c) _____

    d) _____

    e) _____

6. Children must obey their school teachers because the government,
    which owns us, demands that they obey. ☐ True ☐ False

    ▶ *Explain:* _____

    _____

7. What "infirmities" of our superiors must we patiently bear with?

    _____

    _____

8. Match the following:

Leviticus 19:32	Civil government
School teachers	Church rulers
Romans 13:1–7	Parents
Hebrews 13:17	The aged
"Statism"	Number Nine
Neighbor's name	The government owns the people

9. What important restriction must we observe in obeying our superiors? _____

_____

_____

10. Write out Ephesians 6:1–2.

_____

_____

_____

_____

_____

_____

◖ Sixth Commandment: Sanctity of Life

Q105. What does God require in the sixth Commandment?

That I do not revile, hate, insult or kill my neighbor either in thought, word, or gesture, much less in deed, whether by myself or by another, but lay aside all desire of revenge; moreover, that I do not harm myself, nor willfully run into any danger. Wherefore also to restrain murder the magistrate is armed with the sword.

The Sixth Commandment of God's Law demands *respect for our neighbor's life.* Though in so many words it merely forbids murder, it actually goes much further than that: It requires a positive love for our neighbor and the effort "to prevent his hurt as much as possible," and even "to do good unto our enemies" (Question 107). As we have seen (Question 92), the commandments of God have both a *negative* and a *positive* application.

They not only *forbid* certain evil attitudes and actions, but they *require* the opposite attitudes and actions (God-obedient responses).

Question 105 tells us what the Sixth Commandment *forbids;* Question 106 explains what the *root* or *source* of murder is; and question 107 teaches us what the Sixth Commandment *demands.*

There are three matters mentioned in question 105 respecting the forbidding of murder (This commandment is *not* referring to the killing of animals, as some people have interpreted it, but to the taking of *human* life).

1. **God forbids us to have any injurious thoughts against our neighbor, whether for revenge or otherwise.**

Even worse are words and gestures (motions) which indicate a malicious attitude toward another person. And worst of all is the actual taking of his life (the "deed") by ourselves or through some other person. Remember that King David was guilty of murdering Uriah the Hittite, by having Uriah placed in the front line of battle where he would surely be killed (2 Samuel 11:14–17, 26–27).

The "desire for revenge" is the most common motive for murder, and only as we truly fear God and have the Holy Spirit working in our minds can we "lay aside" this powerful, proud desire to "get even" and hurt those whom we feel have treated us unfairly. Our neighbor's life must always be regarded as sacred because he is an image-bearer of God (see Genesis 9:6).

2. **God also forbids us to endanger our own lives, as it is God, not ourselves, who owns our lives.**

What are some forms of willful self-murder? First, there is the sin of suicide (King Saul, Ahithophel, and Judas). Can a true Christian commit this sin? This is a debatable question. There are lesser forms of self-murder, such as recklessly handling firearms, indulging in dangerous speeding, sports, and stunts, and otherwise flirting with danger. Sometimes, risks are involved in the line of duty, but that is different from a careless indifference to our physical well-being. Neither should we forget that self-preservation requires eating healthy food, getting rest and exercise, not abusing alcohol and tobacco, and not using illegal drugs, which are harmful to our bodies (see 3 John 2).

3. **Because of the tendency in everyone to murder others, God has appointed a special punishment for murderers, namely, *capital punishment.***

The "magistrates"—officials of government—are required by the Word of God to put to death those who are guilty of first-degree murder. This duty is stated in Genesis 9:5–6. It is repeated in Romans 13:4. Capital punishment is *God's* punishment, and those who are trying to abolish this punishment are rebelling against the Word of God and defying God

Himself.

Why is murder so wrong? Because, as was stated above, man is made in God's image. To destroy a man is to destroy the image of God which is an attack against God. God alone gives life to man, and only God may take it away. Murder is a heinous sin.

Questions on Number 105

1. The Sixth Commandment demands _____

   _____

2. The command, "You shall not kill," merely means we are not to take the life of a neighbor. ☐ True ☐ False

3. What is the usual motive for injurious and murderous thoughts?

   _____

   _____

4. The four ways that murderous hate expresses itself are: (Q105)
   a) _____
   b) _____
   c) _____
   d) _____

5. Name five ways in which we could commit self-murder:
   a) _____
   b) _____
   c) _____
   d) _____
   e) _____

6. Is smoking a sin? ☐ Yes ☐ No ▶ *Explain:* _____

   _____

   _____

7. Some Christians say that capital punishment is wrong because "two wrongs do not make a right." Comment on this: _____

   _____

   _____

8. How does a person "lay aside all desire of revenge" when someone deliberately hurts him or lies about him? _____

9. Why is human life so priceless? _____
    _____
    _____

10. Write out Genesis 9:6.
    _____
    _____
    _____
    _____
    _____
    _____

❦ The Root of Murder

Q106. Does this Commandment speak only of killing?

No, but in forbidding murder God teaches us that He abhors its very root, namely, envy, hatred, anger, and desire of revenge; and that in His sight all these are hidden murder.

Each year, thousands of people are killed by other people. The murder rate is steadily climbing, faster than the population is increasing. Yet, from 1967 to 1977 there were no executions of any murderers in the United States. In 1930 there were about 130 executions. The Supreme Court had practically abolished the death penalty in the United States.

1. The Root of Murder is hatred.

What lies behind the awful crime of murder? Behind the gun, the knife, the poison, the club, and other murder weapons is human action; and behind the action is the *desire* and *will* to murder. Behind this desire to kill are envy, hatred, anger, lust for revenge, and other motives. Often, in robbery and other crimes, the victim is killed in order to keep him from identifying the attacker. In murder trials, the court always looks for a motive: the reason why the accused person would want to kill the victim.

The Bible tells us that hatred is the basic motive for murder and furthermore, it teaches that all of us have this hatred in our own hearts. We are all potential murderers, and should be regarded as "dangerous persons."

Our Lord explained that when a person hates his neighbor, he is committing spiritual murder! Jesus' words are these: "I say unto you, that whoever is angry with his brother without a cause shall be in danger of the judgment ... and whoever says, 'you fool!' (the language of hate) shall be in danger of hell fire" (Matthew 5:22). The Apostle John teaches the same thing: "Whoever hates his brother is a murderer, and you know that no murderer has eternal life abiding in him" (1 John 3:15).

This spiritual interpretation of the Sixth Commandment not only teaches us that in God's sight there is much more guilt of murder than we suspected, but that every one of us has broken the Sixth Commandment all our lives. God is first of all concerned with the heart, and He sees the hatred and the murderous motives in every human heart. Rather than being a rare crime in our community, spiritual or hidden murder is constantly being committed. It is also true of us that "their feet are swift to shed blood: destruction and misery are in their ways" (Romans 3:15-16).

2. Is it always wrong to hate?

We must not be confused on this matter. Yes, we must hate evil because God hates evil. In fact, some verses in God's Word speak of hating evil men and praying that God will destroy them (see Psalm 5:10; 35:1-8; 59:10; 69:24-28; 139:20, 21; Jeremiah 11:20 and 15:15). The explanation for this is that we must hate the sinful works of men, even while desiring the doers' conversion. But even above the conversion of the wicked, our greatest desire is to see God glorified; and if it takes the destruction of the wicked to glorify God, then we should pray for that too. But we may never hate any person simply because he may be *our* enemy; rather, we hate only *God's* enemies and only because of their evil works against God. And here we must be very cautious of judging sinfully, lest *we* be found guilty.

Only by the regenerating grace of God, by the New Birth, can we be delivered from sinful hate and darkness of heart. We must pray continuously for God's help to love our neighbor and abide in the light of Christ (1 John. 2:10).

Questions on Number 106

1. As the root is necessary for a plant to grow, so hatred is necessary for

   _____ to be committed.

2. What are the four "roots" or motives behind murder, according to this question?

   a) _____

   b) _____

c) _____

d) _____

3. If hate and envy are hidden murder, then actually killing a person is not a greater sin. ☐ True ☐ False ▶ *Explain:* _____

_____

4. According to James 1:14–15, these are the steps in the process of sin: Lust is _____ by an outward object. Then lust is (acted upon), which brings forth _____ . After the *act* of sin, _____ is the consequence.

5. It is ☐ *biblical* or ☐ *unbiblical* to think of obedience to God's commandment as *outward* acts only. ▶ *Explain:* _____

_____

_____

6. It is unbiblical ever to hate a person for any reason.
☐ True ☐ False ▶ *Explain:* _____

_____

_____

_____

7. According to the Sixth Commandment, as God applies it to men, who is guilty of murder? _____

_____

8. Should the death penalty be given to people who are guilty only of "hidden murder"? ☐ True ☐ False ▶ *Explain:* _____

_____

_____

9. Who was the first murderer? (*See John 8:44*). Whom did he murder and how? _____

_____

_____

10. Write out 1 John 3:15.

_____

_____

🌣 The Duty of Loving Our Neighbor

Q107. But is this all that is required: that we do not kill our neighbor?

No, for in condemning envy, hatred, and anger, God requires us to love our neighbor as ourselves, to show patience, peace, meekness, mercy, and kindness toward him, and to prevent his hurt as much as possible: also, to do good even unto our enemies.

This question stresses the positive requirements of the Sixth Commandment—the duty of protecting and preserving the life of one's neighbor.

1. Our Neighbor

Who is our "neighbor"? He is not just the person who lives next door, or just the person who likes us and wants to be friendly. He is any person who comes across our path and with whom we have dealings, directly or indirectly. This is our Lord's teaching in Luke 10:29-37—the parable of the Good Samaritan.

It is impossible to be neutral or indifferent to a fellow human being. Either we love him for the sake of God, or we hate him for the sake of sin. There are eight separate virtues mentioned in this answer which we should show toward our neighbor.

It is not hard to show kindness to those who show kindness to us, but the Sixth Commandment requires more than this. We must show love, patience, peace, meekness, mercy, kindness, and good even to our enemies! This is not possible unless the love of Christ fills our hearts.

2. What Love Means

How are we to show Christian love to all men?

The *first* need that others have is the salvation of their souls. So, to prevent his *spiritual* hurt, we must first be concerned to give the gospel to our neighbor. Apart from this, he will surely perish forever in the lake of fire, which is hell.

Second, we must always speak the truth to Christians and non-Christians alike, even though they may resent it. We are doing them good even though they may think we are unkind and insulting.

Third, we must be ready to aid and to assist our neighbor in any situation where he is in danger of bodily harm or death, even at the risk of our own lives.

Fourth, we must study ways of preserving life against disease and other hazards. Two awful crimes against human life are being promoted today by many persons, including physicians. These crimes are *abortion* and *euthanasia*. Look up these words in a dictionary and you will readily understand why they are condemned by the Sixth Commandment. As God-fearing Christians we must let our voices be heard against these growing forms of murder against the very young and the very old or very ill.

3. Loving our Enemies

Even to our enemies we must seek to do good. The Bible teaches that we are not to return evil for evil (Matthew 5:44–47; Romans 12:17–21). Only the grace of God working in our hearts and minds can enable us to live like that! The question now arises, however, "Is it wrong to fight an enemy in self-defense?" Is it wrong to fight against an attacker, for example, and injure or kill him in the process? Some people have said, No, it is not the biblical thing to do. They even quote Jesus' words attempting to prove their argument (Matthew 5:39–42).

But, on the contrary, it is wrong for us to permit another person to injure or kill us if we can resist him. We must love our own person as much as the neighbor's—not less. Self-defense is biblical (1 Samuel 19:10; Psalm 82:4; Proverbs 24:11–12; Acts 23:17–22).

What Jesus forbids us to do in Matthew 5:39–42 is to retaliate against personal *insults*. He is not forbidding the defense of our persons from harm or death by wicked attackers.

Questions on Number 107

1. Who is the neighbor that we are commanded to love even as ourselves? _____

   Give Scriptural proof: _____

2. It is possible to be neutral toward other people, that is, neither to love nor to hate them. ☐ True ☐ False ▶ *Explain:* _____

3. List the virtues mentioned in this answer that should always be displayed toward our neighbor. _____

4. List four ways in which we should show love to our neighbor's life (*spiritual and physical*):

a) _____

_____

b) _____

_____

c) _____

_____

d) _____

_____

5. Does the Sixth Commandment require us to risk our own lives in order to preserve the life of another? (*See John 15:13.*)
□ True □ False

6. Loving our enemies means that we should not hurt a person, even though he may attack us and seek to kill us. □ True □ False
▶ *Explain:* _____

_____

_____

7. Jesus says, "not to resist an evil person" (Matthew 5:39). What is He referring to? _____

_____

_____

8. The Sixth Commandment requires that: (*which ones?*)
□ a. we warn men against hell
□ b. we administer first aid to an injured person
□ c. we refuse to enter into battle against enemy soldiers
□ d. the sports of boxing and auto racing must be abolished
□ e. we give our bodily organs to others who need them (e.g. kidney)

9. Who demonstrated the greatest love for others, even His enemies (*Romans 5:6-8*)? _____
What did He do for us? _____

_____

10. Write out Romans 12:20-21.

_____

_____

_____

_____

_____

_____

_____

❦ Seventh Commandment: Sanctity of Marriage

Q108. What does the seventh Commandment teach us?

That all unchastity is accursed of God, and that we should therefore loathe it with our whole heart, and live chastely and modestly, whether in holy wedlock or in single life.

Questions 108 and 109 explain the Seventh Commandment—"You shall not commit adultery." This law of God requires that we honor marriage—our neighbor's and our own. Question 108 tells us the ugliness and accursedness of illicit sexual activity, and question 109 explains why adultery is so evil and how it is to be avoided.

God created us male and female (Genesis 1:27) and instituted the bond of marriage for adult men and women. The sex desire is not evil, but it must be controlled and used only in marriage. Marital sex activity is holy and good and necessary. God told Adam and Eve, whom He united in marriage, that they were to be "one flesh" (Genesis 2:24). This means that the husband and wife are to be *one* in love, in religion, in purpose. The sex act is a manifestation of their oneness, as well as a symbol of Christ's oneness with His bride, the Church.

Adultery is the breaking of the marriage bond by either the husband or the wife's becoming "one" with an outsider. Adultery destroys the home; for not only the parents, but the children also are spiritually injured. Adultery is *spiritual* divorce, and it often leads to *actual* divorce. Adultery is not only an attack against the neighbor's marital happiness and one's own happiness, but worst of all, it is an attack against God's ordinance (institution) of marriage and, thus, against God Himself.

Therefore, "All unchastity is accursed of God;" and to please God, we must "loath (despise and hate) it with our whole heart." *Chastity* is sexual purity; we must preserve our sexual cleanliness both before marriage and after marriage. In the Old Testament, sexual sins such as adultery, fornication (sex relations between unmarried persons), prostitution, rape, incest (sex relations between close relatives), and other sins were to be punished by *death* (Leviticus 18:29; 20:10-18; and Deuteronomy 22:21-27). Since these sexual sins are not less accursed in God's eyes today, our civil laws should still punish these crimes with death.

The purposes of marriage and holy sexual activity are:

1. To symbolize the marriage between Christ and His Church (Ephesians 5:23, 30–31)

This is why a Christian must marry only another Christian, so that the marriage will be unified (one) in the Lord (1 Corinthians 7:39).

2. Giving birth to children

God made male and female and told them to be fruitful and multiply and replenish the earth (Genesis 1:28; 9:1). "Birth control" is a very dangerous matter for married couples. God intends them to have children for Him. He blesses His people with children (Psalm 127:3)!

3. To make men and women more complete

Marriage brings happiness and fulfillment to men and women. Adam needed a "helper," so Eve was given to him (Genesis 2:18). It is not good that man should be alone. Husbands and wives and children are needed to help one another along life's road.

Today, the world and even some "churches" are saying that marriage is obsolete (out of fashion) and that sexual activity is all right outside of marriage. This "new morality" is the old immorality of Sodom and Gomorrah, and those who practice it destroy their lives and their homes and tear down their communities. Worst of all, God curses them as He cursed the cities of the plain—if they do not repent.

Questions on Number 108

1. Question 108 tells us what about illicit sexual activity? _____

   _____

   _____

2. Marriage must be regarded as a sacred institution because it was

   instituted by _____ at the creation of man and

   woman. It makes a man and woman "one _____ "

   for life.

3. The sexual intimacy between husband and wife is also sacred because

   it symbolizes the unity of _____ and His

   _____, which is His Bride.

4. The sexual desire that men and women have is evil, but it may be

   expressed in the marriage relationship. ☐ True ☐ False

▶ *Explain:* _____

_____

5. Adultery: (*which ones?*)
   ☐ a. is an attack against another person's marriage
   ☐ b. is an attack against one's own marriage
   ☐ c. can be committed only by a married person
   ☐ d. involves two people only
   ☐ e. is an attack against God Himself

6. Adultery is _____ divorce and often leads
   to _____divorce.

7. What is the only ground for a husband or a wife to obtain a divorce,
   according to Matthew 5:32 and 19:9? _____

   _____

8. If a husband or wife commits adultery, there should be a divorce.
   ☐ True   ☐ False ▶ *Explain:* _____

   _____

   _____

9. What do these words mean?
   a) unchastity _____
   b) loathe _____
   c) chastity _____
   d) modesty _____

10. What are three God-given purposes of marriage?
    a) _____
    b) _____
    c) _____

11. Write out Hebrews 13:4.

   _____

   _____

   _____

   _____

   _____

🔥 The Duty of Purity

Q109. Does God forbid nothing more in this Commandment than adultery and such gross sins?

Since both our body and soul are temples of the Holy Ghost, it is His will that we keep both pure and holy; therefore, He forbids all unchaste actions, gestures, words, thoughts, desires, and whatever may entice thereto.

As is the case with all the commandments of God, the Seventh Commandment requires first of all purity of *heart*. Adultery and sexual sins begin first in the heart, as our Lord explained in Matthew 5:28: "I say unto you, that whoever looks at a woman to lust for her has already committed adultery with her in his heart." This shows that the Seventh Commandment forbids all sexual impurity, whether committed by a married or an unmarried person, or by a man or woman, or by a boy or girl.

Again we are reminded that no person is innocent in this matter. All of us have often transgressed the Seventh Commandment in desire at least, if not by actual deed. Further, we are reminded that it is impossible to keep a pure heart without the strength of the Holy Spirit, and then not perfectly—our wickedness is so great. Our prayer should be that of Psalm 51:10 and 119:9 (Look up these two verses).

Sexual sins, which are thought to bring pleasure, are really sins against ourselves as well as sins against God and our neighbor. 1 Corinthians 6:13–20 teaches that fornication is a sin against one's own body (vs. 18). Our bodies do not belong to ourselves, but to the Lord (vss. 13, 15), Who redeemed us. Further, He has given us His Holy Spirit to live in our bodies (vs. 19), and therefore sexual sins are a defiling of the Temple of the Holy Spirit. We are spiritually married to Christ (vs. 17), and to commit fornication and adultery is to break our spiritual marriage to our spiritual husband, Jesus Christ!

How do we keep our souls and bodies chaste in this wicked world, where sexual temptations are thrown at us from all sides and our evil inclinations toward this sin are so strong?

We are to *avoid* whatever may entice us or others to have sexually sinful thoughts. We must avoid filthy words, stories, pictures, books and magazines. We must avoid immodest clothing, which stimulates lustful thoughts (short skirts, for example!). We must be careful of movies and TV programs—*many of which are too corrupt and indecent for Christians to watch in innocence.* Suggestive dancing, bodily contact and making out are dangerous activities, and often lead to sinful sexual activity. When Christian young people ask God not to lead them into temptation, they must also take steps to *avoid* temptation. God will then enable them to preserve their chastity so that when they enter marriage they can present themselves purely to their husband or wife.

Yes, there is forgiveness for sexual sins; but the *scar* of unchastity can never be removed!

Questions on Number 109

1. The Seventh Commandment requires _____
    of heart, according to _____ in Matthew _____

2. This commandment forbids any kind of wrong sexual activity, and
    not adultery only. ☐ True ☐ False

3. It is possible for a Christian to keep his heart wholly pure from any
    evil sexual desires if he prays hard enough. ☐ True ☐ False
    ▶ *Explain:* _____

    _____

    _____

4. What did Job do to help prevent evil desires in his heart? (*See Job
    31:1*) How are we to practice this today? _____

    _____

    _____

    _____

    _____

5. Why are sexual sins against
    a)Christ? _____

    _____

    b) The Holy Spirit? _____

    _____

6. The Christian is married to _____,
    even if he or she is not married to a wife or husband.

7. Name some things that could easily tempt you to think unchaste
    thoughts: _____

    _____

    _____

    _____

8. What do you think about:
   a) dancing? _____

   b) "going steady?" _____

   c) "making out" and "inappropriate touching"? _____

9. Do you want your future wife or husband to be pure from sexual defilement when you get married? ☐ Yes ☐ No

10. Do you think your future mate will want *you* to be pure?
    ☐ Yes ☐ No

11. Write out Ephesians 5:3-4.

    _____

    _____

    _____

    _____

    _____

    _____

    _____

    _____

❧ The Eighth Commandment: Property Rights

Q110. What does God forbid in the eighth Commandment?

God forbids not only such theft and robbery as are punished by the government, but God views as theft also all wicked tricks and devices, whereby we seek to get our neighbor's goods, whether by force or by deceit, such as unjust weights, lengths, measures, goods, coins, usury, or by any means forbidden of God; also all covetousness and the misuse and waste of His gifts.

1. The Right of Property

"You shall not steal," the Eighth Commandment, demands that we respect our neighbor's property. Behind this commandment is the fact that private ownership of property is a divine right. Property belongs to persons and no one has a right to take another person's property "by force or by deceit."

Actually, all property—the world itself—belongs first of all to God the Creator: "the earth is the Lord's, and all its fullness" (Psalm 24:1). The Lord God gives His property to men as a sacred trust, and each person who legally owns property is responsible to use his property to serve God.

The right of private property, under God, is the foundation of the economic system called "capitalism." Freedom and private property are required by God's Word for man's societal life. The United States of America was founded by men who were steeped in these moral teachings of Scripture received from their Reformed and Puritan heritage. They embodied the basic principles of private property, economic freedom, and honest money (money with real value) into our basic law, the United States Constitution.

Ungodly men have tried to do away with the Eighth Commandment and change the "capitalist" system of freedom and private property for another kind of society in which there is no freedom and the government takes over the land, the property, and businesses with the promise to "help the poor." This ungodly kind of government is called Socialism or Communism or the Welfare State. It has been tried many times in history, and is now being tried by our own government in clear violation of the Constitution. The results will surely be the same as in other countries, namely, the persecution of the church and the enslavement of the people to godless dictators.

The story of Robin Hood is another illustration of stealing from the rich to "help the poor." But no one is really helped, except the Devil, when God's commandments are broken.

You have a God-given right to earn money, to buy things, and to keep your property and possessions as your very own, to use for yourself and to help others. Your neighbor has the same right from God. It is the duty of the government to protect your rights, not take them away by confiscating property, imposing excessive taxes, and curtailing your right to work how and where you wish, by government restrictions. King Ahab sinned against God by taking away Naboth's vineyard (1 Kings 21), and King Rehoboam sinned by taxing the people too heavily (1 Kings 12:3-4, 14, 16) (Note: civil government is to be supported by a tithe [10%] on production, *an income tax,* plus a small head tax [Exodus 30:11-16]; but all other taxes such as land and inheritance taxes are unbiblical!).

Your right to keep your property and wealth is restricted by your duty to God. God gives us the ability to gain property not for our own sake, but for His sake. Never may we call our property or money absolutely our *own,* any more than our bodies and souls are our own, for it all belongs to our faithful Savior. We are always *stewards* or *caretakers* of God's possessions. Our next question will explain this further.

2. Types of Stealing

In this question, we are told of various ways in which this commandment can be broken. Indeed, we are guilty of theft much more than we realize. Six *deceitful* ways of stealing from our neighbor are listed here: unjust weights, lengths, measures, goods, coins, and usury are mentioned. Weights, lengths, and measures refer to business honesty. ("lengths" refers to a measurement for cloth—about 25 inches.) Unjust coins refers to *counterfeit coins* (coins made of a cheap metal which are passed off as precious metal) or *clipped coins* (a piece shaved off silver and gold coins, a trick often practiced in the late Middle Ages). "Usury" is charging *excessive* interest on money loaned to another person, or charging any interest on a loan to a Christian brother in need (Leviticus 25:35–36).

The book of Proverbs has many statements about dealing honestly and justly with our neighbor. "Dishonest scales are an abomination to the Lord: but a just weight is His delight" (Proverbs 11:1; 20:10). "Wealth gained by dishonesty will be diminished, but he who gathers by labor will increase" (Proverbs 13:11; 14:23). Other forms of cheating are false advertising (television has much of this!), receiving stolen goods (Proverbs 29:24), not paying one's debts, not paying wages (Leviticus 19:13; James 5:4) and gambling with cards, dice, lotteries or otherwise (Proverbs 13:11; 16:8; 2 Thessalonians 3:10–12).

Why is the "misuse and waste of" our goods also a transgression of the Eighth Commandment? Because it is stealing from God and ourselves. All that we possess has been given to us by God to be used for His glory. To waste these gifts is to rob both God and ourselves. Even our Lord had the extra food collected after His feeding of the 5,000 (John 6:12).

We see, then, how vitally important this commandment is to the economic well-being of a free people under God!

Questions on Number 110

1. The Eighth Commandment teaches what about "property" and "freedom"? _____

    _____

    _____

2. What do you think of the slogan that "human rights are more important than property rights"? _____

    _____

    _____

3. All property really belongs to
   - ☐ a. the government   ☐ c. God
   - ☐ b. the workers   ☐ d. those having the power to get it

4. How would you evaluate the "communism" in the early church? (*See Acts 2:44, 45; 4:32, 34-35*) _____

   _____

   _____

   _____

   _____

5. Everyone in the United States practices biblical capitalism.
   ☐ True ☐ False ▶ *Explain:* _____

   _____

   _____

6. Match the following:

Private property	"steal from rich to give to the poor"
State owns all property	a capitalist country
Robin Hood	Communism
United States	God's will for man
Naboth	a measurement for cloth
Psalm 24:1	private vineyard
lengths	God, the Owner of all things

7. Name two ways in which money can be falsified to cheat a neighbor.
   a) _____
   b) _____

8. Why are "lotteries" and "raffles" a form of gambling? _____

   _____

   _____

9. Would pitching pennies into a "wishing well" be a proper use of God's money? ☐ Yes ☐ No ▶ *Explain:* _____

_____

_____

10. Write out 1 Corinthians 6:10.

_____

_____

_____

_____

❧ Duties of the Eighth Commandment

Q111. But what does God require of you in this Commandment?

That I further my neighbor's good where I can and may, deal with him as I would have others deal with me, and labor faithfully, so that I may be able to help the poor in their need.

Question 110 tells us what the Eighth Commandment forbids; this one tells us what it requires—or the positive side of the commandment.

We must not only be careful about *not* stealing from or cheating our neighbor; we must also be concerned about *furthering his good* or helping him economically and financially on a voluntary basis, when it is in our power to do so. This answer is obviously referring to Matthew 7:12—the so-called "Golden Rule"—where Jesus told His disciples that "Whatever you want men to do to you, do also to them." This does not mean that we are to give away all our money, even though there would be plenty of men around who would want us to give it to them. It does mean that we are always to deal honestly and give a "square deal" in all business matters; and that is all that we can expect from others also. In cases of real need, we should also be glad to give money or goods to help the poor and distressed.

There are two matters that make charity possible and proper:

1. **We must first of all have our own property.**

The Bible requires every able-bodied man *to work* or else not eat (2 Thessalonians 3:10). Able-bodied people who can work, must work; and it is wicked for the government to support lazy people by means of public welfare money and not require them to work. Each young person is responsible to God to prepare for some kind of vocation or life's work. We owe it to God to prepare ourselves to make a living and to support the financial needs of His Kingdom.

2. **The money that we earn and all our possessions—including our very lives—belong to God, not to ourselves.**

He tells us that we are His *stewards* of these gifts and that we are to manage our money and use it as *God would have it used*. The parable of the Talents (Matthew 25:14–30) and other Scriptures teach us that God holds us responsible for our use of His blessings: our abilities, our opportunities, our possessions, and our money. It is not a sin to be rich, but it is a sin to be a stingy rich person, just as it is a sin to be a stingy poor person. Both covetousness and extravagance (spending money on the wrong things) are a misuse of God's gifts.

What proportion of our income should be directly given to the Lord through almsgiving and offerings in the church? The biblical principle of giving in the Old Testament was the *tithe*—one-tenth of one's earnings. The New Testament does not do away with this principle of giving (see Matthew 23:23). There is still great blessing promised by God to those who do not withhold their tithe (Malachi 3:10). On the other hand, those who do not give God His tithe are said to *rob* God (Malachi 3:8), and they can expect to receive his curse! Does not 1 Corinthians 16:2 indicate that we are to give a certain proportion of our income to God—as God prospers us? Are the New Testament requirements for serving God lower or higher than those of the Old Testament?

"God loves a *cheerful* giver" (2 Corinthians 9:7)!

Questions on Number 111

1. Question 111 tells what the Eighth Commandment _____, namely "That I _____ my neighbor's _____ and labor _____ to help the _____."

2. By minding our own business and not cheating our neighbor, we are keeping this commandment sufficiently. ☐ True ☐ False

   ▶ *Explain:* _____

   _____

3. What verse of Scripture is referred to in question 111? _____

4. To keep the "Golden Rule," we should hand over any of our possessions to any neighbor who asks us for them. ☐ True ☐ False

   ▶ *Explain:* _____

   _____

   _____

5. Whom would you consider a worthy recipient of alms or financial help? _____

_____

_____

6. Anyone who is rich must not be a true Christian, according to 1 Timothy 6:10. ☐ True ☐ False ▶ *Explain:* _____

_____

_____

7. What does the Bible say about work? _____

_____

_____

8. What does it mean that we are *stewards* of God? _____

_____

_____

9. The _____ is one-tenth of our _____.
   God promises to _____ those who refuse to give it to
   Him because they would then be _____
   God according to Malachi 3:8.

10. Write out Ephesians 4:28.

_____

_____

_____

_____

_____

❧ Ninth Commandment: Sanctity of Truth

Q112. What does the ninth Commandment require?

That I bear false witness against no one, twist no one's words, be no backbiter or slanderer, join in condemning no one unheard or rashly; but that on pain of God's heavy wrath, I avoid all lying and deceit as the very works of the devil; and that in matters of judgment and justice and in all other affairs, I love, speak honestly, and confess the truth; also, in so far as I can, defend and promote my neighbor's good name.

The Ninth Commandment requires that we respect our neighbor's name and the truth. The reputation and honor of our neighbor is his sacred right; and it is a grave sin to tear down his reputation and good name by speaking lies, or even by speaking unkindly, about him.

As question 112 is the only question devoted to explaining this commandment, we see that both the *negative* and the *positive* sides of the commandment are taught in this one question.

Behind this commandment of truth-speaking is the fact that God Himself is true and the Source of all truth. In Deuteronomy 6:4 we read: "Hear, O Israel: the Lord our God, the Lord is *one!*" Jesus said: "I am the way, the truth, and the life" (John 14:6), and 1 John 5:6 declares: "The Spirit is truth." Also, 1 John 5:20 states, "We are in Him that is true, in His Son Jesus Christ. This is the true God and eternal life."

To know the truth and to speak the truth, a person must know God and be a Christian! All unbelievers are really against the truth—all truth—because they are in rebellion against the God of truth. Therefore, Paul says of natural men: "Their throat is an open tomb; with their tongues they have practiced deceit; the poison of asps (deadly snakes) is under their lips" (Romans 3:13) and "Let God be true but every man a liar" (3:4). See also Psalm 58:3.

Though the unbeliever may learn many things and become "educated," still all his knowledge is used to serve the Devil, who is called the "father of lies" and in whom is no truth (John 8:44). Satan was the first and worst liar, and all his spiritual children copy his evil works. All men by nature are, therefore, guilty of breaking the Ninth Commandment—not being truth-lovers and truth-speakers in the name of Jesus Christ.

Now let us see the various ways in which this commandment is broken with respect to the neighbor:

1.   *"Bearing false witness"*

This refers to lying, whether in making up a false story or in twisting the facts, so that a wrong impression is given. Especially sinful is lying in a court of justice, when one has taken an oath to speak the truth in the fear of God. This type of lying is called perjury.

2.   *"Twisting another's words"*

This refers to so changing the words of another person that a wrong message is given. This is often done by news reporters who do not accurately or fully quote people; and, therefore, seriously misrepresent the truth. This can cause great harm to everyone involved.

3.   *"Backbiting and slander"*

Backbiting is speaking behind a person's back in an evil and hurtful manner (even though truthful facts are reported), so that injury is done. Slander is telling things about another person which we know to be untrue.

· 4. *"Joining in condemning another person unheard or rashly"*

This refers to our *listening* to the speech of others. This commandment is broken not only by telling a lie, but also in *believing* a lie on insufficient evidence. We must beware of gossip and rumors about other people.

We should warn others who tell us questionable things that they must beware of gossip. Even if we know something evil about another person, we are *not* to speak of it to others before first approaching the person in question *privately* and seeking his repentance—in which case, we should forget the matter, not repeat it. Some persons speak or write falsehoods publicly. They may also be condemned and corrected publicly as their speech is a matter of public knowledge.

Why do people tell lies? There are various motives behind this, such as to "have some fun" and to "entertain" others, or to cover up one's guilt and avoid embarrassment (God is never deceived), or because of hatred and jealousy of another person, or in order to gain advantage, such as in dishonest business dealings. But whatever the reason, there is never any excuse before God to bear false witness. "Little white lies" are also condemned by the God of truth as are so-called "half-truths." Deliberately to give a false impression is a full lie!

In all our words and actions, we are to love the truth, love our neighbor's good name, and detest all lying and deceit, because the God of truth is our Savior and Judge. He who loves lies will land in the fiery lake (Revelation 21:8, 22:15), for this is the very work of the Devil!

Questions on Number 112

1. The Ninth Commandment requires, in general, what duties toward our neighbor? _____

   _____

2. It demands, in general, that we love the _____
   and hate all forms of _____ .

3. The reason that truth is sacred is that it comes from _____ ,
   Who is _____ .
   Give biblical proof (references): _____

   _____

4. Christians and many unbelievers have an equal respect for truth in their hearts. ☐ True ☐ False ▶ *Explain:* _____

_____

_____

5. Is it a lie that George Washington never told a lie? ☐ Yes   ☐ No
    What does the Bible say? _____

    _____

6. "Bearing false witness" is especially wicked under what
    circumstances? _____

    _____

    _____

7. Define the following:
    a) Gossip _____

    _____

    b) Slander _____

    _____

    c) Backbiting _____

    _____

8. Comment on the expression, "it was just a little white lie!"

    _____

    _____

9. In certain situations, it is permissible to lie in order to save life or
    serve the Lord. ☐ True ☐ False (*See Gen. 20:2, 9-12; 27:19;
    Ex. 1:17-20; Josh. 2:4-6*) ▶ *Explain:* _____

    _____

    _____

10. What would you say to your best friend if he or she began to tell you
    a damaging rumor about another person? _____

    _____

    _____

11. Write out Ephesians 4:25. _____

    _____

    _____

    _____

❦ Tenth Commandment: Contentment

Q113. What does the tenth Commandment require?

That not even the least inclination or thought against any commandment of God ever enter our heart, but that with our whole heart we continually hate all sin and take pleasure in all righteousness.

Does anything strike you as rather odd about the Catechism's explanation of the Tenth Commandment? Did you notice that the explanation in the Catechism does not even refer to the particular matters mentioned in the Tenth Commandment? There is nothing said about the neighbor's house or wife or servants or "anything that is your neighbor's." Rather, question 113 tells us what our *heart attitude* should be toward all the other commandments of the Law. The commandment "You shall not covet" speaks directly to our hearts, our inner desires. It shows us that all obedience to God must first spring from the heart.

One might get the impression from reading the first nine commandments that all God is concerned about is external obedience, outward behavior. But this is not so. As the Apostle Paul discovered (Romans 7:7), the Tenth Commandment requires spiritual, heart obedience to *all* the commandments.

The Lord Jesus Christ re-emphasized this truth in His sermon on the Mount (Matthew 5:20-48), that the commandments require heart-purity and heartfelt love to God and our neighbor. The natural, unregenerate man—such as the Pharisees in Jesus' day were proud of their outward obedience and resented Jesus' teaching about the heart. The natural man wants to ignore the Tenth Commandment and the lusts of his heart, even if he is concerned about keeping the other laws of God outwardly.

Thus, the Tenth Commandment condemns the *lust* of the heart, which leads to false religion and the various outward sins against our neighbor, his home, and his property. "Man looks at the outward appearance, but the Lord looks at the heart" (1 Samuel 16:7). Romans 7:14 says: "For we know that the law is spiritual, but I am carnal (fleshly), sold under sin." Sin is first of all in the desires of the heart and, then, secondly in outward behavior.

The Tenth Commandment directs us to live a life of spiritual obedience to God and spiritual contentment with His providence over our lives. The Lord gives us what He wants us to have; and only those things which can be lawfully obtained in submission to God should be desired. We are to desire nothing contrary to God's will for our lives; rather, with our whole heart we must hate all sin and take pleasure in all righteousness.

Does this commandment forbid us to covet under all circumstances? Not if the word covet simply means *desire*. We must desire things continuously. But our desires for our neighbors' property must be within the Law. We must be willing to pay for what he is willing to sell to us. To desire his wife is sinful under any circumstances because that would violate the Seventh Commandment. Thus the word "covet" in this Commandment really means evil, illegal desires in disobedience to the will of God.

Let us consider briefly why we are to keep this commandment and live in Christian contentment before the Lord, without coveting.

1. We must be satisfied with what God gives us because He is free and sovereign, and He gives us what He wishes us to have for our best. He alone is Master of our lives.

2. God is all-wise and infinitely good in giving us His gifts. His love toward us in Christ is perfect. He never withholds from us that which is for our spiritual good and for His glory. To think that God would be unfair to us is folly and unbelief. We deserve nothing, and all that we have, we have received by God's rich mercy.

3. Contentment with God's providence enables us to live in peace and joy, in gratitude and praise. The unsatisfied person is never happy, and is likely to break the commandments of God in order to get what he desires. Having the Lord and His salvation, we need nothing more, and our joy is full.

The Bible says, "Godliness with contentment is great gain ... having food and clothing, with these we shall be content" (1 Timothy 6:6, 8), and, "*Let your* conduct *be* without covetousness; *be* content with such things as you have. For He Himself has said, "*I will never leave you nor forsake you*" (Hebrews 13:5).

What motivates your heart: covetousness or contentment?

Questions on Number 113

1. The Catechism carefully explains the details mentioned in the Tenth Commandment. ☐ True ☐ False

2. The Tenth Commandment:
   ☐ a. has no reference to the other commandments
   ☐ b. is more related to the first table of the Law than to the second
   ☐ c. shows what our heart attitude should be to the whole Decalogue

3. The Tenth Commandment shows us that God requires obedience that is

☐ a. outward only   ☐ b. inward and outward   ☐ c. inward only

4. Name two biblical preachers who emphasized that the Law of God requires heart-love and obedience to God.

a) _____

b) _____

5. The natural, unregenerate man is never concerned about outward, external obedience to the commandments.   ☐ True   ☐ False

6. Coveting (desiring another person's property) is always sinful.
☐ True   ☐ False ▶ *Explain:* _____

_____

_____

_____

7. Is man responsible to control the "least inclinations" of his heart?
☐ True   ☐ False ▶ Can he do so? _____
▶ *Explain:* _____

_____

_____

8. The civil government should enforce obedience to the Tenth Commandment. ☐ True   ☐ False ▶ *Explain:* _____

_____

_____

9. Give three reasons why covetousness is wrong and godly contentment is right:

a) _____

_____

b) _____

_____

c) _____

_____

10. Write out Philippians 4:11. _____

_____

_____

_____

❦ *Christian Obedience to the Law is Imperfect*

Q114. Can those who are converted to God keep these Commandments perfectly?

No, but even the holiest men, while in this life, have only a small beginning of such obedience, yet so that with earnest purpose they begin to live not only according to some, but according to all the Commandments of God.

In this question and the next one, we have two concluding statements concerning the Law of God. Question 114 explains *the nature of Christian obedience to the* Law.

The natural man, who is unregenerated, is not able to obey God's holy will in any degree. Romans 8:7 says that the unsaved person's mind is "enmity (hatred) against God: for it is not subject to the law of God, nor indeed can be." But the question asks if the *converted* or regenerated person can keep God's holy commandments perfectly.

We have seen that perfect obedience to God requires a perfect heart-love for God and a perfect heart-hatred for sin (see Questions 4, 5 and 113). Since the regenerated saint of God still has his "old man," the old nature of sin, he is unable to give God perfect obedience. Indeed, as question 60 states it: we are "still prone always to all evil."

Therefore, "even the holiest men, while in this life, have only a small beginning of this obedience." The most sanctified Christians, such as the Apostles, are still sinful and not perfect. The Scriptures tell us of Noah's drunkenness, Job's cursing the day of his birth (3:1–2), David's acts of adultery and murder (2 Samuel 11), Peter's shameful denial of his Lord (Luke 22:54–62), and Paul's confession of indwelling sin (Romans 7:21).

But though it is true that even the most godly Christians still have sin in their hearts, and commit various acts of sin (1 John 1:8), yet they are called *saints* by God and not sinners. As born-again persons, indwelt by the Holy Spirit, Christians do produce a sincere and unreserved obedience. Note these two facts about Christian obedience:

1. It is with earnest purpose.

There is a deep and genuine desire to be holy in thought, word, and deed. In contrast with the Pharisee, who is satisfied with a mere outward show of righteousness, the true believer has a deep heart-hunger for righteousness and, in David's words, his soul pants after God (Psalm 42:1). Paul said, "I press (run) toward the goal for the prize of the upward call of God in Christ Jesus" (Philippians 3:14). The real Christian seeks to put every thing aside in order to obey his blessed Lord and Savior, even as a runner has only one thing in mind, to reach the goal line.

2. It is a complete obedience.

That is, the true believer does not pick and choose among the commandments and precepts of God and keep only those things which suit him; rather, he desires to keep all the Word of God without exception. He wants to obey all that God requires, simply because it is God Who requires it. We must respect all of God's Word because we love God and delight to do His will, regardless of personal likes and dislikes. Christian obedience involves *total* obedience—even though it is never perfect obedience.

3. It is not perfectionism.

We must mention in connection with this question the false teaching of "perfectionism" or "entire sanctification" or "the second work of grace," which is believed by many professing Christians today. This doctrine was taught by the early Anabaptist groups during the Reformation period, and later by John Wesley, the founder of the Methodist Church. The Pentecostal churches also teach "perfectionism." These people, using such verses as Matthew 5:8; Philippians 3:15; 1 John 3:6, 9 and 5:18, say that a Christian may become perfectly sanctified in his soul and cease sinning.

One Evangelical United Brethren pastor said in a letter: "It was through divine grace that God saved me. Three years later, He led me into the Wesleyan experience of holiness ... the gift of a pure heart which He gave me on August 6, 1949... I was nearly an hour parked along the road under that soul-transforming experience." He described his experience as follows: "Suddenly God poured out the Holy Spirit upon me. Wave after wave went through me from head to foot. My eyes were instantly full of tears."

What are we to say about such a testimony?

1. The emotional experiences which Christians sometimes have do *not* prove that sin has been eradicated and completely removed from their hearts.

2. The Scriptures clearly teach that the most holy men still have their old nature of sin (see the examples given above).

3. Those who say that they have no sin deceive themselves, according to 1 John 1:8 (the Apostle includes himself!); and Christ taught us to pray for *daily* forgiveness, even as we pray for our *daily* bread (Matthew 6:11–12). The perfectionists do not have a correct view of sin. They forget the Tenth Commandment, which condemns the *slightest inclination toward covetousness and spiritual pride!*

4. The verses that they use to prove "perfectionism" do not prove sinless perfection, but, rather, they teach our perfection in Christ and the completeness of the work of the Holy Spirit in us to sanctify us in both body and soul. 1 John 3:9 and 5:18 mean that the child of God does not *practice* sin and *delight* in it—not that he never commits acts of sin (1 John 2:1 teaches otherwise).

The Christian believer is a *saint;* he loves God and God's will, and daily he seeks God's grace to make him more obedient and holy. But he never rests in his own holiness; rather, his only plea of righteousness before God is the righteousness of his Savior Jesus Christ. His constant lament is, "O wretched man that I am! Who will deliver me from this body of death?" (Romans 7:24).

Questions on Number 114

1. Questions 114 and 115 give _____

    _____

2. Question 114 is very important respecting the nature of our obedience to the Law of God. It instructs us concerning:

    a) Our imperfection—that we achieve only _____

    _____

    b) Our purpose—that we desire _____

    _____

3. Perfect obedience to God's Law requires perfect _____ for God and perfect _____ of sin every moment of our lives.

4. Several saints in the Old and New Testaments reached perfection of heart. ☐ True ☐ False

5. Born-again Christians are called:
    ☐ a. *saints,* because they do not sin
    ☐ b. *sinners,* because they still love sin
    ☐ c. *saints,* because they love holiness

6. Sanctification is the teaching that (*which ones?*):

☐ a. Christians are declared righteous in Christ.

☐ b. Christians are progressively made more holy in this life.

☐ c. Christians seek to reach perfect obedience by the Holy Spirit.

☐ d. Christians reach sinless perfection before they die.

☐ e. Christians may receive a "second work of grace" which enables them to have a pure heart

7. The professing Christian who claims to love the gospel and the law of God, but who remains in a liberal church, appears to lack an "_____ purpose to live according to _____ the commandments of God."

8. What is "perfectionism"? _____

_____

_____

9. Name some groups who believe in it: _____

_____

_____

10. Give two reasons why the doctrine of sinless perfection is unscriptural:

a) _____

b) _____

11. Write out 1 John 2:4–5: _____

_____

_____

_____

_____

_____

_____

❦ The Role of the Law in the Christian Life

Q115. Why then does God so strictly enjoin the Ten Commandments upon us, since in this life no one can keep them?

First, that as long as we live we may learn more and more to know our sinful nature, and so the more earnestly seek forgiveness of sins and righteousness in Christ; second, that without ceasing we diligently ask God for the grace of the Holy Spirit, that we be renewed more and more after the image of God, until we attain the goal of perfection after this life.

This concluding question on the Law of God (which began with question 92) tells us *the two-fold function of the Law in the Christian's experience.*

The unbeliever, of course, must first hear the demands of God's Law in order to be convicted of sin. "By the law is the knowledge of sin" (Romans 3:20). The law then brings the convicted sinner to Jesus Christ for salvation (Galatians 3:24).

What is true for the sinner is also true for the saint. The law always keeps teaching us our sinfulness and keeps leading us to Jesus Christ for forgiveness. The first purpose of the law is to show us the holy requirements of God, to cause us to see how far short we fall of perfectly glorifying God (Romans 3:23).

The law was never intended by God to be a means of salvation, a way of earning eternal life by human obedience. Rather, it is a looking-glass (James 1:23), which shows us what we are before God—dirty, polluted, and sinful and in need of daily spiritual cleansing. This cleansing comes not from the law (the mirror), but from Christ and His Spirit, through the blood of the Cross. The Apostle Paul says that "the law is good if a man use it lawfully" (1 Timothy 1:8).

1. The First Use of the Law

The *first* use of the law is to learn more and more our sinfulness in thoughts, words, and deeds. As we meditate on the Scriptures daily, we will discover not only what we do wrong, but we will also learn more of our sins of *omission,* what we fail to do in the service of Christ. The law convicts us of sin and directs us to Christ alone for His righteousness.

2. The Second Use of the Law

The *second* use of the law in the life of the believer is positive; that is, it shows us *what* God wants us to be in our heart and life—perfect. The goal of the Christian is to be like Jesus Christ, his Head. Again, Paul says that the purpose of God in redeeming His people is that they might "be conformed to the image of His Son" (Romans 8:29). And, with Paul, we say in our hearts: "Not that I have already attained, or am already perfected; but I press on, that I may lay hold of that for which Christ Jesus has also laid hold of me" (Philippians 3:12). Our goal is absolute perfection and though we will not attain it in this life, we must nevertheless follow after it in this life. How do we seek perfection of heart and life? The Catechism gives the answer: By diligently asking God for the grace of the Holy Spirit. The Spirit of Christ is our Sanctifier: the power to live according to God's law comes only from the Holy Spirit (Romans 8:4).

We see, then, that there are two uses of the law in our Christian experience: a)*negatively*, the law shows us our sins and imperfection, and, b) *positively*, it gives us the goal of perfection, what the infinitely righteous God would have us to be by His grace—sinlessly holy, even as He is holy (1 Peter 1:15–16).

There is constant need, then, to be reminded of the law of God. The law should be learned when we are young and should be read to the congregation continually. Our prayer should always be: "Open my eyes, that I may see wondrous things from Your law" (Psalm 119:18). The law is *strictly enjoined upon us!*

Questions on Number 115

1. Question 115 tells us _____

   _____

2. A modern system of theology called "Dispensationalism" teaches that the New Testament believer is not under the law, but under grace alone (Romans 6:14). ☐ True ☐ False ▶ *Explain:* _____

   _____

   _____

3. God does not require of us perfect obedience to His law, because this is impossible for us. ☐ True ☐ False ▶ *Explain:* _____

   _____

   _____

4. There are two purposes of the law in our Christian life:
   a) to show us our _____
   b) to show us the goal of _____

5. The law is likened to a _____ in James 1:23, which means that the law ☐ *reveals sin* ☐ *cleanses away sin.*

6. What is an *improper* use of the law? _____

   _____

   _____

7. Match the following:

Law of God	No Law, only Grace
Dispensationalists	Provides our spiritual power
Paul's desire	The goal of perfection is attained
The Holy Spirit	Strictly enjoined on us
After this life	To strive to be like Christ

8. What are sins of omission? _____

   _____

   _____

9. The Ten Commandments should be read in public worship services.
   ☐ True ☐ False ▶ *Explain:* _____

   _____

10. Write out Psalm 119:4–5. _____

    _____

    _____

    _____

    _____

    _____

❧ *The Necessity of Prayer*

Q116. Why is prayer necessary for Christians?

Because it is the chief part of thankfulness which God requires
of us, and because God will give His grace and Holy Spirit only to
those who earnestly and without ceasing ask them of Him, and
render thanks unto Him for them.

Having carefully explained the law of God, which tells us *how* to obey
God and serve Him in thankfulness, the Catechism closes by explaining
the subject of prayer. Prayer, says the Catechism, is the chief part of

thankfulness. The law and prayer go together to make up our life of sanctification and thankfulness. We are not justified by either the law or prayer, but we are justified and converted in order to pray and obey. Our obedience to the law must be prayerful obedience, and our prayers to God must be for grace to obey His law and do His will.

Questions 116 and 117 give us an important introduction to the subject of Christian prayer; and the remainder of the Catechism is devoted to explaining the so-called "Lord's Prayer"—the perfect model for God-honoring prayer.

Question 116 tells us the *necessity* for prayer, and question 117 tells us the *nature* of prayer.

Prayer is necessary for the Christian for two basic reasons, according to this question:

1. It is the chief part of thankfulness.

It is our primary way of thanking God. True, we *show* God our thankfulness by living holy and loving lives before Him and others, but in prayer we personally *tell* God that we are thankful. He first of all wants to hear us talk to Him and tell Him what is in our hearts. We read of the thankful leper who, after receiving healing from the Lord, turned to Jesus and "with a loud voice glorified God, and fell down on his face at His feet, giving Him thanks" (Luke 17:15-16).

The Psalmist said, "Bless the Lord, O my soul: and all that is within me, bless His holy name" (Psalm 103:1). Only the Christian can truly pray to the Lord, and every true Christian does pray. A prayerless Christian is no Christian at all. God requires His people to pray, and His Holy Spirit works in us to pray: "*When You said, 'Seek My face,' My heart said to You, 'Your face, LORD, I will seek'*" (Psalm 27:8). Adoring prayer is the highest honor that we can pay to God.

2. It is the means by which God gives us His grace and Holy Spirit.

God promises to give us His grace, but not apart from our supplication (asking) for it. The Lord certainly knows all our needs—better than we do (Matthew 6:8)—but still He requires us to ask Him to satisfy those needs.

Jesus taught His disciples two parables showing that God requires prayer before He grants His grace to His people. Luke 11:5-13 is the parable of the "Persistent Friend," which teaches us that if we keep asking God, He will be moved to give us His Holy Spirit (vss. 8, 13). Luke 18:1-8 is the parable of the "Persistent Widow" who likewise was so insistent on receiving a favor that she finally got what she wanted. "God shall avenge His own elect which cry day and night unto Him, though He bear long with them" (vs. 7). It may seem strange to us, but God wants us to keep asking, to keep seeking, to keep knocking, and then He will give us what we desire (Luke 11:9-10).

What do we need most of all, every moment of every day? We need the Holy Spirit of Christ. He is God's Greatest Gift to us. He brings with Him God's grace and favor, and He sanctifies to us all the other gifts of God. We must daily plead with God to give us His Spirit and grace.

Is prayer, like your food and air, a necessary part of your life?

Questions on Number 116

1. What is the relation of prayer to:

   a) our justification? _____

   _____

   b) our sanctification? _____

   _____

   c) our thankfulness? _____

   _____

2. Our obedience to the holy law and will of God must be _____ _____ obedience. And our prayers to God must be for _____ to _____ His law.

3. Questions 116 and 117 give an _____ to the subject of prayer. Question 116 tells of the _____ of prayer, and 117 explains the _____ of prayer.

4. The two main reasons why prayer is necessary for the Christian are:

   a) _____

   _____

   b) _____

   _____

5. If God sees us living a good and holy life, this is sufficient to show our thankfulness to Him. ☐ True ☐ False ▶ *Explain:* _____

   _____

   _____

6. A prayerless Christian is:

   ☐ a. a contradiction   ☐ c. an impossibility

   ☐ b. a sad person   ☐ d. all too common today

7. What does "persistence" mean in Luke 11:8? _____

_____

_____

8. The Holy Spirit
   - ☐ a. enables us to pray
   - ☐ b. is the primary object of our prayer
   - ☐ c. is not always present in true prayer
   - ☐ d. is the best answer to our prayer

9. God is more willing to give than we are to receive, but He will not give us His Spirit and grace if we don't bother to ask.
   ☐ True ☐ False

10. Write out Deuteronomy 4:29. _____

_____

_____

_____

_____

_____

◖ Aspects of Acceptable Prayer

Q117. What belongs to such prayer which is acceptable to God and which He will hear?

First, that with our whole heart we call only upon the one true God, who has revealed Himself to us in His Word, for all that He has commanded us to ask of Him; second, that we thoroughly know our need and misery, so as to humble ourselves in the presence of His divine Majesty; third, that we be firmly assured that notwithstanding our unworthiness He will, for the sake of Christ our Lord, certainly hear our prayer, as He has promised us in His Word.

Have you heard a prayer that did not really seem like a prayer to you? Can you remember saying a prayer in the past that you now feel was really not a prayer? Perhaps we are even ashamed of some of our past prayers.

Prayer should never be a mechanical thing; that is, it must always come from the heart and be the sincere desire of the heart. On the other hand, it must come from our hearts *as they are instructed by Scripture* concerning the will of God. Prayer must express what God Himself has said to us: "This is the confidence that we have in Him, that if we ask anything according to His will, He hears us" (1 John 5:14).

So prayer is really a spiritual *art* that is perfected as we learn the Scriptures and speak continuously to God, using His Word. The Apostles needed to be taught to pray, and so does every Christian (Luke 11:1; Romans 8:26–27). The Holy Spirit must teach us *how* to pray and *what* to pray for, according to Scripture.

In this question, *the nature of true prayer* is explained. Three things are necessary for a prayer to be true prayer that God will hear and answer.

1. **Prayer must be addressed with the whole heart to the Triune God revealed in the Bible.**

Any prayer which does not recognize the Sovereign God of Scripture or that is not in the name of the Trinity is false prayer. Therefore, all prayers by Jews and Modernists and others who deny the Deity of Christ are false prayers. A Roman Catholic prayer in the name of Mary or other "saints" is false prayer. Prayer must be to the Father, through the Son, and by the grace of the Holy Spirit. Praying to God must be wholehearted, that is, sincere and believing. God hates double-mindedness (James 1:6–7). We are also here reminded that we are to ask for all that He has commanded us to ask of Him. This phrase will be fully explained when we discuss the "Lord's Prayer" (see Q118).

2. **Prayer must be marked by humility and contrition.**

To pray with a self-righteous attitude or in self-confidence and pride is to violate the very nature of prayer. Prayer is the recognition before the "Divine Majesty" that I am a sinful, unworthy person and not worthy of any good thing from God, and that I am completely dependent on God's mercy. The story of the Pharisee and the Publican (Luke 18:9–14) shows the difference between self-righteous and self-condemning prayers.

3. **Prayer must be grounded only on the merit and worthiness of Christ.**

Jesus Christ is the only Mediator between God and man. He is our only High Priest, Who always lives to make intercession for us with the Father (Hebrews 7:25). No one comes to the Father except through Him (John 14:6). Does this mean that after every prayer we must add "In Jesus name"? Not necessarily. It *does* mean that in all our prayer we are conscious that God is hearing us only through Jesus Christ, our Great High Priest, Who redeemed us and brings us to the Father.

These three features mark every true prayer. There are *different aspects* of prayer, such as adoration, confession, thanksgiving, and supplication; but whatever the content of any particular prayer, whether it be long or short, it must come from a humble heart and go to the Majestic

God through Jesus Christ, the only Mediator and Intercessor with the Father.

We often "say our prayers," but how often do we really *pray?*

Questions on Number 117

1. All prayers are good, and no one should be critical of any prayer.
   ☐ True ☐ False ▶ *Explain:* _____
   _____

2. Prayer, to be acceptable to God, must:
   ☐ a. be heartfelt
   ☐ b. have good grammar
   ☐ c. be in the name of a god
   ☐ d. be based on God's promises of Scripture
   ☐ e. always ended, "in Jesus' name, Amen."

3. What is God's judgment of the prayer of the hypocrite or unsaved person, according to Proverbs 15:8, 26, 29 _____
   _____
   _____
   _____

4. What are the three conditions for God-honoring prayer?
   a) _____
   _____
   b) _____
   _____
   c) _____
   _____

5. Comment on these so-called "prayers":
   a) "Lord, give me a new car; and Lord, give me a new suit; and a new digital TV, and help me win a million dollars so I won't have to work any more. Amen." _____
   _____
   _____

   b) "Oh God, I'm glad I'm not as bad and ugly as Suzy, and that I always try to be good to everyone. In Your name. Amen." _____

_____

_____

c) "God, if there is a real God, please keep me from getting killed in
this war. Amen." _____

_____

_____

6. Match the following:

   Confession and Praise   The object of true prayer

   God   Content of prayer

   Humility   Attitude in prayer

7. True prayer must be through _____, Who is the only
   _____ between the believer and the Father,
   and our only High _____.

8. What do these phrases mean in this question:
   a) "Whole heart" _____

   _____

   b) "know our need and misery" _____

   _____

   c) "Divine Majesty" _____

   _____

9. What are the four main aspects of prayer?
   a) _____
   b) _____
   c) _____
   d) _____

10. Write out John 14:13–14. _____

   _____

   _____

   _____

   _____

   _____

◖ *The Nature of Prayer*

Q118. What has God commanded us to ask of Him?

All things necessary for soul and body, which Christ our Lord comprised in the prayer which He Himself taught us.

"What has God commanded us to ask of Him?" This question will explain what was said in the first part of question 117: We call upon God "for all that He has commanded us to ask of Him." It is very important that in our prayers we ask of God only what He tells us to ask. We are not free to request anything contrary to God's holy will.

James rebukes those who pray for selfish reasons: "You ask, and do not receive, because you ask amiss, that you may spend it on your pleasures" (James 4:3). Some have said that if a Christian will only pray with strong enough faith, he will receive what he asks for. This is not true. Only if we ask *according* to *God's will,* will He hear us and answer us (1 John 5:14).

This question tells us the *content of true supplication,* that is, what God wants us to ask of Him in our daily prayers. Remember that supplication (asking) is not the only element in our prayers (we also must praise and thank God and confess our sins), but it is a necessary part of prayer, a duty *commanded* of us!

Notice that this answer limits our supplications (requests) to our own personal needs—our souls and our bodies. But there is something even more important than our needs, and that is God's glory. As the "Lord's Prayer" teaches, we must first ask God to glorify Himself and extend His Kingdom and, then, secondly, we may ask for our personal needs. They are the following:

1. Spiritual needs

Our primary spiritual need is grace to do the will of God and to be patient and resigned to God's dealings with us. Naturally we think that our most important needs are physical and earthly, but really they are not. It is not healing of body or earthly enjoyments that are first, but the Kingdom of God and His righteousness.

This is the great lesson that Jesus taught. To be concerned most about our earthly happiness and prosperity is to be like "the Gentiles," the unbelievers (see Matthew 6:32–33), who are concerned only about their earthly life, not about their relationship to God. Our spiritual needs include the forgiveness of daily sins, the renewing of the Holy Spirit, abiding in Christ, and bringing forth fruits of Christian thankfulness, *especially* when we are suffering and in distress.

2. Bodily needs

These needs are always second and less important. As we shall see in question 125, there is a petition in the Lord's Prayer concerning our bodily needs—health, food, clothing, possession, a peaceful life, etc. (Proverbs 30:8; James 5:15). Yet, in praying for bodily needs, we must never demand them of God, but remember to add, "If it be Your will." This is what our Lord Himself did (Matthew 26:39; Luke 22:42). In asking for our spiritual needs, such as grace and the Holy Spirit, we need not say, "If it be Your will," because we know it is always His will to give us these essential gifts for our salvation.

Jesus said that men "always ought to pray and not lose heart" (Luke 18:1). You must more and more learn to live in daily prayer to your Lord, realizing that He is concerned about everything that concerns you: your health, your education, your dating, your family, your relations with others, your work—all your problems, big and small.

Questions on Number 118

1. Question 118 tells us the _____ of true _____.
    Other parts of true prayer are _____

    _____

2. According to _____ (*Bible reference*), selfish prayer to
    satisfy our own pleasures will be treated how by God? _____

    _____

3. The content of true supplication includes both our _____
    and our _____ needs.

4. What does the word "supplication" mean? _____

    _____

    _____

5. Even more important than our own personal needs is _____
    _____ , which is also taught in the _____.

6. What are your spiritual needs at all times? _____

    _____

    _____

7. What are your bodily needs? _____

    _____

    _____

8. God always answers our requests for spiritual needs, but does not always grant our bodily requests. ☐ True ☐ False

   ▶ *Explain:* _____

   _____

   _____

9. If God does not answer our prayer to heal someone, then we must conclude that we did not pray in faith. ☐ True ☐ False

10. Mark which kinds of needs these verses refer to:

Matthew 6:33a	☐ spiritual	☐ bodily
James 5:14	☐ spiritual	☐ bodily
2 Corinthians 12:9	☐ spiritual	☐ bodily
Proverbs 30:8	☐ spiritual	☐ bodily
Ephesians 1:17	☐ spiritual	☐ bodily
2 Kings 20:5	☐ spiritual	☐ bodily

11. Write out Philippians 4:6. _____

    _____

    _____

    _____

    _____

❧ The Pattern of the Lord's Prayer

Q119. What is the Lord's Prayer?

Our Father who art in heaven, Hallowed be Thy name. Thy kingdom come. Thy will be done in earth, as it is in heaven. Give us this day our daily bread. And forgive us our debts, as we forgive our debtors. And lead us not into temptation, but deliver us from evil: for Thine is the kingdom, and the power, and the glory forever. Amen.

"What is the Lord's Prayer?" Actually, the prayer before us could be called, more accurately, the "Disciples' Prayer," as it is not the prayer our Lord Himself prayed (at least, not all of it), but the prayer He taught His disciples to use. Our Lord's prayers are recorded in Matthew 11:25–27; John 17; Luke 22:41–45; 23:34, 46. Why could not Jesus have used this so-called "Lord's Prayer?" Because the fifth petition is a request for forgiveness of sins, and Jesus had no sins to be forgiven.

But this prayer is indeed the perfect prayer and was taught by our Lord in order to give us a pattern or model for our prayers. "In this manner, therefore, pray" (Matthew 6:9). This does not mean that this is the only prayer that we may use. The remainder of the New Testament shows the Apostles praying other prayers also. Luke 11:1-4 gives us another version of this prayer but with some differences, as one can see. This shows us that the version in Matthew 6:9-13 is not the only acceptable prayer. It is even possible to use this model prayer in the wrong way. Some people recite it mechanically and superstitiously, never entering into the spirit of the words; and this is a sinful use of the Lord's Prayer—using "vain repetitions" (6:7).

Consider some of the important features of this prayer that make it a perfect model for *all* prayers:

1. It is a prayer for converted people only.

The words, "Our Father," can be used only by the children of God, those who know God as their Father through Christ Jesus. It is not proper to use this prayer in a worldly gathering. The only prayer that the sinner may pray is for forgiveness and salvation.

2. It is brief and yet complete.

It can be prayed in a few seconds, even by a child, and it contains all the essential parts of true prayer to God. This does not mean that all prayers must be this short (Solomon's prayer in 2 Chronicles 6:12-42 is seven times as long), but it does mean that prayers need not be long to be effective. God is not impressed with many beautiful words; He *does* want us to speak directly to Him, however, and as frankly and honestly as we can.

3. Its order is perfect.

The opening words are an address to God, then follow three petitions which promote God's honor and the coming of His Kingdom. Then follow three more petitions which concern our needs as God's children. The prayer is concluded by a meaningful doxology and the solemn Amen. It is God-centered throughout, not man-centered.

4. It is a supplication for others also.

Notice that it is in the plural form. The plural pronouns "our," "we," and "us" indicate that in our prayers we must always remember the needs of other Christians as well as our own.

We might also mention some other biblical rules concerning prayer:

a. Our prayers must always be *God-centered,* that is, they must aim at His glory alone. He and His Kingdom are always first, and we pray for ourselves only to glorify Him.

b. Our prayers must be *in faith*. Without faith it is impossible to please God or to receive answers from Him (Matthew 21:21–22; Hebrews 11:6).

c. Our prayers should be *specific*. We should not pray in vague generalities, but we should speak to God about specific, definite matters—people, things, and events (1 Timothy 2:1–2). For example, pray for missionaries by name, for the conversion of your friends, also by name.

d. Our language must be *respectful*. Slang and slovenly speech are not becoming to the King of kings. We should ever remember that God deserves our greatest respect. Some people use the old English pronouns, "Thee" and "Thou" and "Thine" when referring to God in prayer. These old English forms are not normal today, and it is not necessary to use them. But if you feel that they are more respectful, then you may use the old English.

e. Prayers should be both *regular* and *spontaneous*. This means that we should have set times for daily prayer (Daniel prayed three times a day regularly—Daniel 6:13). But, also, in emergency situations we should breathe a prayer to the Lord, as did David (Psalm 38:22; 69:1). Our minds should always be on the alert to speak to our Heavenly Father. "Pray without ceasing" (1 Thessalonians 5:17).

Questions on Number 119

1. The "Lord's Prayer" is really the _____ _____ , because Jesus never prayed it as such. Why not? _____

   _____

   _____

2. This prayer was intended to serve what purpose? _____

   _____

3. It has been wrongly used in what way? _____

   _____

4. The "Lord's Prayer" is a good one to use in non-church groups because it is the perfect prayer. ☐ True ☐ False

   ▶ *Explain:* _____

   _____

   _____

5. The other version of the Lord's Prayer is found where? _____
    _____

6. The four important features of the "Lord's Prayer" are these:

    a) _____

    b) _____

    c) _____

    d) _____

7. What is meant by God-centered prayer? _____
    _____
    _____

8. True prayer must always be:

    ☐ a. short   ☐ c. man-centered

    ☐ b. sincere   ☐ d. in "Old English"

9. Match the following:

    Vain repetitions   Fifth petition

    Solomon   An emergency petition

    Forgiveness   A long prayer

    "Help me, Lord!"   Automatic words

10. What are the following? (*Give examples*)

    a) A specific prayer? _____
    _____
    _____

    b) A regular prayer? _____
    _____
    _____

    c) An emergency prayer? _____
    _____
    _____

11. Write out Matthew 6:6 _____
    _____
    _____

_____

_____

_____

_____

❦ *Addressing God in Prayer*

Q120. Why did Christ command us to address God thus: "Our Father"?

To awaken in us at the very beginning of our prayer that childlike reverence for and trust in God, which are to be the ground of our prayer, namely, that God has become our Father through Christ, and will much less deny us what we ask of Him in faith than our parents refuse us earthly things.

With question 120, the Catechism begins the explanation of the Lord's Prayer. The three divisions of this prayer are: (1) the Address, (2) the Six Petitions, and (3) the Doxology.

This question and the next explain the opening address of the prayer: "Our Father who art in heaven."

It is certainly important that we address God correctly when we speak to Him. Only in the Christian religion is God spoken of as a "Father." The term father is very significant, and by the Holy Spirit it "awakens in us" an awareness of our spiritual relationship to the Almighty God. It is true that God is the Judge, the Punisher of the Wicked, the Almighty Creator, the infinite and incomprehensible Sovereign, and we must respect His greatness and majesty (see the next question). But how precious that this great God actually wants us to know Him and to speak to Him as Father!

Not only in the New Testament, but in the Old Testament also, God had revealed Himself as a Father to His people. "I am a Father to Israel" (Jeremiah 31:9); "You, O Lord, are our Father" (Isaiah 63:16). See also Psalm 103:13 and 1 Chronicles 29:10. This shows that the Modernists are wrong when they say that Jesus taught a new idea of God that had not been known in the Old Testament.

Is God the Father of all men? The Modernists say, "Yes." But the Bible tells us that by nature we are of our "father, the Devil" (John 8:44). God is Father only to those who are in Christ (John 1:12). Thus, only Christians may pray this prayer or speak to the living God as Father.

Think of the preciousness of the Fatherhood of God to us when we pray.

1. God is Father to us because He *chose* us to be His children even

before He created the world (Ephesians 1:4), because He *redeemed* us by the death of Christ (Galatians 4:5), because He *regenerated* us by His Spirit (Galatians 4:6) and because He *adopted* us into the heavenly family (Galatians 4:5). As His children, we are members of the Family of God and joint-heirs with Christ of all the riches of heavenly glory (Romans 8:17).

2. When we pray, we are to speak directly to our Father. Prayer must always be personal conversation. It is dangerous to use prayers written by others. They are not necessarily wrong, but how would our earthly father feel if we just read the words of others when we spoke to him?

3. We are to love and revere God as Father. Children are to respect their earthly fathers (Fifth Commandment), how much more must they love and respect their Heavenly Father.

4. We are to trust in God to take care of us and protect us. Our earthly fathers try to take care of us and they will make great sacrifices to help and protect us. How much more does our Heavenly Father look after us and supply His beloved children with what *we* need when we "ask of Him in faith." Our Catechism authors were thinking of Matthew 7:9–11 and Luke 11:11–13 when they wrote of the Heavenly Father's being more willing to give us good gifts than our earthly parents are willing to give us earthly things.

Is the address, "our Father who art in heaven," referring to the first Person of the Trinity or to the entire Trinity? Some Reformed authorities think that the name Father here refers to the entire Trinity (and also in the Apostles' Creed). We pray to God, and this God is Father to us through Jesus Christ by the operation of the Holy Spirit (Galatians 4:6). The Catechism seems to take this position also: "God [the Trinity] has become our Father through Christ."

At any rate, how blessed it is for us prodigal sons to return to God and call Him, "My Father."

Questions on Number 120

1. What are the divisions of the "Lord's Prayer"?

    a) _____

    b) _____

    c) _____

    Write out the first division: " _____

    _____."

2. What is God's relationship to unbelievers? _____

   _____

3. May unbelievers then use the term "our Father"? ☐ Yes ☐ No

4. Should unbelievers pray at all? ☐ Yes ☐ No ▶ *Explain:* _____

   _____

   _____

5. The "Fatherhood of God" is a new truth revealed first by Jesus
   Christ. ☐ True ☐ False ▶ *Explain:* _____

   _____

   _____

6. Who teaches the "universal Fatherhood of God and the universal
   Brotherhood of Man?" _____.
   Is it true? ☐ Yes ☐ No

7. How does a person become a child of God? _____

   _____

   _____

8. Since we speak directly to our heavenly Father in prayer, must we be
   careful about using other people's prayers? ☐ Yes ☐ No
   ▶ *Explain:* _____

   _____

9. "Childlike reverence" for God means that:
   ☐ a. we must be afraid to pray
   ☐ b. we fear that we may be damned
   ☐ c. we respect Him as the Almighty God

10. In Matthew 7:9–11, what two gifts would an earthly father give to his
    child? _____ and _____.
    Earthly fathers are _____ but the heavenly Father is good.
    God gives _____ to them who _____ Him.

11. Who is the heavenly Father, the Trinity or the First Person of the
    Trinity? _____
    What is your Biblical proof? _____

12. Write out Luke 11:13 _____

_____

_____

_____

_____

_____

❦ *The Majesty of God in Prayer*

Q121. Why is it added: "Who art in heaven"?

That we might have no earthly thought of the heavenly majesty of God, and from His almighty power expect all things necessary for body and soul.

The second part of the opening address is "Who art in heaven." This means "that we may have no earthly thought of the heavenly majesty of God and from His almighty power expect all things necessary for body and soul."

The two parts of this address to God carefully balance each other. On the one hand He is *our* Father, but He is also the Father *in heaven*. He is not an earthly Father, and we must always remember that He is God. In our prayers, we must never have human ideas of God. We sometimes have a tendency to talk to God on equal terms, as if He is like a schoolmate or a mere man. He is, indeed, our Father, but He is always the majestic God, also.

We have a good example of this balance of spiritual thought about God in the case of Abraham. God revealed His Fatherly character to His child Abraham when He said, "Shall I hide from Abraham what I am doing?" (Genesis 18:17); and God called Abraham His "friend" (James 2:23). Yet, Abraham, realizing that God is almighty and infinitely glorious, humbly said to the Heavenly Father: "Indeed now, I who am but dust and ashes have taken it upon myself to speak to the Lord" (Genesis 18:27).

Are we to have some kind of picture of God in our minds when we pray? Do you dimly think of a figure of a man when you close your eyes to pray? This is the natural thing to do, for we are earthly. But it is wrong. The Scriptures teach that we are not even to think of our Savior in earthly terms: "Even though we have known Christ according to the flesh, yet now we know Him thus no longer" (2 Corinthians 5:16). The Apostle Peter says of Christ in heaven: "Whom having not seen you love. Though now you do not see Him, yet believing, you rejoice with joy inexpressible and full of glory" (1 Peter 1:8). We must fight against the tendency to have earthly thoughts of the heavenly Father and of Christ.

Twice the "Lord's Prayer" speaks of heaven. Where is heaven? The Bible speaks of three different heavens—see 2 Corinthians 12:2. The first heaven is the sky, the atmosphere above the earth where the clouds float (Psalm 104:12). The second heaven is outer space, where the planets and stars are located (Genesis 1:14; Psalm 33:6). The third heaven is the place of the glory of God (Psalm 103:19; 1 Kings 8:27) and the abode of the glorified Christ, His angels and His saints. God indeed is everywhere, even in hell (Psalm 139:8), but His glory is especially manifested in the place called heaven.

Being in heaven and being God, our Father can give us all things necessary for body and soul through Jesus Christ; and we can confidently expect Him to do so. Nothing is too hard for Him.

Questions on Number 121

1. The opening address of this prayer shows us the proper *balance* between reverence and trust, between godly fear and hope.
   ☐ True ☐ False

2. What is meant by "earthly thoughts" of God? _____

   _____

   _____

3. Comment on the popular expression, "Talk to the man upstairs."

   _____

   _____

4. Abraham was called the _____ of God, and God was Abraham's heavenly _____ . Yet Abraham revered God when he said: " _____

   _____

   _____ ."

5. What New Testament proof do we have that we should not have earthly thoughts of Christ in our prayers? _____

   _____

6. It is ☐ *easy* ☐ *hard* ☐ *impossible* to speak to someone without having any picture in our minds as to how they look.

7. The Bible uses the word "heaven" in what three ways? (*Give references*)

a) _____

_____

b) _____

_____

c) _____

_____

8. Since our heavenly Father is the Almighty God, we can confidently expect what from Him? _____

_____

_____

9. In what way is God in heaven and not in earth or in hell? _____

_____

_____

10. Write out Revelation 5:13. _____

_____

_____

_____

_____

_____

_____

_____

_____

❧ *The First Petition: God's Name*

Q122. What is the first petition?

"Hallowed be Thy name;" that is, grant us, first, rightly to know Thee, and to hallow, magnify and praise Thee in all Thy works, in which Thy power, goodness, justice, mercy and truth shine forth; and further, that we so order our whole life, our thoughts, words, and deeds, that Thy name may not be blasphemed, but honored and praised on our account.

We now begin our study of the six petitions of the Lord's Prayer. These six petitions, or requests, are divided into two groups:

a. *Petitions, 1, 2, and 3 are concerned with God Himself—His Name, His Kingdom, and His will.*

b. *Petitions 4, 5, and 6 are concerned with ourselves—our physical needs, forgiveness, and spiritual protection.*

God is to be first in our prayers and desires, and ourselves second. This is always the proper order of biblical Christianity.

The first petition is "Hallowed be Thy name," that is, "Cause Your name to be regarded as holy." What does this mean? First, we should be clear as to what God's "name" refers to. Refer back to our study of question 99 on the Third Commandment. There we saw that God's name refers to His Person. In Scripture, God calls Himself by various descriptive names and titles such as "Lord," "God," "Almighty," "Father," "Son," Jesus," "Christ," "Holy Spirit," and many more. God also reveals His Person in nature, in His works of creation and providence: "Oh Lord, our Lord, how excellent is Your name in all the earth" (Psalm 8:1). Thus, God's name stands for Himself and all that He does as He reveals Himself in His Word and in His works. Now God is perfectly glorious and holy in Himself, and no creature can possibly add more glory to God. So this is not a prayer for God to become more holy than He is already!

Rather, when we pray this petition, we are asking that God's holiness shall be recognized and properly honored by all creatures, especially by ourselves. The Catechism speaks of two ways in which God's holy name—Himself—is to be hallowed and honored:

1. By a true knowledge of God

To properly glorify God and worship Him, we must first of all rightly know God. We learn of God first from the Scriptures. Then, as we look at nature as God's creation through the truth of Scripture, we learn more of God: "The heavens declare the glory of God" (Psalm 19:1).

It is impossible to know God and glorify Him except as we are born again and believe on His Son, the Lord Jesus Christ. As we rightly learn of God, we find that He is a God of infinite "power, goodness, justice, mercy, and truth." The highest objective of prayer is to praise God for His glory and majesty, and pray that we may increasingly know Him and hallow His name.

2. By a life of consecration to God

Not only do our words count to declare God's glory, but our lives also must serve to hallow God's name. Words without the life are meaningless and hypocritical, because they do not come from a sincere heart. Notice that our "thoughts, words, and deeds" will serve either to honor God's name or blaspheme and dishonor God's name. We are never *neutral* to the glory of God. "Therefore, whether you eat or drink, or whatever you do, do all to the glory of God" (1 Corinthians 10:31).

How do we "order our whole life" to hallow God's name? By

continuously learning the Scriptures through daily reading and by attending church services; by observing God's commandments in all situations; by being concerned to spread the gospel to others. And last, but not least, by praying this petition to God each day.

In heaven, the saints and angels sing to God "holy, holy, holy" (Revelation 4:8) continuously; and so should our hearts and lives be ever devoted to God's holy name.

Questions on Number 122

1. The Lord's Prayer contains _____ petitions. How are they divided?

    a) _____

    _____

    b) _____

    _____

2. The "name" of God refers to:

    ☐ a. His proper titles only, such as "The Almighty"

    ☐ b. His great work of creation and providence and not Himself

    ☐ c. His Person as expressed in His Word and His works

3. To hallow God's name means that we:

    ☐ a. make God's name holy

    ☐ b. keep God's name holy

4. We can actually add to God's perfect glory by our holy words and works. ☐ True ☐ False ▶ *Explain:* _____

    _____

    _____

5. Seeking the hallowing of God's name is our highest objective it is even more important than winning souls to Christ.

    ☐ True ☐ False

6. What are the two basic ways in which we want God's name to be hallowed?

    a) _____

    b) _____

7. Which attributes and glories of God are mentioned in these verses:

    Psalm 36:5 _____

Psalm 119:137 _____

Romans 1:20 _____

Psalm 104:24 _____

Nahum 1:3 _____

1 John 4:8 _____

8. To glorify God, a person must first of all experience what great benefit?

_____

_____

9. Name three ways in which we order our lives to glorify God's name: (Q122)

a) _____

b) _____

c) _____

10. Write out Psalm 115:1 _____

_____

_____

_____

_____

_____

❦ The Second Petition: God's Kingdom

Q123. What is the second petition?

"Thy kingdom come;" that is, so govern us by Thy Word and Spirit, that we submit ourselves to Thee always more and more; preserve and increase Thy Church; destroy the works of the devil, every power that exalts itself against Thee, and all wicked devices formed against Thy Holy Word, until the fullness of Thy kingdom come, wherein Thou shalt be all in all.

"Thy Kingdom come," the second petition of the Model Prayer, is full of important truth which we must seek to understand and about which we must pray daily. What is the *Kingdom of God* for which we are to pray?

The Kingdom of God refers to God's rule over His creation. A king is one who has authority and power to rule over subjects. God has all authority and power to rule over all things. Therefore, we read, "The Lord has established His throne in heaven, and His kingdom rules over all" (Psalm 103:19).

But because of the rebellion of the evil angels and the fall of man into sin, most of God's Kingdom has turned against Him and set up a rebel kingdom under the rule of Satan. Therefore, God has established another Kingdom, wherein men willingly turn back to Him and once again acknowledge His rule over them. This is the Kingdom of Grace, also called the Kingdom of heaven or the Kingdom of God.

This Kingdom of God is based on the Person and Work of Jesus Christ, Whom God has made to be King. By means of His redemptive work, Christ the King is in the process of establishing His rule over the hearts of all the elect of God. When we pray, "Your Kingdom come," we are asking God to extend that rule of Christ and to bring it to completion so that it may stand victorious over against the kingdom of Satan.

The Catechism speaks of three things relating to the Kingdom of God:

1. The nature of the Kingdom of God

The Kingdom is present wherever there is voluntary submission to the rule of God in Christ. It is a spiritual Kingdom, involving the *heart* of man primarily. Our Lord told Pilate that His "Kingdom is not of this world" (John 18:36), that is, it does not consist of physical power and compulsion, as do the kingdoms of this world; but rather it is a matter of love for the truth (vs. 37). We are in the Kingdom when the Kingdom is in us, as we submit to the Word and the Spirit of Christ (Romans 14:17).

Are the Church and the Kingdom the same thing? The Catechism speaks here of the Church as being the Kingdom. This is true when we think of the Church in the universal and invisible sense. The Kingdom of heaven indeed includes the visible Church, but it involves much more than the organized churches; it includes all men and organizations and human efforts which recognize the authority and rule of Christ. Thus Christian civil rulers, Christian homes, Christian schools, Christian hospitals, and other Christian institutions and activities—which are not under the government of the church—are truly Kingdom activities. All of life: farming, medicine, plumbing, politics, art, etc., must be made Kingdom activities by the Lord's people, who have received the Word and Spirit in their hearts (Col. 3:23-24).

It should be noted that the Kingdom of heaven on this earth even includes false Christians and hypocrites. The Lord taught many parables to show that not all who profess to be His servants really belong to Him. They shall be cast out of the Kingdom and burned (Matthew 13:30, 41, 49; 25:1, 14).

2. The enemies of the Kingdom of God

As we pray for the Kingdom to be preserved and to increase, we must also pray that all opposition to the Kingdom will be destroyed. Who are the enemies of Christ's Kingdom? First is Satan, who has set up his own kingdom of darkness (Matthew 4:8-9; John 12:31; Ephesians 2:2). There is a fierce battle going on between the two kingdoms. As Christians, "We do not wrestle against flesh and blood, but against principalities, against powers, against the rulers of darkness of this world, against spiritual hosts of wickedness in the heavenly places" (Ephesians 6:12). *Inside* the Kingdom, Satan seeks to bring in false doctrine and evil works in order to corrupt and destroy the people of God. Fighting and bitterness among Christians are also attacks from the enemy (Psalm 83:2-3; 1 John 3:10; 4:11). *Outside* the Kingdom are enemies who try to destroy us by persecution (1 Peter 4:12-14). Against all these enemies of God's Kingdom we must pray and fight, using the spiritual weapons that God has given to us (see 2 Corinthians 10:4-5 and Ephesians 6:13-18).

3. The goal of the Kingdom of God

The Kingdom of grace in this world is but the temporary phase of the Kingdom of God. When Christ returns the fullness of the Kingdom will have come. Then the Kingdom will be the Kingdom of glory. Then the hearts of all the elect will be perfectly sanctified and subject to the rule of God. At that time Christ Himself will turn over the Kingdom to the Father: "Then comes the end, when He delivers the kingdom to God the Father, when He puts down all rule and authority and power" (1 Corinthians 15:24). All Christ's enemies will at that time be made to confess that He is the only true and all-powerful King (Of course, we do not agree with the premillenialists, who teach that the Kingdom will fully come when Christ returns to Jerusalem and sets up a 1000-year earthly kingdom! Study the lesson on Question 52 for this point).

We must pray daily for God's Kingdom to come in greater power into our hearts and lives. We must pray that the churches will become more pure and biblical. We must pray that the work of missions will increase so that the elect will be brought into the Kingdom. We must pray that the laws of Christ may more and more be acknowledged by the civil governments. And we must pray that the Kingdom of grace will soon become the Kingdom of eternal glory.

Questions on Number 123

1. The Kingdom of God is the rule of God over His creation.
   ☐ True ☐ False

2. Christ established a new Kingdom of God by His _____
   on the cross, and only _____ are in this Kingdom.

3. Christ's Kingdom is one of:
    ☐ a. nature   ☐ b. grace   ☐ c. nature and grace

4. As King, Jesus Christ is ruling from _____, using His
    _____ and Spirit. His rule is primarily in the
    _____ of His people.

5. How is the Kingdom of heaven different from the visible churches?

    _____

    _____

    _____

    _____

    _____

6. The Catechism question speaks of what three matters relating to the
    Kingdom of God?
    a) _____
    b) _____
    c) _____

7. Only the elect may be said to be in the Kingdom of heaven in this
    world. ☐ True ☐ False ▶ *Explain:* _____

    _____

    _____

8. Name some of the enemies of the Kingdom of God.
    a) inside the Kingdom _____

    _____

    b) outside the Kingdom _____

    _____

9. Ephesians 6:13–18 tells us what our spiritual armor is, with which to
    fight off our spiritual enemies. Describe the following:
    a) Helmet _____
    b) Shoes _____
    c) Breastplate _____
    d) Shield _____

e) Girdle or belt _____

f) Sword _____

10. According to 1 Corinthians 15, Christ is now reigning as King and putting His enemies under His _____ (vs. 25). The last enemy that shall be destroyed is _____ (vs. 26). After Christ completes His conquest of "all _____ and all _____ and _____ " (vs. 24), He shall turn over the completed Kingdom to " _____ even the _____." (vs. 24). Then the Son shall Himself be " _____ unto Him that put _____ _____ under Him, that God may be _____ in _____ " (vs. 28).

11. Write out Hebrews 12:28. _____

_____

_____

_____

_____

❦ The Third Petition: God's Will

Q124. What is the third petition?

"Thy will be done in earth, as it is in heaven;" that is, grant that we and all men renounce our own will, and without gainsaying obey Thy will, which alone is good; that so every one may fulfill his office and calling as willingly and faithfully as the angels do in heaven.

We now come to the third petition of the Model Prayer: "Thy will be done in earth as it is in heaven." We must keep in mind that these first three petitions are concerned with the glory of God. There is also a progression to be seen in these petitions. The name of God is honored as His Kingdom comes to men's hearts, and His Kingdom comes to men's hearts as His will is done. These three things: The Name, the Kingdom, and the Will of God all go together and cannot be separated.

Two Ways to Speak of God's Will

To understand this petition, and this Catechism question, we need first to understand what the *will* of God is.

We must see that the Bible speaks of the will of God in two ways, not that God has two wills. God is *One*. Still, *we* must distinguish between God's will of *decree,* and God's will of *command.* Or, we can call them the *secret* will of God, and the *revealed* will of God. (See Deuteronomy 29:29.) God's secret will or will of decree refers to God's plan for all things. This will or plan was determined by God before He began the work of creation. This will is always performed perfectly in heaven, on earth, and in hell! God says, "My counsel shall stand, and I will do all My pleasure" (Isaiah 46:10). "For who has resisted His will?" (Romans 9:19). See also Daniel 4:35, and re-read questions 26, 27, and 28 on the providence of God.

We do not need to pray that God's decrees may be kept—they cannot possibly fail; but we must pray constantly that His commands, His instructions, His precepts may be kept by ourselves and all men. We must be intensely concerned about having our lives regulated by God's holy commandments; and we must pray for grace to obey God's Word under all circumstances. The *secret* will of God requires submission; the *revealed* will of God requires obedience. This third petition refers not to the secret will of God's predestination, but to His will of command.

Note the three main points made in this question:

1. **We must renounce our own will.**

Our will, our desires, and our decisions are always wrong and evil when we act by ourselves. Fallen, sinful men can never will to do good apart from the knowledge of God's will. "Good" is what God's Word requires; all else is evil. To renounce our own will means to recognize that by nature our wills are totally depraved, and to ask God to give us grace to make us surrender to His will entirely.

2. **We must do God's will.**

To obey God's will is our calling and service as Christians. Our Lord said, "For whoever does the will of My Father in heaven is My brother and sister and mother" (Matthew 12:50). Those who are not desirous of doing the will of God will never enter the eternal Kingdom of heaven (Matthew 7:21). We were created to do the will of God and nothing else. We truly live and find joy when we obey God. Jesus said, "My food is to do the will of Him who sent Me" (John 4:34).

3. **How God's will is to be done.**

God requires perfect obedience on earth even as there is perfect obedience in heaven. He has never lowered His standards.

a. God's will is to be obeyed "without gainsaying" or "murmuring." This sounds easy, but it is often very hard when the temptation to disobey is very strong. Sometimes we think that it would be to our advantage to forget the will of God for a moment and go ahead and do our own will. This is the whisper of Satan, however, and can only bring us into sin and sorrow. Always, God's will "alone is good" and for our welfare.

b. God's will is to be obeyed in our "office and calling." This means in our daily work and routine, not just on some special occasions. Life is made up of a lot of little things mostly; and it is in these common duties that we must be especially concerned about God's commandments, keeping them in thought, word, and deed. We must first make sure that our "offices" (our jobs, our activities) are proper ones to begin with.

c. God's will is to be obeyed as the angels and saints in heaven obey— "willingly and faithfully." The heavenly obedience, as performed by the angels and glorified saints, is performed:

1) *willingly*—without any complaints

2) *faithfully*—without alterations

3) *instantly*—without postponement

4) *constantly*—without interruptions

How do you find out the will of God in certain difficult situations? For example, which hat should you buy? Which girl should you date? Which college should you attend? There are many matters which require close prayerful study in the light of the *general principles* of Scripture in order for us to know what is the right thing to do. Some choices are *indifferent* in themselves, and a decision either way would be in keeping with the will of God. We are to eat and drink to the glory of God (1 Corinthians 10:30), and this may be *either* pancakes or cereal, carrots or peas. Of course, when any decision would involve our transgressing some law in God's Word, it is automatically wrong.

Scripture is the only infallible rule for practice, and we must never resort to extra-biblical "revelations," such as dreams, visions, tongues, etc., to find the will of God. There are many people today who are trying to do just that. They are in serious error.

May we in all things say with our Lord, "Not My will, but Yours be done" (Luke 22:42).

Questions on Number 124

1. What is meant when we say that the first three petitions of the Lord's Prayer are a progression? _____

_____

_____

_____

2. What does the Bible mean by the "will" of God? _____

_____

_____

3. God has two separate wills. ☐ True ☐ False
   ▶ *Explain:* _____

_____

_____

4. The third petition is a request that God will perform His eternal decrees. ☐ True ☐ False

5. The will of God's command has never been kept perfectly on earth.
   ☐ True ☐ False ▶ *Explain:* _____

_____

6. Question 124 tells us what three things?
   a) _____
   b) _____
   c) _____

7. Why must we first renounce our own will in order to do the will of God? _____

_____

_____

8. In our "office and _____," we should seek God's strength to obey Him perfectly, which means obeying Him in what way?
   a) _____
   b) _____
   c) _____
   d) _____

9. How do we decide the will of God between:
   a) Telling a lie and not telling a lie? _____

_____

   b) Spending one's little money for needed food, or for cigarettes?

_____

c) Ordering a hamburger or a hot dog? _____

d) Joining a Baptist Church or a Reformed Church? _____

_____

10. Write out Romans 12:2. _____

_____

_____

_____

_____

_____

❧ The Fourth Petition: Our Daily Bread

Q125. What is the fourth petition?

"Give us this day our daily bread;" that is, be pleased to provide for all our bodily need, so that we may thereby acknowledge Thou art the only fountain of all good, and that without Thy blessing neither our care and labor, nor Thy gifts, can profit us; that we may therefore withdraw our trust from all creatures and place it alone in Thee.

The last three petitions of the Lord's Prayer concern the needs of God's children here on earth. This fourth petition concerns our material needs, and the last two deal with our spiritual needs.

The Catechism correctly understands the term "daily bread" to refer to "all our bodily need." Some people have felt that Christ is not speaking of physical bread but of spiritual bread, and that we should not pray for such earthly matters as material bread. However, the Lord *does* want us to pray for our bodily needs and for *very spiritual reasons*. It is wrong to separate the material and the spiritual as if they had no connection. Unless our physical lives are sustained day by day, we cannot engage in any spiritual service to God on earth, for we will soon die.

Indeed, this may be the reason that this petition is put *before* the other two. This order of the petitions seems to be wrong, for we would expect our spiritual needs to be mentioned first. Yet, in order of *time*, though not in *value*, the physical does come first. But, of course, our concern and prayers for material needs must always be *in order* to hallow God's name, to seek His Kingdom, and to do His will. God's glory is primary in all things.

What is included in the expression "daily bread"? All bodily needs: food, clothes, health, shelter, work and harvests. These things are essential to human life on earth. Note that bread is not a luxury but a need. We must beware of praying covetous prayers—asking for what we do not need. Paul says, "Having food and clothing, with these we shall be content" (1 Timothy 6:8). See also Proverbs 30:8-9. Christ uses the adjective "daily" to remind us that we do not need a large surplus for the future (we may not live very far into the future), but to look to *Him* daily, rather than to any surpluses. Daily prayer will prevent daily worry about the future.

The reasons that God requires us to pray for our earthly needs—even though He mercifully grants them to people who never pray (Matthew 5:45) and to animals, which cannot pray (Psalm 47:9)—are three, according to question 125:

1. That we may acknowledge God as the Fountain of all good

Behind nature stands God, and we must remind ourselves every day that it is not "Mother Nature" who feeds us and takes care of our needs, but it is God by His providence (see Q27). How often we speak of nature as an "it." We say, "It rains," "It snows," "It was a good year," when actually it is God Who sends us these things. The Bible writers always attribute material benefits to God's hand, not to "Nature." How great is the ingratitude of men who use God's gifts and never even acknowledge Him!

2. That we may seek the blessing of God along with His gifts

To receive God's physical gifts and not receive His blessing and grace with them, results in these gifts becoming *curses* to us! "The curse of the Lord is on the house of the wicked, but He blesses the home of the just" (Proverbs 3:33); see also Psalm 37:16; 73:7, 18; 78:29-30; James 5:5. God expects us to show "care and labor" to provide for our needs. But we should never be content with only the gifts that we earn; rather, we must ask God to sanctify them to us, that our strength and health and energy may be used to serve Him and not our own selfish desires. Therefore, there should be prayer to God before or after each meal. Along with our bodily food, we should also have spiritual food for our souls by the reading of God's Word. *Is this the practice in your home?*

3. That we may place our trust in God alone

We are by nature inclined to trust in the creature rather than the Creator. We need food, air, water, clothing, etc. to survive physically. But surviving physically is not the most important thing. Sooner or later these things will not support our bodies and we shall die. But if we are trusting only in the Son of God for our righteousness and salvation, we shall never die (John 6:49–50). Our necessary bread must not become an idol to us, a false god (see Question 95).

A word should be said about "divine healing." By this is meant the healing of the body by supernatural intervention, through prayer and faith. Do we have a right to expect God to heal us of incurable diseases, to cause bones to heal correctly without medical care, to heal us without using medicines and physicians? Today there are some "Divine Healers," who go about trying to convince people that they have the power of God to heal people miraculously. How should we regard this so-called "divine healing"?

a. We must always look to God first for any and all healing. It is sinful first to seek a physician's care before praying to the Lord about the matter (2 Chronicles 16:12–13; James 5:13).

b. It is not always God's will that we be healed quickly (and perhaps not at all). We must entrust ourselves to God's sovereign plans (2 Timothy 4:20; 2 Corinthians 12:7).

c. God does use medicine and medical practice to minister to our bodily needs. Instead of despising such means, we should thank God for them (1 Timothy 5:23).

d. We must be careful about using medicine. Some medicines and drugs can actually do harm to our bodies, and some doctors tend to load their patients with drugs. Don't trust in any doctor as if he were a god (Mark 5:26).

e. Don't trust in any "healer" either, because these "healing preachers" are not part of the New Testament ministry for us today. They are false prophets (Ephesians 4:11–12).

Questions on Number 125

1. The fourth petition is the first of the last group of petitions, all of which concern _____.

2. Some people think that this petition refers only to what kind of "bread"? _____.

3. In order of _____, our physical needs are first. In order of _____

   _____, our spiritual needs are more important.

4. What is included in the expression "bread"? _____

   _____.

5. The word "daily" teaches us what about our physical needs?

   _____

   _____

6. Who supplies the physical needs of unbelievers and animals that do not or cannot pray? _____

7. The three reasons that we should pray for our physical needs are these:

   a) _____

   _____

   b) _____

   _____

   c) _____

   _____

8. Match the following:

   "Mother Nature"   Temporary food

   Spiritual food   The Bread of Life

   Physical bread   A false god

   The Lord Jesus Christ   God's Word

9. What would you do (spiritually) if you:

   a) Scratched your finger _____

   _____

   b) Broke your leg _____

   _____

   c) Had a headache _____

   _____

   d) Got incurable cancer _____

   _____

10. Write out Proverbs 30:8-9. _____

   _____

   _____

   _____

_____

_____

_____

_____

_____

_____

_____

❧ The Fifth Petition: Forgive Our Debts

Q126. What is the fifth petition?

"And forgive us our debts, as we forgive our debtors;" that is, be pleased, for the sake of Christ's blood, not to impute to us miserable sinners our manifold transgressions, nor the evil which still always cleaves to us; as we also find this witness of Thy grace in us, that it is our full purpose heartily to forgive our neighbor.

"Forgive us our debts as we forgive our debtors." This fifth petition of the Model Prayer can easily be misunderstood. For example, is it referring to money debts? Why do we need to keep asking forgiveness if Christ died for our sins and we asked for pardon before? Will God not forgive us if we don't forgive others? If He *does* forgive us because we forgive others, are we not *meriting* His forgiveness? These are some of the problems that arise with this fifth petition. Let us study the following points:

1. God's Forgiveness

"Debts" does not refer to *money*, but rather, to *sins*, as Luke 11:4 explains it: "Forgive us our sins." Our sins are called "debts" because they represent our failure to pay to God perfect love and obedience as His law requires. As the Catechism explains in many places, our failure to pay God our debt of obedience means that we must pay God a debt of punishment (see Questions 12 and 16, for example). This debt can never be paid by ourselves; but God in His grace provided His Son to pay our full debt of love and punishment so that we might be forgiven our debts to God. This question makes it clear once more that forgiveness of sins is *only for the sake of Christ's blood* (His sacrificial death) and for *no other reason*. We could never begin to merit forgiveness before God.

What sins does God freely forgive? "Our manifold transgressions" (our actual sins of thought, word, and deed) and our evil, depraved nature, which always clings to us. We may speak of sins of *commission* (doing evil), sins of *omission* (failing to do good), sins that are *private*, sins that are *public*, sins that are done *consciously*, sins that are done *unconsciously* (without our being aware of them), sins against *God* only, against *ourselves,* against *others.*

2. The Conditions of Forgiveness

Why do we have to repeatedly ask for forgiveness when Christ's blood washed away all our sins—past, present, and future sins? It is true that once we are justified by God, this act of God's grace forever settles our account with God (Romans 5:1; 8:33). Yet, our daily sins are in themselves worthy of damnation, and God requires of us, as moral creatures, that we acknowledge them to be so. *Our personal assurance of justification in Christ* depends on our personal repentance and confession of sins continuously. God has appointed that confession of sin and *assurance* of forgiveness go together (Psalm 32:3-5; 1 John 1:9).

This petition also speaks of our forgiving others their debts. Again, this refers to the sins committed against us by others, not to the money debts that others may have to us. We must be willing heartily to forgive our neighbor any sin that he may have committed against us. This willingness to forgive others is caused by the grace of God in our own heart. It is this same grace that causes us to beg of God His forgiveness. The verse really reads, "As we have forgiven our debtors."

In Matthew 6:14-15 Jesus explains this matter further: "But if you do not forgive men their trespasses, neither will your Father forgive your trespasses." Refusal to forgive indicates that the grace of God is lacking in the heart. To forgive another person's sins means not to hold them against him any longer. And though we cannot forget injuries done to us, we should try not to think about them and not talk about them. We must also assure the forgiven person that we have forgiven him.

Are we to forgive every sin committed against us? Some people think so. However, Luke 17:3-4 clearly teach that we are to forgive only those persons who repent: if he "returns to you saying, 'I repent,' you shall forgive him." However, before we can expect such a humble request, we must first speak to the offender and "rebuke" him in a loving fashion. If we refuse to discuss the matter in question with the so-called offender, we have no right to expect him to seek our forgiveness. Those who refuse to repent when informed of their sin are not to be forgiven by us because they certainly are not forgiven by God. "*If we confess our sins,* He is faithful and just to forgive us our sins" (1 John 1:9).

Of course we must always pray for our enemies that God will work His grace in their hearts to cause them to repent (Matthew 5:44). *Never may we return evil for evil to those who have sinned against us, but rather we must always show a sincere desire to forgive them.*

Questions on Number 126

1. This petition can easily be misunderstood if a person does not understand the other Scriptures well. ☐ True ☐ False

2. What does "debts" mean in this petition? How does this term apply to our relationship to God? _____

   _____

   _____

3. Does this petition refer to all sins? ☐ Yes ☐ No
   Name some *types* of sins that we must confess to God.

   _____

   _____

   _____

4. The ground or merit for our forgiveness is
   ☐ a. our repentance   ☐ c. Christ's righteousness imputed to us
   ☐ b. our prayer   ☐ d. our forgiveness of others

5. "The evil which still always cleaves to us" refers to what? _____

   _____

   _____

6. Why does God require us to ask for daily forgiveness if Christ paid for *all* our sins? _____

   _____

   _____

7. God will forgive us only if we first _____ others.
   Our willingness to forgive the worst injuries against ourselves shows
   the witness of God's _____ in our _____.

8. If we are unwilling to forgive others who are sorry that they have
   sinned against us, God ☐ *will* ☐ *will not* forgive us.

9. In Jesus' parable in Matthew 18:23–35, a certain king freely _____
   _____ his servant a debt of _____ (vs. 24) when the
   servant _____ him, saying, "Lord, have _____
   _____ with me" (vs. 26).
   Later, this same servant refused to have patience with a fellow-
   servant who owed him only _____ (vs. 28), but had him
   " _____ into _____ ." (vs. 30).
   When the King heard about this, he delivered the servant to the

_____ till he also pay

_____ that was _____ unto _____ (vs. 34).

10. We need not ☐ *pray for* ☐ *forgive* our enemies if they show no
signs of repentance. ▶ *Explain:* _____

_____

_____

11. Write out Psalm 51:1. _____

_____

_____

❧ The Sixth Petition: Deliverance from Evil

Q127. What is the sixth petition?

"And lead us not into temptation, but deliver us from evil;" that is,
since we are so weak in ourselves that we cannot stand a moment,
and besides, our deadly enemies, the devil, the world, and our
own flesh, assail us without ceasing, be pleased to preserve and
strengthen us by the power of Thy Holy Spirit, that we may make
firm stand against them and not be overcome in this spiritual
warfare, until finally complete victory is ours.

This sixth and last petition of the Lord's Prayer is a petition that we may
be kept from sin. In the fifth petition, we ask God to forgive us our sins
already committed; in this one we ask God to keep us from committing
sins. This petition also needs to be carefully explained by other Scriptures,
or we may get a false idea of what it teaches.

We first need to get the correct meaning of the word "temptation."
The Bible uses this word in two ways:

1. Temptation sometimes means *trial, proving, testing.* God definitely
   does "tempt" men in this sense. He so tested Adam and Eve; He
   tested Abraham (Genesis 22:1); He so "tempted" Job (1:12; 2:6);
   and Jesus thus tested Philip (John 6:5–6).

2. Temptation may also mean an *enticement* or *inducement to sin.* In this
   sense, God cannot tempt any man. Only Satan and evil persons and
   evil things can incline us to sin.

James in his epistle speaks of these two kinds of temptation in
chapter one. *First,* he says, "Count it all joy when you fall into various

trials" (vs. 2); but *then* he says, "God cannot be tempted by evil, nor does He Himself tempt any man," that is, He causes no man to sin (vs. 13). Trials are sent by God, but He never tempts or induces us to sin. The very same situation is both a temptation to sin and test from God not to sin.

In this petition, the second meaning is the one Christ used. This is clear if we take the whole petition as a unit. We are to ask God for protection from the "Evil One," who seeks to cause us to sin. One reliable Greek scholar translates it: "Do not allow us to be led into temptation"— by the Evil One. (Note: "Evil" should be translated "Evil One"—Satan.)

This question tells us two important things about our struggle against Satan's efforts to cause us to sin.

1. Why we need God's protection

a. Because we are utterly weak in ourselves and cannot stand a moment against our spiritual enemies in our own strength, we must beware of self-confidence. There is not one Christian who has strength in himself—apart from God—to fight the spiritual war against the temptation to sin.

b. Our enemies who constantly seek to tempt us to sin are the wicked trinity: the Devil, the world, and our flesh. Satan is behind the world and our flesh to make them even more powerful. Satan tempted Adam and Eve; he tempted Job; he caused David to number the children of Israel (1 Chronicles 21:1); he assaulted Christ (Matthew 4) and Peter (Luke 22:31); and he continues to stalk the earth as a roaring lion, seeking whom he may devour (1 Peter 5:8). There is no let-up, no truce, no furlough in this deadly struggle against our spiritual enemies. They "assail us without ceasing" and daily we must watch and pray, and not sleep, lest we enter into temptation (Matthew 26:41).

2. The help that God promises

We will find ourselves in situations and circumstances that will surely lead us to sin unless God intervenes with His powerful Holy Spirit, Word, and grace. If Christ told us to pray for protection and deliverance from the Evil One and his forces, then we can confidently expect God to answer this petition. God has promised: "I will never leave you nor forsake you" (Hebrews 13:5). The trusting Christian need not yield to temptation, because He who is He in you (Christ's Spirit) is greater than he who is in the world, (Satan) (1 John 4:4); and "he who is born of God (born again) does not sin; but he who is born of God keeps himself, and the wicked one does not touch him" (1 John 5:18). Yes, we can expect to overcome our spiritual enemies by the power of Christ in us. Joseph did (Genesis 39:10-12); Job did (Job 42:12); and so did the Apostles (Romans 8:37).

Now this is not to say that if we pray this petition every day we will be happy and triumphant Christian warriors, living sinless lives. No, the Lord will permit us to be sorely tested and tried, as were Abraham, Job, David, Peter, etc., and we will on some occasions fall into sin, perhaps even denying our Savior as did Peter. But the Lord will give us His grace to repent in sorrow and return to Him. Complete victory will be ours in Christ at death, though we may lose some battles once in a while in life. One reason for this is that we do not practice what we pray! We don't always *flee* temptation.

Needless to say, when we pray this petition, it is sheer mockery to go out and expose ourselves to wicked influences in defiance of God. We need not expect God to answer this petition under such conditions.

What are some of the tempting influences in your life?

Questions on Number 127

1. In what two ways does the Bible use the word "temptation"?

   a) _____

   b) _____

2. God permits our faith to be tried, but He never urges us to sin.

   ☐ True   ☐ False

3. God "tempts" us in order to:

   ☐ a. reveal our weakness   ☐ c. show us His grace

   ☐ b. make us fall   ☐ d. show others spiritual lessons

4. Temptations come to

   ☐ a. some Christians   ☐ c. weak Christians

   ☐ b. all Christians   ☐ d. strong Christians

5. The proper translation of this petition is "deliver us from

   _____."

6. The unholy trinity that seeks to make us sin against God are:

   a) _____

   b) _____

   c) _____

7. The _____ is called a "roaring _____"

   who seeks to _____ Christians (1 Peter 5:8). He tempted

   _____ to eat the forbidden fruit; _____

   to number the Israelites; and _____ to deny Christ.

8. Check the verses that teach us that God's grace is sufficient for us in our trials and temptations?

☐ Luke 5:2　　　　　　　　　☐ 2 Corinthians 12:9

☐ Galatians 4:10　　　　　　☐ Philippians 4:13

☐ 2 Thessalonians 1:12　　　☐ 1 Timothy 1:14

☐ 3 John 13.

9. The person who purposely exposes himself to sinful temptations cannot really pray this petition sincerely. ☐ True ☐ False

10. Write out 1 Thessalonians 5:23. _____

_____

_____

_____

_____

❧ Close of the Lord's Prayer

Q128. How do you close this Prayer?

"For Thine is the kingdom, and the power, and the glory, for ever;" that is, all this we ask of Thee, because as our King, having power over all things, Thou art willing and able to give us all good; and that thereby not we, but Thy holy name may be glorified for ever.

The closing statement of this Perfect Prayer is the *doxology*. This word comes from the Greek word *doxologia,* which means "to speak glory or praise." The hymn we often sing in church, "Praise God from Whom all Blessings Flow" is also called "The Doxology."

You will be surprised to learn that the modern Bible translations, such as the American Standard Version, the Revised Standard Version, the New International Version, the Catholic Bibles, and others do not include this beautiful doxology at the close of the Lord's Prayer, nor even the "Amen." The reasons that the translators give are (1) that the oldest manuscript copies do not include this doxology and (2) that the version of the Lord's Prayer in Luke 11:4 does not include the doxology.

We prefer to abide by the manuscript copies that do include this doxology and follow the Heidelberg Catechism.

Certainly our Lord could have used this doxology, as it is obviously based on 1 Chronicles 29:11, a part of King David's prayer: "Yours, O Lord, is the greatness, the power and the glory, the victory and the majesty; for all that is in the heaven and in the earth is Yours; Yours is the kingdom, O Lord, and You are exalted as head over all." Notice that the same words "power," "glory," and "kingdom" are in David's doxology.

This doxology is really the foundation on which the entire Lord's Prayer, and all true prayer, rests. Notice that it is introduced by the word "for," which explains the reason or basis for the prayer. Our Savior here teaches us that prayers to God can be answered and will be answered because:

1. "Yours is the Kingdom."

God, our heavenly Father, is also King over all things; and he has given Christ all authority in heaven and earth (Matthew 28:18) (Refer back to question 123 for the discussion of God's Kingdom). Being the King because He is Creator, Provider, Redeemer, and Judge, God has the *authority* to grant all petitions made for the advancement of His name and His Kingdom. He is the absolute Lord and Ruler, reigning in righteousness, truth, and love; and we pray to Him for that reason.

2. "Yours is the Power."

Not only does God hear us because we are His children, but He has all power to answer our true prayers. All power belongs to God. He has the ability to enforce His holy will. No power can stay His hand or resist Him. This fact should fill our hearts with perfect confidence when we pray. We are not talking to a weak or helpless god, but to the Almighty, Who will answer every petition that advances His Kingdom. The original Greek word for "power" in this doxology is *dynamis,* which means "energy" (our word "dynamite" is taken from this word!). God has more power than all the energy of the universe! He can even change the hard, stubborn hearts of sinners and cause them to believe His Word!

3. "Yours is the Glory."

If God is King over all, and if He has all power and might, then He must be the God of all glory. When we say that God is glorious, we are saying that He is infinitely perfect in His whole Being as Three Persons. So glorious is God because of His goodness, power, love, righteousness, and other virtues, that we shall forever stand in awe and wonder before Him. In our prayers, we are concerned above all that God's holy name may be glorified.

The closing word of this doxology is "forever." This word modifies all three nouns. God's Kingdom is forever, His power is forever, and His glory is forever. Because God is eternal, His faithfulness is forever (Psalm 89:2; 146:10). Because God is eternal, He is not limited to our time, and He is ready with answers to our prayers even before we ask Him! (Isaiah 65:24).

Questions on Number 128

1. What is a "doxology?" _____

   _____

   The word comes from which Greek word? _____

2. This last statement of the Lord's Prayer is:
   ☐ a. a request   ☐ c. a confession of praise
   ☐ b. a petition   ☐ d. the basis for true prayer

3. People who read many modern versions of the Bible will discover
   what about this prayer? _____

   _____

   Why? _____

   _____

4. What Old Testament passage provides a basis for this doxology?

   _____

   What was the occasion? _____

   _____

5. The little conjunction "for" indicates that the doxology is not the
   ground or basis of prayer. ☐ True ☐ False ▶ *Explain:* _____

   _____

   _____

   _____

6. We know that God through Christ will answer all true prayer for
   which three reasons.

   a) _____
   b) _____
   c) _____

7. Because our God reveals Himself in this Model Prayer as our
   heavenly _____ and as the _____ over all
   creation, we may have confidence that He will hear our prayers.

8. The Greek word for "power" is _____ and means
   _____. God has more _____
   than all the nuclear bombs that man can make.

9. The word "forever" refers to what? _____

_____

10. Write out Psalm 115:1. _____

_____

_____

_____

_____

❧ *The Meaning of "Amen"*

Q129. What is the meaning of the word "Amen"?

"Amen" means: so shall it truly and surely be. For my prayer is much more certainly heard of God than I feel in my heart that I desire these things of Him.

We come now to the last word of the Lord's Prayer, the solemn "Amen." It makes no difference whether you pronounce the word with a long a, or a short a, or some other way, the idea is the same! The word means "firmness," "security," "certainty," "so let it be," "it shall be."

"Amen" is a Hebrew word that has been carried over literally into the Greek New Testament and then into the English translation. In the Old Testament, "Amen" was used to indicate a person's solemn agreement to a truth or law (see Numbers 5:25; Deuteronomy 27:15, etc.) In the New Testament, it is used after declarations of blessing (Romans 1:25), praise (Romans 11:36), benedictions (Romans 15:33; 16:24), and prayers.

The Savior often used "Amen" to introduce a statement. When thus used, it is translated "verily." In the Gospel of John, Jesus used the word twice in succession to signify the great importance and truthfulness of what He was about to say. This phrase, "Verily, *verily,* (Literally, *"Amen, amen"*), I say unto you ... " is used in John's Gospel 25 times! No other New Testament speaker used "Amen" in this way, which indicates that Christ spoke with special authority. He is the Truth, the Amen of God (John 14:6; Revelation 3:14), the faithful and true Witness.

"Amen" means certainty and truth. The Catechism sums up its meaning: "So shall it truly and surely be." As the ending for our prayers, there is a double application of this meaning of certainty and truth. The two things included, according to question 129, are these:

1. **"Amen" is God's assurance to us that He will certainly hear and answer our prayer.**

    In His Word, God has promised to answer our prayers as we pray in the Name of Jesus Christ our great High Priest according to His will. "All the promises of God in Him [Christ] are Yes, and in Him *Amen* [certain and unbreakable], to the glory of God through us" (2 Corinthians 1:20). God cannot break His covenant promises to us in Christ when we claim them by faith and use them as our prayers. We should use this word (Amen) most thoughtfully and carefully, because we are reminding the Living God to give us what He has promised to us. "So shall it truly and surely be." The certainty of our prayer is based not on our "feelings" or "good will," but on God's unbreakable promises.

2. "Amen" is our solemn promise to God that we prayed a sincere, heartfelt prayer.

We dare not pray as hypocrites or pray insincerely. Our prayers must come from our inmost hearts. By this little word, we express our desire to glorify God alone in our prayer and to pray only according to His holy will as revealed in Scripture. It is saying, "Oh, Father, Who knows my heart and inmost thoughts, You know that my prayer was sincere, and that I earnestly desire these things of You."

Amen, then, is a sign and seal to both God and ourselves that our Bible-based prayers are valid and deserve to be answered for the sake of Christ's merits.

Our prayers are not a waste of time, as unbelievers think; but they are used by God as part of His eternal plan to save us, to build up His Kingdom and to bring in the new heavens and the new earth. Our secret petitions, uttered in the depths of our hearts, ascend to the throne of God and are stored in golden vials as sweet incense for the Lord (Revelation 5:8).

With this question, we not only finish the subject of the Lord's Prayer, but we also finish the Catechism. How fitting that "Amen" finishes the Catechism also, for we feel that the matters we have studied are truly and surely so. We say a hearty "Amen" to our threefold comfort of learning of our *sins,* learning of our *salvation,* and learning of our *service* to our blessed Redeemer.

May the great, eternal truths of this little book ever be precious to you, in life and in death. And may your church ever embrace the *Heidelberg Catechism* as her confession of faith.

Questions on Number 129

1. The word "Amen" may be pronounced

    ☐ a. only one correct way   ☐ b. in various ways

2. The meaning of "Amen" is _____

_____.

3. "Amen" is the English *translation* of a Hebrew word.
    ☐ True ☐ False ▶ *Explain:* _____

    _____

4. In the Old Testament, "Amen" was used only after prayers, as
    Deuteronomy 27:15 indicates. ☐ True ☐ False

    ▶ *Explain:* _____

    _____

5. In the New Testament, "Amen" is used in connection with
    declarations of _____

    _____

6. Our Lord, in the Book of _____, often said,
    " _____ , _____ I say unto you."
    The word used is actually _____

7. In what way is Jesus Himself "the Amen"? _____

    _____

    _____

8. What is the double meaning of the "Amen" of our prayers?
    a) _____

    _____

    b) _____

    _____

9. "Amen" means: (*check the correct answers*)
    ☐ a. God has promised to answer true prayer.
    ☐ b. So shall it truly and surely be.
    ☐ c. My feelings make my prayers true and certain.
    ☐ d. I have prayed sincerely to the glory of God.
    ☐ e. Verily
    ☐ f. I truly desire these things of You.

10. How important should this Catechism be
    a) to you? _____

    _____

b) to your church? _____

_____

11. Write out 2 Corinthians 1:20. _____

_____

_____

_____

_____

_____

Outline of the Catechism

I. The Theme: My Only Comfort in Life and Death Q.1

II. The Christian's Three-fold Knowledge Q.2

III. MY SINFULNESS (Questions 3–11)
A. The Definition of Sin Q3, 4
B. The Fact of Sin Q5
C. The Origin of Sin Q6, 7
D. The Extent of Sin (Total Depravity) Q8
E. The Responsibility for Sin Q9
F. The Consequences of Sin Q10, 11

IV. MY REDEMPTION (Questions 12–85)
A. The Nature of Redemption (Satisfying the Justice of God) Q12
B. The Impossibility of Self-redemption Q13, 14
C. The Kind of Redeemer Needed Q15–17
D. The Redeemer Identified Q18
E. The Redeemer Revealed Q19
F. The Place of Faith in Redemption Q20, 21
   1. The Necessity of Faith Q20
   2. The Nature of Faith Q21
   3. The Content of Faith (as summarized in the Apostles' Creed) Q22
G. An Exposition of the Apostles' Creed Q23–58
   1. Introduction Q23-25
   2. God the Father in Creation and Providence Q26-28
   3. God the Son Q29-52
      a. His Titles Q29-34

Glossary of Terms

This glossary, with slight changes (indicated by *), is taken from Dr. Alexander C. De Jong's manual, *An Introduction to Biblical Truths* (Baker Book House, Grand Rapids, Michigan, 1978), originally entitled, *What I Confess*.

A

Adiaphora. Matters of conduct which are neither sinful nor righteous in themselves but which may become legitimate or illegitimate in the Christian life according to circumstances.

Adoption. The act of God's love whereby He takes saved sinners into His family and bestows all the rights of sonship upon them as children of God.

Apocrypha. Those fifteen religious books which were written in the period between the Old and New Testaments, and officially accepted by the Roman Catholic Church in 1548 as inspired Scripture. They should not be included in the Holy Bible because they were not inspired by God, the Holy Spirit.*

Apostasy. A falling away from the truth of God as revealed in the Bible, in words and deeds, by one person, a church, or a nation.

Arminianism. A system of doctrine which regards God's actions as limited by and dependent upon the free actions of man. This system derives its name from a Dutch theologian named Jacobus Arminius who died in 1609. Arminian theology was adopted by John Wesley, the founder of the Methodist Church and is popular in Fundamentalist churches. It was condemned by the Reformed Churches at the Synod of Dordt in 1618.

Assurance. The conviction that a person is presently saved by grace and will surely enter into heaven, which a believer may attain as he rightly uses the means of grace and knows the witness of the Holy Spirit in his heart.

Atonement. The satisfaction of God's justice made by the sacrificial death of Jesus Christ, which was necessary for the forgiveness of sinners. The Old Testament ritual of bloody sacrifices foreshadowed the One Sacrifice of Christ to put away the guilt of sin.*

C

Calvinism. The system of truth which acknowledges the absolute sovereignty of God, and man's total dependence on God for every part of his life, faith, and salvation. It is consistent biblical Christianity, which received its basic expression in the writings of the Genevan Reformer, John Calvin (died 1564). It stands opposed to Arminianism.*

Canon of Scripture. The list of the books of the Bible which are recognized as inspired by God, the Holy Spirit. These 66 Books were given Apostolic approval in the early church.*

Catholic Church. The universal, world-wide church of God as distinguished from any special congregation or denomination. When the word "Roman" is used with it, it refers to a special organization of churches under the control of a Pope who lives in Vatican City at Rome.

Congregation. A group of Christ-confessing repentant sinners of like faith gathered in one place for the purpose of worship.*

Conscience. The function of a human being which registers approval when a person's actions fit in with his standards of conduct, and disapproval when his actions violate his standards of what is right and wrong.

Conversion. The sinner's turning from sin to God, which is the effect of regeneration and which includes repentance and faith.

Covenant of Grace. That gracious arrangement of God made with believers and their children, in which God promises eternal salvation in the way of repentance and the obedience of faith.*

Creation. A series of acts of God's will in the six-day creation week by which He made all things good for the praise and glory of His Name. *

D

Deity of Christ. The truth that Jesus of Nazareth was and is the only true God, One in Whom dwells all the fullness of the Godhead bodily.

Depravity, Total. The truth that the unsaved sinner is corrupted by sin in every part of his personality and completely unable and unwilling to do any good which is well pleasing to God. This corruption of nature is inherited from Adam.*

Divine Decrees. God's eternal purpose, in which He has foreordained whatsoever comes to pass. All of God's decrees form the counsel of His will.

E

Election. God's unconditional and sovereign choice of certain persons in Christ unto final salvation.

Eschatology. The biblical teaching concerning the last things. These teachings include such matters as the state of man after death, the return of Christ, the signs announcing His second coming, the resurrection, the judgment and eternal life.

Exaltation of Christ. The life of Jesus Christ which He now lives as having been rewarded by God for His perfect work. It consists of His resurrection from the dead, His ascension into heaven, His sitting at the right hand of God, and His return at the end of time.

Excommunication. The final step in Christian discipline, in which the unrepentant church member is solemnly excluded from the fellowship of the church until such a time as he turns from his sins.

F

Faith, Historical. A mere agreement with the truths of the Bible as a matter of historical fact, without personal trust in God and Jesus Christ for salvation.

Faith, Temporary. A faith which resembles true faith but which does not proceed from a new-born life and which withers and disappears under the pressures of sin and persecution.

Faith, True. See *Heidelberg Catechism, Q21.*

Fall of Man. The act which took place when Adam and Eve ate of the forbidden fruit in the garden of Eden and which plunged mankind from the situation of perfection and joy into the death of sin and misery.

Five Points of Calvinism. Five interrelated biblical truths explained in the Canons of Dordt, a Reformed confession written in 1618–19 to refute the errors of James Arminius. These five truths are: (1) unconditional election; (2) limited or definite atonement; (3) total depravity; (4) irresistible grace; (5) perseverance of the saints.*

Foreordination. God's determination from all eternity of everything that takes place in time.

Forgiveness of Sins. The act of God by which the sinner's guilt is no longer charged to him and he is thus released from paying the penalty of his sins. It is also called *pardon.*

G

Glorification. The final state of salvation of God's elect, at which time they are taken to heaven in the moment of death and receive a new body and a new universe when Christ comes again.

Good Works. Those acts of man which proceed from a true faith, according to the Law of God and which are dedicated to God's glory.

Gospel. The good news of salvation which God provides for sinners in the work of Jesus Christ.

Grace of God. The unmerited goodness and favor of God which God gives to those people who deserve His wrath and punishment because of sin. Man's salvation is ascribed solely to the grace of God. *

H

Heaven. This place refers to (1) the celestial world (Genesis 1:1); (2) that place where God's presence and glory are concentrated; (3) the future home of the saved (2 Corinthians 5:1).

Hell. The place of eternal punishment prepared particularly for Satan and his angels where all unsaved sinners will be banished from the blessed presence of God.

Heresy. An unbiblical doctrine, which is contrary to the accepted creeds or doctrinal standards of a church, which, if left unchallenged, would eventually destroy the witness of that church to God's truth.

Hope. The believer's eager expectation of final glory and joy in a recreated universe, which shall be given to him when Christ returns. It is based on the certainty of God's unchangeable promises.*

Humiliation of Christ. The position which Christ took under the Law of

God at the time of His birth. While in this position, He experienced the wrath of God, the miseries of life, and final banishment from this life in His death and burial. This position ended for Jesus at the time of His resurrection from the dead.

I

Incarnation. The act of God the Son in taking to Himself a complete human nature, body and soul, to win salvation for sinners.

Independence of God. That perfection by which God is perfectly sufficient to Himself and in no way whatever dependent on anyone or anything.

Infallibility of Scripture. The biblical teaching that the Bible is absolutely trustworthy and free from all errors because inspired by God the Holy Spirit.*

Infinity of God. That perfection of God by which He is completely boundless, without any limits as to space and time.

Immanence of God. That perfection of God by which He is everywhere present in the created world. It is also called His omnipresence.

Imputation. The act of a judge by which something is reckoned over unto one's account or laid to the charge or credit of someone. What is reckoned or charged forms the basis for a declaration by the judge either unto acquittal or condemnation. The Bible speaks of three major imputations: (1) of Adam's sin to the whole human race; (2) of the elect's sin to Jesus Christ; (3) of Christ's righteousness to the believing sinner.

Iniquity. A word for sin which includes the ideas of perverseness, the absence of justice, and wickedness.

Inspiration of the Bible. The act of God, the Holy Spirit, by which He influenced the writers of the Bible books to write the exact words and thoughts which God intended them to write.

Intercession of Christ. The work of the exalted Savior in heaven whereby He pleads before His Father the cause of each and every true child of God.*

J

Justification. An act of God, the Judge, in which He graciously forgives sins and declares us perfectly righteous. This declaration is based on the perfect righteousness of Christ, which is reckoned or imputed to the believer's life. This blessing can be received only in the way of faith.

K

Keys of the Kingdom. The authority of church government and discipline, which Christ, the Head and King of the Church, has given to the lawfully elected officers of His church.

Kingdom of God. The rulership of God established in and acknowledged by the heart of the regenerated sinner, which is partly realized in this age but which shall reach its full realization when Christ comes a second time.

L

Legalism. The wrong theory that one can become right with God by obeying the Law of God. This error is seen clearly in the lives of the Pharisees who thought their obedience was acceptable to God.

Liberty, Christian. The freedom of the saved sinner from the wrath of God, the guilt and power of sin, the curse of the Law, the bondage of Satan, and the power of man's vain traditions and superstitions. *

Longsuffering of God. That perfection of God by which He patiently bears with man's long-continued disobedience.*

M

Means of Grace. The ordinary means which Christ Jesus uses to bring the blessings of salvation into sinner's lives. Christ uses especially the Word, the sacraments, and prayer to apply effectively His work in the lives of the elect.

Mediator. One who stands between two parties who are at odds. Jesus Christ is the only Mediator between the offended God and the offending sinner.

Merit. That which is earned. Merit is in contrast with grace, which cannot be earned by man's work. Christ merited salvation and graciously gives salvation to whom He will.

Messiah. A Hebrew word meaning "anointed." An anointed person was set apart to perform a certain work. Christ is the Greek term meaning the same thing. Jesus Christ was anointed to be the perfect Prophet, Priest, and King.

Millennium. The thousand-year period spoken of in Revelation 20:1–10. During this period Christ reigns, and Satan is kept in check. We believe this thousand-year period to refer to the time between Christ's ascension into heaven and His final return at the end of time.

Miracle. A special event in the physical world caused by the direct activity of God, which points beyond itself to the saving work of God in Jesus Christ through the Holy Spirit.

N

Natures of Christ. The mystery of Jesus who is both perfectly human and perfectly divine. Though our Lord has two natures as the result of the Incarnation, He is one Person—the second Person of the Trinity. *

O

Obedience of Christ. The work of Jesus Christ in which He took care of the guilt of sin and met the penal requirements of God's Law. This is often called Christ's *passive* obedience. Christ also perfectly fulfilled the demands of God's Law. This is often called Christ's *active* obedience. This two-fold obedience is the ground for forgiveness of sins and all His saving benefits to us.*

Original Guilt. The liability to punishment which was Adam's because of his first sin and which is reckoned or imputed by God to all members of the human race.

Original Sin. The first sin of Adam, which became the root out of which all the sin and misery of the world has come.

P

Perfectionism. The teaching that it is possible for a Christian, in this life, to reach a position where he no longer commits any sin.

Perseverance of the Saints. The biblical teaching that the regenerated sinner can neither totally nor finally fall away from salvation but shall be preserved in faith and holiness by the abiding grace of God.*

Predestination. God's eternal determination of the final end of every individual among angels and men.

Propitiation. The removing of God's displeasure and wrath by Jesus Christ as He fully satisfied the justice and holiness of God. Christ is the propitiation for our sins.

Providence. The everywhere-present activity of God whereby He preserves the whole order of creation and governs all things and events unto their appointed end.

R

Reconciliation. The root idea is to change thoroughly from one position to another. By virtue of Christ's perfect work, the elect are removed from a position of estrangement and alienation into a position of friendship and companionship with God.

Redemption. God's work of delivering sinners from the bondage of sin by paying a ransom. The ransom price paid to deliver elect sinners is the blood of Jesus Christ which satisfies God's justice.*

Regeneration. The act of God, the Holy Spirit, by which He makes the spiritually dead sinner alive. It is also called the *New Birth*.

Reprobation. God's sovereign act of passing by certain sinners not chosen to salvation and His righteous condemnation of such sinners to endure the just punishment of their sins.*

Revelation. God's activity by which He makes known truth to men.

Revelation, General. God's action of communicating truth to man through the created world of nature, the history of man, and man's own conscience.

Revelation, Special. God's action of communicating truth to some men in and through the Scriptures.

Righteousness. Conformity to what is right, namely, the Law of God.

Righteousness of God. That perfection of God by which He as the Holy One acts in perfect harmony with His Law. It is also called the Justice of God, by which He rewards good and punishes evil.

S

Sacrament. A holy, religious ceremony instituted by Christ, in which the grace of God in Christ and the blessings of the covenant of grace are pictured, sealed, and applied to believers who respond in faith and loyalty to God. The New Testament Church observes the sacraments of baptism and the Lord's Supper which replace the Old Testament sacraments of circumcision and the Passover. *

Salvation. The deliverance of man from the guilt, power and penalty of sin; and from the captivity of the Devil, by the gracious provision of God in the work of Christ for sinners and the work of the Holy Spirit in the sinner.

Sanctification. The work of God whereby the saved sinner is refashioned in the whole man after the ways of God so that he dies more and more to sin and lives unto righteousness.

Satisfaction of Christ. Christ's act of sacrificing Himself in order to meet the demands of God's justice, which required that the penalty of the broken Law of God be paid, in the place of each one of the elect. It is also called the *Vicarious Atonement* and *Substitutionary Atonement*. See also Obedience of Christ.

Sovereignty of God. That perfection of God's absolute authority over His created universe by which He does everything for His own glory according to the counsel of His will.

T

Temptation. The enticement of a person by Satan, the sinful world, or the sinful nature of man, to commit sin by offering some seeming advantage to the person being tempted.

Transgression. A word meaning sin which describes the act as a stepping over the line laid down in God's Law.

Trinity. The biblical teaching that the One God exists in three separate Persons, the Father, the Son, and the Holy Spirit, Who are the same in substance and equal in glory.

Truth. That which is in harmony with God's nature and revelation.

W

Wrath of God. God's perfectly righteous anger at sin and His act of inflicting deserved punishments upon guilty sinners.